I0887153

GENDER VIOLENCE IN AUSTRALIA

Gender Violence in Australia

Historical Perspectives

Edited by Alana Piper and Ana Stevenson

MONASH University
Publishing

Gender Violence in Australia: Historical Perspectives

Monash University Publishing
Matheson Library Annexe
40 Exhibition Walk
Monash University
Clayton, Victoria 3800, Australia
www.publishing.monash.edu

Monash University Publishing brings to the world publications which advance the best traditions of humane and enlightened thought.

Monash University Publishing titles pass through a rigorous process of independent peer review.

ISBN: 9781925835304 (pb)
ISBN: 9781925835311 (pdf)
ISBN: 9781925835328 (epub)

www.publishing.monash.edu/books/gva-9781925835304.html

Series: Australian History
Series editor: Sean Scalmer

Design: Les Thomas

Cover image: *The Drunk*. Lithograph by George Bellows, circa 1923.
Image courtesy of the US Library of Congress.

A catalogue record for this book is available from the National Library of Australia.

Printed in Australia by Griffin Press an Accredited ISO AS/NZS 14001:2004 Environmental Management System printer.

The paper this book is printed on is certified against the Forest Stewardship Council ® Standards. Griffin Press holds FSC chain of custody certification SGS-COC-005088. FSC promotes environmentally responsible, socially beneficial and economically viable management of the world's forests.

CONTENTS

INTRODUCTION

Challenging gender violence

Alana Piper and Ana Stevenson

In 2015, the Australian federal government proclaimed that violence against women had become a national crisis.[1] Despite widespread social and economic advances in the status of women since the 1970s, including growing awareness and action around gender violence, its prevalence remains alarming. A third of all women in Australia have been assaulted physically; a fifth of all women have been assaulted sexually.[2] Intimate partner violence is significantly more prevalent in Australia than western Europe or North America.[3] One woman each week is murdered by an intimate partner,[4] and recent research suggests that nearly forty per cent of all women who suicide have a history of domestic or family violence.[5] Domestic violence is a precipitating factor in a third of all homelessness.[6] The resulting strain on government services and lost productivity means that family violence has been estimated as costing the Australian economy around $13.6 billion a year.[7]

---

1 Michaelia Cash, "We have a national crisis when it comes to violence against women in Australia," *HuffPost*, 12 November 2015.

2 Peta Cox, *Violence Against Women: Additional analysis of the Australian Bureau of Statistics' personal safety survey, 2012*, Horizons Research Report, no. 1 (Sydney: ANROWs Horizons, 2015), 22.

3 World Health Organisation, Department of Reproductive Health and Research, London School of Hygiene and Tropical Medicine and South African Medical Research Council, *Global and regional estimates of violence against women: prevalence and health effects of intimate partner violence and non-partner sexual violence* (Italy: World Health Organisation Reports, 2013), 47.

4 Willow Bryant and Tracy Cussen, *Homicide in Australia: 2010–11 to 2011–12: National homicide monitoring program report*, Monitoring Reports, no. 23 (Canberra: Australian Institute of Criminology, 2015), 16.

5 NSW Government, *NSW Domestic Violence Death Review Team Report, 2015–2017* (Sydney: Domestic Violence Death Review Team, 2017), xiv.

6 Selina Tually, Debbie Faulkner, Cecile Cutler and Michele Slatter, *Women, Domestic and Family Violence and Homelessness: A Synthesis Report* (Adelaide: Flinders Institute for Housing, Urban and Regional Research, 2008), 14.

7 National Council to Reduce Violence against Women and their Children, *Economic cost of violence against women and their children* (Canberra: Commonwealth of Australia, 2009), 4.

Australia likewise has one of the highest reported rates of sexual violence in the world, with the region only surpassed by some areas of sub-Saharan Africa.[8] Research further suggests that the vast majority of cases of sexual assault – like other forms of gender violence – still go unreported.[9] Sexual harassment has been increasing according to the Australian Bureau of Statistics, which in 2016 found that nearly a fifth of adult women had been sexually harassed in the last twelve months, while over half had experienced sexual harassment at some point overall.[10] A 2017 report by the Australian Human Rights Commission uncovered overwhelming levels of sexual harassment and assault across the nation's universities.[11] Furthermore, as Michael Salter observes, the minimisation and disbelief typically faced by women who experience gender-based violence should be understood as a type of abuse in itself, one with serious physical and mental health effects.[12]

These experiences are by no means limited to women. Men, while at far less risk, can also be victims of family or sexual violence, with their abusers often other men.[13] Such violence needs and deserves acknowledgement, although it should also be recognised that the claims of men's rights campaigners that one in three victims of family violence are male is a myth, one perpetuated largely as a distraction from violence against women.[14] Gender violence towards men can also result from aggression towards those who do not adhere to normative ideals of hegemonic, heterosexual gender stereotypes. The Australian Research Centre in Sex, Health and Society found in its 2012 study that nearly half of all gay, lesbian, bisexual and transgender people hide their sexuality or gender

---

8 Naeemah Abrahams, Karen Devries, Charlotte Watts, Christina Pallitto, Max Petzold, Simukai Shamu and Claudia Garcia-Moreno, "Worldwide prevalence of non-partner sexual violence: a systematic review," *The Lancet* 383, no. 9929 (2014): 1684–1654.

9 Australian Bureau of Statistics, *Personal Safety Survey, 2005* (2006), 8.

10 Australian Bureau of Statistics, *Personal Safety Survey, 2016* (2017).

11 Australian Human Rights Commission, *Change the Course: National Report on Sexual Assault and Sexual Harassment at Australian Universities* (Sydney: Australian Human Rights Commission, 2017).

12 Michael Salter, "Invalidation: A neglected dimension of gender-based violence and inequality," *International Journal of Crime, Justice and Social Democracy* 1, no. 1 (2012): 3–13.

13 Cox, *Violence Against Women*, 43.

14 Lucy Nicholas and Christine Aguis, *The Persistence of Global Masculinism: Discourse, Gender and Neo-Colonial Re-Articulations of Violence* (Cham: Palgrave Macmillan, 2018), 52.

identity for fear of experiencing "heterosexist violence or discrimination" in public.[15]

Gender violence thus seems to have reached a particularly significant historical moment in Australia. At the same time, violence against women has been declared a timeless and universal phenomenon.[16] This can make the challenge of eliminating gender-based violence seem overwhelming, perhaps creating a perception that the problem is too large to expect substantial or fast-moving changes, or that a triage approach should be adopted in which only the most egregious forms of abuse are worthy of attention. A notable feature in some of the backlash commentary against the publicity that violence against women has recently received is the idea that there is a continuum of seriousness when it comes to gender violence, which makes all but the very worst behaviours seem trivial. This fallacy can be particularly visible in the case of high-profile women who otherwise lead privileged and even powerful professional and public lives – a conspicuous example being the gendered, misogynistic media commentary surrounding Australia's first female prime minister, Julia Gillard.[17]

High-profile news stories about female crime victims likewise highlight larger patterns about gender violence. But rarely does such commentary reveal the relationships between the present moment and the broader historical and cultural context – connections that would demonstrate how such cases are not mere outliers. The disappearance of 29-year-old Jill Meagher in 2012 led to an outpouring of grief, but also frustration. Her death at the hands of a stranger led the media to characterise her "ill fate as 'random'."[18] Yet at least two other women had been threatened in the same area during previous months. One had gone to the authorities on both occasions, though police pursued no follow up or official incident report; the other did not view her experience as serious enough to report until after

---

15 William Leonard, Marian Pitts, Anne Mitchell, Anthony Lyons, Anthony Smith, Sunil Patel, Murray Couch and Anna Barrett, *Private Lives 2: The second national survey of the health and wellbeing of gay, lesbian, bisexual and transgender (GLBT) Australians* (Melbourne: The Australian Research Centre in Sex, Health & Society, La Trobe University, 2012), viii.

16 United Nations Department of Economic and Social Affairs, "Violence against women," *The World's Women 2015*.

17 Anne Summers, "Her rights at work: The political persecution of Australia's first female Prime Minister," *The Economic and Labour Relations Review* 23, no. 4 (2012): 115–126; Marian Sawer, "Misogyny and misrepresentation: Women in Australian Parliaments," *Political Science* 65, no. 1 (2013): 105–117.

18 David L. Richards and Jillienne Haglund, *Violence against Women and the Law* (Milton Park: Routledge, 2015), ix.

Meagher's disappearance. Meagher's rape and murder might thus be seen as a confluence of factors, from failures of the legal system to the extent of public apathy and cynicism towards violence against women.[19]

Meagher, a married cisgender white woman, attracted an outpouring of public empathy in part because she personified a type of ideal victim. In contrast, the media often characterises women of colour, migrant women, and the LGBTQIA+ community as culpable for their own victimisation. The 2014 murder of Mayang Prasetyo by husband Marcus Wolke was a case in point. Brisbane's *Courier Mail* quickly sensationalised the tragedy by focusing on certain facts about the victim's life and death: first, that the horrific murder involved Wolke cooking Prasetyo's dismembered remains; and second, that the 27-year-old was Balinese, a transgender woman, and a former sex worker.[20] "Monster Chef and the She Male," the front page of the *Courier Mail* read; "Ladyboy and the Butcher," it continued inside, further describing Prasetyo as a "top high-class Asian shemale".[21] The media turned Prasetyo into "an aberrant object whose intimate life and tragic demise could then serve as the targets of fascination and titillation as much, if not more, than they could as prompts for empathy."[22]

Other recent cases further illustrate the interlocking abuses of the heteropatriarchal colonial State over racialised and gendered bodies. One particularly arresting case was that of Ms. Dhu, a Yamatji woman from regional Western Australia. In August 2014, after calling the police for help over her partner's violation of an apprehended domestic violence order, Ms. Dhu was herself arrested for fine default. Upon her incarceration, the 22-year-old had broken ribs and developing cases of septicaemia and pneumonia. Days later Ms. Dhu died; assuming her to be experiencing drug-related withdrawal symptoms, police and health professionals failed to properly attend to her medical needs. The CCTV footage which illustrated the extent of this neglect was shown repeatedly during the resulting coronial inquest; her family's request for it to be made public so as to reveal the depth of her suffering was refused.[23]

---

19 Ibid., ix-x.

20 Matthew Ball, *Criminology and Queer Theory: Dangerous Bedfellows?* (Basingstoke: Palgrave Macmillan, 2016), 1–2.

21 Thomas Chamberlin and Rose Brennan, "Monster chef and the she male," *Courier Mail*, 7 October 2014; Rose Brennan, Thomas Chamberlin, and Kate McKenna, "Ladyboy and the butcher," *Courier Mail*, 7 October 2014.

22 Ball, *Criminology and Queer Theory*, 2.

23 Ethan Blue, "Seeing Ms. Dhu: Inquest, conquest, and (in)visibility in black women's deaths in custody," *Settler Colonial Studies* 7, no. 3 (2017): 299–320.

As *Gender Violence in Australia* repeatedly demonstrates, connections between different types of violence frequently illustrate the complex underpinnings of gender violence. Ms. Dhu, a victim of domestic violence in one circumstance, was callously rendered a victim of state violence in another. Such patterns are a direct challenge to the idea that Australia has arrived at a particular moment of crisis that appeared out of nowhere. The histories presented in this collection indicate exactly where these violent behaviours come from and how they have been rationalised over time, to the detriment of women, children and men themselves.

This is why it is so troubling when the more "innocuous" instances of misogyny problematised by feminists are derided for detracting energy from more serious issues, or dismissed as the hysteria of a minority of easily-offended individuals who should be glad they are not living in more oppressive nations, or a hundred years ago. There is a failure to recognise that historical gains against gender violence in Australia have only occurred because of the willingness of some to stand against community complacency. There is also a failure to recognise that violent behaviours on this "continuum" are ultimately rooted in the same racist, heteropatriarchal cultural legacies. By undervaluing the socially constructed nature of gendered relations, ahistorical understandings of gender violence insinuate that society should resign itself to some level of gender violence as part of the human condition. How then, this collection asks, can histories of violence transform contemporary perceptions of gender violence in Australia?

Historians are uniquely empowered to challenge complacency about the inevitability of such phenomena by revealing the socio-historic contexts that have allowed gender violence to flourish, as well as periods when significant, fast-paced progress was made. Several chapters in this collection focus on the hard-won victories of the 1970s and 1980s, from the criminalisation of marital rape to the growth of domestic violence refuge services. As Zora Simic chronicles in the opening chapter, it is no coincidence that this period also saw the flourishing of Australian historical scholarship on gender violence. Influenced by women's liberation politics, early feminist historians made the historical significance of violence against women visible for the first time.[24] The *national* significance of gender violence was also explored, with it posited that colonial conditions had led to a particularly virulently androcentric culture that exacerbated family and sexual violence into the

24 Anne Summers, *Damned Whores and God's Police: The Colonization of Women in Australia* (Ringwood: Penguin, 1975); Miriam Dixson, *The Real Matilda: Woman and Identity in Australia, 1788 to 1975* (Ringwood: Penguin, 1976).

present day.[25] The dark side of mateship and the homosocial culture of the colonial frontier, historians suggested, enabled a type of hyper-masculinity among Australian men, which in eschewing feminine characteristics and company inevitably produced attitudes that facilitated gender violence.[26]

Historical research on gender violence was more limited during the late 1990s and 2000s; as Jacqui Theobald and Suellen Murray's chapter intimates, governmental approaches to domestic violence started to vacillate in this period and social activism around gender violence declined. Scholarship emerged in a piecemeal fashion rather than in a context of lively collegial interchange, with works more narrowly-focused in topic and scope.[27] Important work was conducted, however, particularly in relation to intersectional experiences of violence. New analyses of settler colonialism drew greater attention to interracial sexual violence, and its role in enacting imperialist agendas.[28] Histories of gender-based violence within queer com-

25 Judith Allen, "The invention of the pathological family: A historical study of family violence in NSW," in *Family Violence in Australia*, ed. Carol O'Donnell and Jan Craney (Melbourne: Longman Cheshire, 1982), 1–27; Kay Saunders, "The study of domestic violence in Colonial Queensland: Sources and problems," *Historical Studies* 21, no. 82 (1984): 68–84; Marilyn Lake, "Historical Reconsiderations IV: The politics of respectability: Identifying the masculinist context," *Historical Studies* 22, no. 86 (1986): 116–131; Judith A. Allen, *Sex & Secrets: Crimes Involving Australian Women since 1880* (Oxford: Oxford University Press, 1990); Anne-Maree Collins, "Testimonies of sex: Rape in Queensland, 1880–1919," *Journal of Australian Studies* 15, no. 29 (1991): 50–63; Moira Carmody, "Uniting all women: A historical look at attitudes to rape," in *Crimes of Violence: Australian Responses to Rape and Child Sexual Assault*, ed. Jan Breckenridge and Moira Carmody (Sydney: Allen & Unwin, 1992), 3–17; Jill Bavin-Mizzi, *Ravished: Sexual Violence in Victorian Australia* (Sydney: University of New South Wales Press, 1995).

26 Raymond Evans, "A gun in the oven: Masculinism and gendered violence," in *Gender Relations in Australia: Domination and Negotiation*, ed. Kay Saunders and Raymond Evans (Marrickville: Harcourt Brace Jovanovich, 1992), 205.

27 Ann Genovese, "The battered body," *Australian Feminist Studies* 12, no. 25 (1997): 91–103; Sue Doyle, "The pyjama girl," *Journal of Australian Studies* 24, no. 64 (2000): 34–41; Constance Backhouse, "'Her protests were unavailing': Australian legal understandings of rape, consent and sexuality in the 'roaring twenties,'" *Journal of Australian Studies* 24, no. 64 (2000): 14–33; Jo Aitken, "'The horrors of matrimony among the masses': Feminist representations of wife beating in England and Australia, 1870–1914," *Journal of Women's History* 19, no. 4 (2007): 107–31; Jacqui Theobald, "The beginnings of the Victorian women's refuge movement: Difference, equality and protectionism, 1974–1979," *Lilith: A Feminist History Journal*, no. 21 (2015): 48–62; Elizabeth Nelson, *Homefront Hostilities: The First World War and Domestic Violence* (Kew, Vic.: Australian Scholarly Publishing, 2014).

28 Larissa Behrendt, "Consent in a (neo)colonial society: Aboriginal women as sexual and legal 'other'," *Australian Feminist Studies* 15, no. 33 (2000): 353–367; Lynette Russell, ed. *Colonial Frontiers: Indigenous-European Encounters in Settler Societies* (Manchester: Manchester University Press, 2001); Victoria Haskins, "'A better chance'? – sexual Abuse and the apprenticeship of Aboriginal girls under the NSW

munities also emerged.[29] Where past feminist scholarship mostly focused on adult victims, contemporary disclosures of past child abuse began stimulating a considerable literature on child victims of both sexes.[30] Recent scholarship further suggests a returning interest in gender violence more generally.[31] Analyses of past criminal justice responses to family and sexual violence in particular have expanded significantly in the last few years, driven both by historians and legal scholars.[32] This collection is itself the

---

Aborigines Protection Board," *Aboriginal History* 28 (2004): 33–58; Victoria Haskins, "'Down in the gully and just outside the garden walk': White women and the sexual abuse of Aboriginal women on a colonial Australian frontier," *History Australia* 10, no. 1 (2013): 11–34; Victoria Haskins, "'A troublesome gin like Annie': Masculinity, race and intimate violence in Federation-era North Queensland," *law&history* 4, no. 2 (2017): 125–150; Libby Connors, "Uncovering the shameful: Sexual violence on an Australian colonial frontier," in *Legacies of Violence: Rendering the Unspeakable Past in Modern Australia*, ed. Robert Mason (New York: Berghan Books, 2017), 34.

29 Shirleene Robinson, ed. *Homophobia: an Australian History* (Annandale, NSW: The Federation Press, 2000); Graham Willett and Yorick Smaal, ed. *Intimacy, Violence and Activism: Gay and Lesbian Perspectives on Australasian History and Society* (Melbourne: Monash University Publishing, 2013).

30 Shurlee Swain, "Confronting cruelty: Writing a history of the detection and treatment of child abuse," *Victorian Historical Journal* 71, no. 1 (2000): 7–18; Dorothy Scott and Shurlee Swain, *Confronting Cruelty: Historical Perspectives on Child Abuse* (Carlton South, Vic.: Melbourne University Press, 2002); Yorick Smaal, "Historical perspectives on child sexual abuse, Part 1," *History Compass* 11, no. 9 (2013): 702–714; Yorick Smaal, "Historical perspectives on child sexual abuse, Part 2," *History Compass* 11, no. 9 (2013): 715–726; Nell Musgrove, *The Long History of Forgotten Australians and Children's Institutions* (North Melbourne, Vic.: Australian Scholarly Publishing, 2013); Yorick Smaal, "Boys and homosex: Danger and possibility in Queensland, 1890–1914," in *Children, Childhood and Youth in the British World*, ed. Shirleene Robinson and Simon Sleight (Basingstoke: Palgrave Macmillan, 2015), 221–236; Amanda Kaladelfos, "The dark side of the family: Paternal child homicide in Australia," *Journal of Australian Studies* 37, no. 3 (2013): 333–348; Nell Musgrove, "Abuse of foster children in nineteenth-century Australia: Why did it happen then, and why does it matter now?" *History of Education* 45, no. 4 (2016): 460–476; Yorick Smaal, Andy Kaladelfos, and Mark Finnane, ed. *The Sexual Abuse of Children: Recognition and Redress*, ed. (Clayton, Vic.: Monash University Publishing, 2016).

31 Amanda Kaladelfos and Lisa Featherstone, "Editorial: Sexual and gender-based violence: Definitions, contexts, meanings," *Australian Feminist Studies* 29, no. 81 (2014): 233–237.

32 Amanda Kaladelfos, "The politics of punishment: Rape and the death penalty in colonial Australia, 1841–1901," *History Australia* 9, no. 1 (2012): 155–175; Amanda Kaladelfos, "The 'condemned criminals': Sexual violence, race and manliness in colonial Australia," *Women's History Review* 21, no. 5 (2012): 697–714; Simon Bronitt and Wendy Kukulies-Smith, "Crime, punishment, family violence, and the cloak of legal invisibility," *Journal of Australian Studies* 37, no. 3 (2013): 390–401; Yorick Smaal, "Keeping it in the family: Prosecuting incest in colonial Queensland," *Journal of Australian Studies* 37, no. 3 (2013): 316–332; Lisa Featherstone and Amanda Kaladelfos, *Sex Crimes in the Fifties* (Melbourne: Melbourne University Publishing,

product of an era of both fast-paced change as well as increased scrutiny and awareness about the reality of gender violence, past and present.

Such continued work is not only desirable, but necessary. Histories of gender violence cannot be static because contemporary understandings of its meanings are constantly evolving, evident in changing terminology alone. "The term 'domestic violence' is, of course, of recent coinage," the *Journal of Women's History* 2007 special edition on the subject recognises; it appears anachronistic if discussed before the late twentieth century.[33] Yet, as Tanya Evans's chapter explores, while applying modern terminology and standards to historical behaviour can create tensions, not doing so can inadvertently normalise past violence. Moving away from euphemistic discussions of gender violence can represent a more open acknowledgement of the problem, which can then enable a more comprehensive approach to solutions. A recent shift away from "refuge" and "shelter" to discussions of domestic and family violence services, for example, reflects the diversity of programmes needed to assist those escaping such violence.[34] Similarly, calls by sexual abuse and domestic violence support groups to replace the term "victim" with "survivor" act as a reminder to historians of the need to recognise not just women's oppression, but their agency, an aspect that early feminist histories of gender violence tended to overlook.[35] The chapters in this volume thus consider historical questions about gender violence in ways informed by current perspectives and knowledge.

Section I of this volume interrogates violence within the home. Some may be surprised by the extent to which family violence was acknowledged as a problem in previous centuries (figure 1); then as now, however, motivation and solutions to confront it have been less forthcoming. Moreover, while its general existence was admitted, specific instances have remained more concealed, both as a result of the coercive control abusers exerted over their victims and a disinclination from the wider community to interfere in matters occurring within the privacy of the home. Particular forms of family violence,

---

2016); Michelle Arrow, "Making family violence public in the Royal Commission on Human Relationships, 1974–1977," *Australian Feminist Studies* 33, no. 95 (2018): 81–96; Heather Douglas, Francesca Bartlett, Trish Luker and Rosemary Hunter, *Australian Feminist Judgments: Righting and Rewriting Law* (Oxford: Hart Publishing, 2014).

33 Megan McLaughlin and Elizabeth H. Pleck, "Editor's note," *Journal of Women's History* 19, no. 4 (2007): 7–11.

34 Jacqui Theobald, "Feminist oral history and the Victorian domestic violence services movement," *Australian Feminist Studies* 28, no. 78 (2013): 372.

35 Ann Curthoys, "Race and gender in recent Australian historiography," *Journal of Interdisciplinary Gender Studies* 1, no. 1 (1995): 8.

such as psychological abuse, were not yet recognised as abuse, perhaps even by victims themselves. An enduring problem, for historians and the justice system alike, is how to establish evidence in such cases.

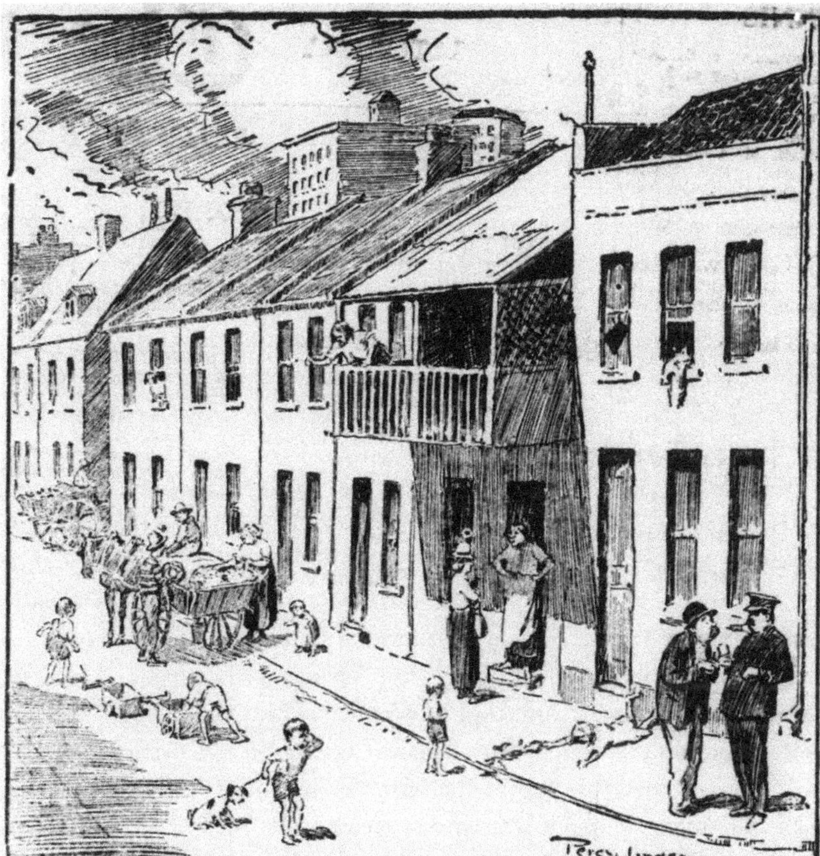

"Which is the house where a man's been beating his wife?"
"Take y'r pick, sergeant."

Figure 1. Contemporaries recognised the pervasiveness of wife-beating in the average neighbourhood.
Cartoon by Percy Lindsay, published in *Recorder*, 19 May 1934, 3.
Image courtesy of the National Library of Australia.

The silences over family violence and the power of history to break that silence thus acts as a linking theme across the chapters in this section. The first chapter illustrates how feminist historians first named gender violence as an issue. Without such interventions, Zora Simic intimates, it would be difficult – if not impossible – for commentators today to discuss these questions in a systematic manner. Simic calls for an overarching history of gender violence, and this volume offers a crucial step towards that aim. Family history in particular, Tanya Evans' chapter then suggests, offers a means for breaking continuing silences surrounding domestic violence by revealing the invisible personal and social legacies past gender violence has for many Australians.

By outlining the operation of domestic economic abuse in 1890s' Queensland, Alana Piper's chapter illustrates how gendered power dynamics produced attitudes that continue to allow less overt forms of gender violence by encoding expectations of female dependency and submissiveness against male independence and assertiveness. Women and children, she shows, are both liable to become victims of the relationship between family and structural violence. Lisa Durnian's chapter on patricide further explores how children have been victims of gender violence by proxy. As with battered wife syndrome, silence and lack of intervention regarding family violence has the potential to erupt into other forms of violence, such as children killing their mothers' abusers.

That family violence often comprises the whole family is further borne out by Andy Kaladelfos's chapter on incest, which reveals that the inequality of power relations between husband and wife as well as parent and child has contributed to the difficulties in standing up for child victims. Finally, Lisa Featherstone examines another form of familial sexual violence in her chapter about the long-time legal invisibility of marital rape, and how the late-twentieth-century campaign to criminalise this act confronted deep-rooted community beliefs that female consent became irrelevant inside marriage. A cursory search of the term "spousal rape" on Reddit reveals such conceptions have not entirely disappeared.

Section II reflects on the increased risk of gender violence faced by particular communities. From the colonial frontier to the contemporary workplace, certain contexts have made individuals vulnerable to particular forms of gender violence. While the diversity and specificity of experiences needs to be recognised, the commonalities across many contexts are equally important. Chapters in this section demonstrate how misogynistic attitudes and unequal power relations both lead to the victimisation of particular groups, and increase the struggle to have their voices heard thereafter.

Liz Conor examines how Indigenous stockwomen, often isolated from kinship networks through spatial, language, and culture barriers, were not only exploited for their sexual and economic labour, but continue to be exploited by romanticised contemporary reimaginings. Raelene Frances offers a chapter on the vexed issue of female agency within sex work, in particular the past and ongoing government approaches to migrant women in Australia. Frances traces the evolution from an abolitionist approach to the sex trade that failed to distinguish between trafficked women and migrant sex workers, to a human rights approach that supports the rights of sex workers and recognises the importance of such support in preventing abusive practices. Shurlee Swain likewise directly connects the past and present by examining the various forms of gender-based violence revealed by the series of governmental inquiries into historical institutional abuse held since the 1990s. While such recognition is a step in the right direction, Swain argues, future abuses will not be prevented until the patriarchal structures underpinning such violence – including the attitude that some children are less worthy than others – are addressed.

Rebecca Jennings illustrates how the queer community has also faced attitudes that served to legitimate violence for failing to conform to expected binary gender roles. Again demonstrating the interconnections between different types of violence, Jennings describes how such oppression sometimes led to silences about violence within intimate relationships. Tanya Fitzgerald's chapter examines how women with greater cultural and social power are still at risk in professional contexts. Specifically, while women's representation in academia has improved, Fitzgerald shows that many continue to experience the same dilemmas as their foremothers when it comes to abusive or discriminatory workplace environments. This analysis of gendered micro-aggressions against women working in universities therefore acts as a case study for the types of insidious gender violence faced by working women more generally.

Section III looks to histories of activism against gender violence. Many people, most especially women's rights reformers, have long sought ways to tackle gender violence, at least as it manifests in certain contexts. While the State and the legal establishment have periodically expressed concern about instances of gender violence, these institutions have similarly been reluctant to acknowledge a systemic problem in gender relations. The realisation that gender violence is not just a feminist issue is increasingly accepted today. This section demonstrates how the importance of emphasising the interconnects between different gender violence issues cannot be underestimated.

Ana Stevenson and Brigitte Lewis's chapter explores the evolution of cultural attitudes to gender violence in Australia, a transformation equally connected to how feminist messages have been communicated to the public technologically. Mary Tomsic illustrates how the Australian feminist films of the 1970s were an important site for calling out gender violence, although the extent of their circulation and impact was limited when compared to the global resonance of recent works like the television adaptation of Margaret Atwood's *The Handmaid's Tale*.[36] The digital age has made it easier for activists to circulate information quickly, but often made it more difficult to maintain community focus and get actual feet on the ground. This is a particular concern, given that research suggests that by the early 2000s, many of the inroads feminists had previously made in governmental approaches to domestic violence began to backslide.[37] Jacqui Theobald and Suellen Murray's chapter reveals both the benefits and limitations of engaging with government bodies with respect to domestic violence services. Since the State is seemingly never as feminist in its vision as activists themselves, perhaps we as feminist historians might profitably indulge in visions with utopian possibilities here.

A focus throughout this collection is how history can be used to illuminate the current national crisis. Explicit connections between past and present are drawn in terms of tracking the changes and continuities in experiences of, and social and legal responses to, domestic, family, sexual, institutional, economic, psychological, emotional, and structural violence. This collection makes significant inroads into uncovering these histories, yet its compilation has also revealed how much there is left to do. For example, further historical inquiry into questions such as transgender violence, disability abuse, elder abuse, emotional abuse, and sentencing policies, as well as the experiences of Indigenous peoples, immigrants, refugees, and the stateless, remains critical. So, too, do investigation of the experiences and perspectives of the perpetrators themselves. Additionally, histories that seek to elucidate such a diversity of experience in the past need to be mirrored in the present by increased diversity among historians themselves. In exploring the prevalence and devastating impact of varied abuses from the nineteenth to the twenty-first century, *Gender Violence in Australia* provides another step towards greater historical insight into the changing attitudes towards and nature of gender violence.

This history is not a comforting narrative in which social progress has gradually led to an amelioration of gender-based violence. Neither is

---

36 *The Handmaid's Tale* (Hulu, 2017–).

37 Ruth Phillips, "Undoing an activist response: Feminism and the Australian government's domestic violence policy," *Critical Social Policy* 26, no. 1 (2006): 192–219; Marian Sawer and Gwendolyn Gray Jamieson, "The women's movement and government: Feminist fading?" *Australian Feminist Studies* 29, no. 82 (2014): 403–418.

it a confirmation that gender violence is historically inescapable, a social constant that legal and cultural shifts have failed to alter. This history is a rallying cry. The chapters in this collection confirm that gender violence comes in many forms, all of which are endemic and interconnected – but, most importantly, are able to be challenged.

Section I

Gender Violence in the Home

Chapter 1

HISTORICISING A "NATIONAL DISGRACE"

Towards a feminist history of domestic violence since 1788

Zora Simic

In Australia, domestic violence has been a highly visible public issue in recent years, particularly since 2015 with the appointment of bereaved survivor Rosie Batty as Australian of the Year,[1] the establishment of the Australian "Counting Dead Women Project",[2] and the launch of a Royal Commission into Family Violence in Victoria. The Royal Commission's 2016 report found that support systems were overwhelmed although front line services continue to be cut, signalling a tension between increased publicity and ongoing denial and inaction.[3]

While domestic violence has been described as a "national shame" by Prime Minister Malcolm Turnbull,[4] it is far from a new problem. The term itself is typically dated to the late 1970s, yet various precursors including

1 Rosie Batty's 11 year-old son Luke was the victim of domestic violence at the hands of his father. Rosie went on to become a high-profile family violence campaigner.

2 Destroy the Joint, an online feminist organisation, began its Counting Dead Women campaign in 2014. See: *Destroy the Joint*, Facebook, 2012-present, accessed June 14, 2018, https://www.facebook.com/DestroyTheJoint/.

3 The Royal Commission into Family Violence began in Victoria in February 2015. The final report was tabled in State Parliament in March 2016. See: *Royal Commission into Family Violence: Report and Recommendations* (Melbourne: Victoria Government Printer, 2016).

4 At a state leaders summit held in October 2016 to combat gendered violence, Turnbull described rates of violence against women by their partners as a "national shame" and a "disgrace". See: Daniela Ritorto, "Turnbull calls Australia's domestic

"wife-beating" in the nineteenth century and "battered wife" in the mid-twentieth, serve as reminders that such activity has never remained entirely behind closed doors, but been part of public discourse. Cognisant of both the enduring nature of this problem, and the fact that there is currently no over-arching history of domestic violence in Australia, this chapter makes a case that the time is right for one. I make this argument not only or even because of the (relatively) high visibility of the issue. Rather, I argue, via an examination of developments in the feminist historiography of domestic violence in Australia, that feminist historians are now better positioned to attempt such a project. Indeed, this collection is testimony to the increasing sophistication and diversification of histories of gender violence. Relatedly, I contend that any such overarching history should be an explicitly feminist project in both political and methodological terms.

The larger purpose of this chapter is to reflect on what it means to advance feminist history of domestic violence now – that is, in the context of unprecedented local and global awareness of this issue, and in terms of developments in Australian historiography. To do this, I revisit the trailblazing work of feminist historians Kay Saunders and Judith Allen whose early scholarship on the problems and possibilities of historicising domestic violence remain instructive and pertinent. Yet it is also the case that we are researching in a different historical moment – not only is domestic violence more visible as a social problem, but Australian historians are now addressing violence as a key theme in greater numbers and depth than ever before.[5] Australian history has come a long way since 1992 when Raymond Evans argued that researchers "intent on pursuing the origins of the notionally connected themes of violence and masculinity in this country are [in the first instance] disadvantaged by a general tendency among historians to ignore, underplay or marginalize violence in their nation's past."[6] Indeed, when Saunders and Allen began their research and

---

violence 'a disgrace'," *SBS News*, 28 October 2016, accessed June 14, 2018, http://www.sbs.com.au/news/article/2016/10/28/turnbull-calls-australias-domestic-violence-disgrace.

5 This work includes two research centres producing longitudinal data and analysis – the Prosecution Project at Griffith University (1850–1960 coverage of criminal trials in various Australian archives) and the Centre for the History of Violence at Newcastle. See: *The Prosecution Project*, Griffith University, 2014–2018, accessed June 14, 2018, https://prosecutionproject.griffith.edu.au/; The Centre for the History of Violence, University of Newcastle, accessed June 14, 2018, https://www.newcastle.edu.au/research-and-innovation/centre/chov/about-us.

6 Raymond Evans, "A Gun in the Oven: Masculinism and Gendered Violence," in *Gender Relations in Australia: Domination and Negotiation*, ed. Raymond Evans and Kay Saunders (Sydney: Harcourt Brace Jovanovich, 1992), 197.

writing on this topic in the early 1980s, "domestic violence" had only very recently been named as such and historians – including feminist ones – had only just started to properly historicise family life, masculinism and other phenomena relevant to comprehending family violence in the past and present.

The first and most substantial part of this chapter is mainly a historiographical exploration of how feminist historians, namely Saunders and Allen, came to write of domestic violence and the context in which they did so – the early years of feminist knowledge production about this issue. In focusing primarily on feminist histories of domestic violence, I also trace the emergence of a feminist critique of it. The final section of this chapter briefly elaborates on what a feminist history of domestic violence might look like, with the caveat that any such history would be envisioned as a collaborative project, both in the narrow sense of a co-authored history and in the wider sense of building respectfully on the work already done. A feminist history of domestic violence would also ideally contribute to feminist activism around this issue, just as earlier scholarship did in the past. It was within activist forums, and the emerging domestic violence sector – not the usual spaces of Australian history – that Allen and Saunders found their first receptive audience, as well as useful critical tools to analyse the material they had found in the archives. In doing so, they each anticipated major developments and debates within Australian historiography from the mid-1980s. And while each were sensibly cautious in their claims and methodology – stressing the limits of the archive and existing analytical frameworks – over thirty years later, their work remains some of the most ambitious undertaken on the topic of domestic violence in Australian history.

Early histories of domestic violence in Australia

The naming of domestic violence in the late 1970s opened up the topic to historical investigation. Key pioneering works of Australian history and anthropology had already acknowledged violence against women as a discernible feature of Australian society, as part of Indigenous-settler relations and a consequence of colonialism.[7] However it was not until the mid-1970s that gendered violence was addressed more substantially, with the first feminist histories of Australia, notably those by Anne Summers and Miriam

7 Manning Clark, *A History of Australia* (Carlton: Melbourne University Press, 1962); C.D. Rowley, *The Remote Aborigines* (Ringwood, Vic.: Penguin, 1972).

Dixson, suggesting a particularly Australian misogyny placed women at increased risk of male violence.[8] Summers' book *Damned Whores and God's Police* (1975), along with American texts such as Susan Brownmiller's *Against Our Will* (1975), would inform the framework of feminist interventions against violence which developed in the 1970s.[9] Still, as Summers would note in her introduction to the revised twentieth anniversary edition of *Damned Whores*, "much of the language we use today to describe everyday exploitation did not even exist then. The term sexual harassment had yet to be coined; [and] we had not begun to speak of domestic violence although we were becoming depressingly aware of how widespread what we referred to as wife-bashing was".[10]

In Australia, Judith Allen would become the first historian to publish substantial work on the topic, but I begin here with Kay Saunders in order to emphasise the significance of the naming of domestic violence in the late 1970s. In 1977 and 1978, while conducting post-doctoral research on indentured labourers in the Queensland State Archives, Saunders noticed that in the Supreme and local court records, "there were many 'assault and battery' cases where a husband attacked his wife." At that point, she later wrote, "she was unable to intellectually locate and interpret this material". However, the significance of these sources dawned on her a year later, and she was back in the archive, going through every file again. A talk on the topic to a non-academic audience in 1980 spurred her along, though in her own field "social historians generally and feminist historians specifically had not yet identified masculinism and violence as a problem to be analysed". For Saunders, the first historiographical breakthrough in Australia came with the publication of Judith Allen's chapter "The invention of the pathological family: An historical study of domestic violence in NSW, 1880–1939," published in 1982. Saunders found Allen's work "an inspiring piece of scholarship."[11] Two years later Saunders' own article "The study of

8 Anne Summers, *Damned Whores and God's Police* (Ringwood: Penguin, 1975); Miriam Dixson, *The Real Matilda: Woman and Identity in Australia 1788 to the Present* (Ringwood: Penguin, 1976).

9 Gail Mason, "Violence," in *Australian Feminism: A Companion*, ed. Barbara Caine, Moira Gatens, Emma Grahame, Jan Larbalestier, Sophie Watson, and Elizabeth Webby (Melbourne: Oxford University Press, 1999), 337.

10 Anne Summers, *Damned Whores and God's Police*, updated edition (Ringwood: Penguin, 1994), 1.

11 Kay Saunders, Reflective preface to republication of her 1984 article, in *Pastiche I: Reflections on 19th Century Australia*, ed. Penny Russell and Richard White (St Leonards: Allen & Unwin, 1994), 201–202.

domestic violence in Queensland: Sources and problems" was published in *Historical Studies*.[12]

Saunders' article remains an obligatory citation for any historian working on domestic violence in Australia, not only because it is one of the earliest such publications. Saunders framed domestic violence within wider patterns of institutionalised violence in colonial Queensland 1859–1900 (including frontier violence, a brutal convict system, exploitation of indentured labourers), while also making a persuasive case for it as a special kind of violence, easily obscured in the historical record and in the present day because of, she argued, the enduring ideology of the bourgeois family. Further, Saunders navigated the various court records – which collectively "yielded a surprising abundance of primary sources" – to reveal two different routes typically pursued by working-class and middle-class parties respectively: the criminal courts for working-class couples and divorce and judicial separation proceedings for middle and petit bourgeois class women, where female petitioners "invariably cited gross physical abuse in their petitions". In identifying these patterns, Saunders proposed to use history to challenge what she called the "enduring and inaccurate stereotype in Western culture… [of the] wife batterer as a low income earner with few economic, social or psychological skills".[13] Here she drew on then-current research in Britain, the United States and Australia that indicated perpetrators could be found in all classes, ethnic groups and regions, an indication of how the "naming" of domestic violence and the research that came in its wake had provided both impetus and interpretative tools for her historical study. For later historians, we can discern here too what would become prevailing orthodoxy in the domestic violence sphere: that it is a practice that cuts across class, race and ethnicity, an influential argument that has informed both activism and service provision, while also being routinely contested on various grounds, including the contention that while domestic violence features in all class contexts, it is more common in working or lower-class ones, and to argue otherwise is a policy failure.

In her 1984 article, Saunders nodded to Judith Allen's argument that domestic violence has "been a practice without a history". Allen's chapter, "The invention of the pathological family", opens the 1982 interdisciplinary edited collection *Family Violence in Australia*, edited by Carol O'Donnell

12 Kay Saunders, "The study of domestic violence in colonial Queensland: Sources and problems," *Historical Studies*, 21, no. 82 (1984): 68–84. (Note: *Historical Studies* is now titled *Australian Historical Studies*.)

13 Ibid., 72.

and Jane Craney.[14] This ground-breaking collection was mostly full of articles by criminologists and lawyers – including by Jocelynne A. Scutt, who in various capacities would later be part of changing laws in regards to rape and domestic violence in both Victoria and New South Wales. A year later Scutt also published one of the first books on domestic violence aimed at a broader audience, *Even in the Best of Homes: Violence in the Family* (1983).[15] The use of "family violence" in the title of the edited collection was explicitly presented in the introduction as part of a wider feminist critique of the ideology of the family and the public/private divide which the editors argued "prevents people from talking about their experiences and feelings and thus discovering common elements in apparently individual lives".[16] Various contributors also used the term "domestic violence" throughout, including Scutt and Allen, suggesting that at this stage the terms were largely interchangeable.[17] Also observable, however, are seeds of a later debate about the efficacy of one term over the other; evident in one criticism directed at feminism in an otherwise explicitly feminist introduction – which is that feminism had thus far, in the abiding focus on the oppression of women, "found it necessary to ignore children's problems".[18]

Another contributor was activist Wendy Bacon, then a freelance journalist and recent law graduate fresh from the feminist campaign to free Violet and Bruce Roberts. In 1976, Roberts and her son Bruce were imprisoned for the murder of her long-time abusive husband Eric. Four years later they were released at the discretion of the New South Wales government, following a high-profile campaign mobilised by feminists. The campaign for their release has been credited with bringing domestic violence to public consciousness, including as a "feminist" concern. Her initial trial, meanwhile, has been persuasively historicised by Ann Genovese as "pre-domestic violence" – in the sense there was neither the language, law or political will to recognise what Roberts had endured as "a battered wife". The personal histories of Violet and Bruce were reduced to a paragraph in their unsworn testimonies and none of the witnesses they identified were called in to

14 Judith Allen, "The invention of the pathological family: a historical study of family violence in NSW," in *Family Violence in Australia*, ed. Carol O'Donnell and Jan Craney (Melbourne: Longman Chesire, 1982), 1–27.

15 Jocelynne A. Scutt, *Even in the Best of Homes: violence in the family* (Ringwood: Penguin, 1983).

16 Carol O'Donnell and Jan Craney, ed. *Family Violence in Australia*, viii.

17 Jocelynne A. Scutt, "Domestic violence: The police response," in *Family Violence in Australia*, 110–120.

18 O'Donnell and Craney, ed. *Family Violence in Australia*, xi.

testify.[19] The Free Violet Roberts campaign informed Bacon's chapter, co-written with lawyer Robyn Landsdowne, on "Women who kill husbands: The battered wife on trial".[20] In the early 1980s, in their triple capacity as activists, solicitors and researchers, Bacon and Landsdowne conducted interviews with a number of incarcerated women, including Roberts. In doing so, they helped to bring "domestic violence into the topography of public discourse" and to drive legal change, notably an amendment to the New South Wales *Criminal Act* recognising the impact and effects of domestic violence.[21]

The *Family Violence in Australia* collection as a whole had its origins in a foundational moment in feminist knowledge production about domestic violence in Australia: a Federal Government International Women's Year Grant to produce a statistical study of "violence in the home", conducted by sociologists Carol O'Donnell and Heather Saville, and released in 1979 to coincide with the agenda-setting Conference for Family Violence, convened by the Australian Institute of Criminology. One of the goals and outcomes of this conference was to provide a social constructivist – rather than pathological – framing of domestic violence. Participant and convenor Jocelynne Scutt praised the strength of the feminist analysis presented,[22] and as Janet Ramsey would later historicise, the conference "turned out to be the venue for the Australian confrontation between professionals supporting the individual psychology framing of family violence and the feminist social structures framing".[23] In the edited collection that followed, previous researchers on family violence (which in this instance incorporated incest and child abuse) were condemned for representing it as somehow aberrant rather than common and for attempting to show that victims somehow deserved it. The editors hazarded a guess "that most research into domestic violence has been carried out by economically independent middle class males whose children were primarily looked after by their wives".[24]

---

19 Ann Genovese, "The battered body," *Australian Feminist Studies* 12, no. 25 (1997): 91–103.

20 Wendy Bacon and Robyn Landsdowne, "Women who kill husbands: The battered wife on trial," in *Family Violence in Australia,* 67–94.

21 Genovese, "The battered body," 93.

22 Jocelynne Scutt, ed. *Violence in the Family: a collection of conference papers* (Canberra: Australian Institute of Criminology, 1980).

23 Janet Ramsay, "Policy activism on a 'wicked issue': The building of Australian feminist policy on domestic violence in the 1970s," *Australian Feminist Studies* 22, no. 53 (2007): 247–264, 255–256.

24 O'Donnell and Craney, ed. *Family Violence in Australia.*

Judith Allen was still a PhD student in history at Macquarie University when she researched and wrote her contribution, a chapter whose arguments she would develop and refine for another historical paper presented in the context of a major conference on domestic violence in 1985 titled "Desperately seeking solutions: Changing battered women's options since 1880",[25] and her 1990 book *Sex and Secrets: Crimes Involving Australian Women Since 1880*.[26] As for Saunders, it was the criminal and divorce courts that formed the basis of her archive and without making large claims for this evidence – "it is not possible", she wrote, "to speak of increases or declines in a meaningful sense" – she did argue that "these extant records can reveal not only the personal context of domestic violence, but also the changing priorities of the state, as to the scale, means and class selection of responses to state violence".[27] The changes Allen discerned over time – for instance in how the law and other institutions managed domestic violence and in women's options or lack thereof for escaping it – she partly accounted for by elaborating on "a number of developments in the social history of women": the dramatic reduction of married women's fertility from an average total of seven lives births in 1880 to three by 1920, changing expectations about marital and sexual satisfaction and new post-war opportunities for paid employment. Prior to these developments, "few women achieved sufficient independence to prosecute their attackers",[28] or to leave their marriages. Allen boldly argued that the self-promoting "modernisers" of nineteenth-century divorce laws had failed to account for female dependence: until well into the twentieth century, even those women who did manage to leave their violent marriages found their most feasible option was to enter another one, hopefully violence-free. Fewer children theoretically decreased dependence, but exacerbated the likelihood that a young wife with no or few children would die at the hands of her husband. Moving closer to her present, Allen argued for the "re-privatisation" of domestic violence from the inter-war years on: policing and legal recourse declined as medical authorities gained ground through the "psychologisation of the batterer and the blaming of the victim".[29]

---

25 Judith Allen, "Desperately seeking solutions: Changing battered women's options Since 1880," in *National Conference on Domestic Violence: Proceedings*, Vol. 1, ed. Suzanne E. Hatty (Canberra: Australian Institute of Criminology, 1986), 119–136.

26 Judith Allen, *Sex and Secrets: Crimes Involving Australian Women Since 1880* (Melbourne: Oxford University Press, 1990).

27 Allen, "The Invention of the pathological family," 1.

28 Allen, "Desperately seeking solutions," 121.

29 Ibid., 130.

At the 1985 National Conference on Domestic Violence, again conducted by the Australian Institute of Criminology, Allen extended her case for a *feminist* history of domestic violence. Feminism, she argued, had challenged the psychological redefinition of family violence – the paradigmatic example of which was "battered wife syndrome" – by exposing the endemic character of women battering, and had brought women's experiences to the centre of analysis and policy. It should now be a minimum requirement, suggested Allen, that "locating woman battering as an aspect of overall social relations between the sexes is a minimum requirement for all scholarship on the question". Yet even feminists had yet to properly grapple with what she identified as the "real problem – masculinity". In politicising the issue, feminism had only gone half way – masculinism and its history had yet to be comprehended as "intensely political". If the historical record shows nothing else, she posited, it reveals the "wily and adaptive politics of masculinity", the historical memory of which must inform future policy.[30]

The organisers of the 1985 National Conference also argued for the necessity of "adopting a feminist perspective when addressing the issue of male violence" and planned accordingly, with starting points that explicitly modelled a feminist approach. Firstly, they argued for a definition of "woman battering" that encompassed both "physical assault and the various forms of psychological violation which usually precede or accompany this violence". (Terminology appears in transition at the conference, with an explanatory note flagging that "woman/wife battering, female partner assault and domestic violence" were each used throughout the conference and the proceedings.[31]) Secondly, the conference itself was organised on the premise that "woman battering, despite being enacted between individuals, is both shaped and legitimised by the gender-based structural equalities within society." However, the feminist approaches presented were heterogeneous, with Allen's empirically rich historical paper, for example, rounding up a "theoretical" section in which two of her fellow Macquarie colleagues presented radically different analyses: Alicia Lee offered a sprawling, wildly interdisciplinary and crudely historical account of misogyny against women, with a discernible radical feminist bent,[32] while sociologist Vivien Johnson – a former refuge worker – questioned what had already become orthodoxy in the feminist refuge movement

30 Ibid., 120.

31 Suzanne E. Hatty, "Preface," in *National Conference on Domestic Violence*, xvii-xviv.

32 Alicia Lee, "The foreigner within the walls," in *National Conference on Domestic Violence*, 67–84.

– that women stay in violent relationships because they have nowhere else to go – by using Freud to "examine more honestly the very real problems of heterosexual intimacy".[33] Scutt, meanwhile, proposed anti-pornography measures, within her broader agenda of criminal and legal reform;[34] this aspect of her activism, however, never gained much traction in Australia where governments were reluctant to legislate and where pornography was a never as significant a feminist issue as it was in the United States.[35]

The 1985 National Conference also featured papers from migrant and Aboriginal perspectives, the latter from Beverly Ridgeway of the South Australian Health Commission who proposed that any understanding of domestic violence within Aboriginal communities must begin with "background information on the historical role of Aboriginal women within traditional societies" and the recognition that Aboriginal people are "survivors of white domination and oppression."[36] These were arguments that would come to preface many subsequent reports and studies of domestic violence in Indigenous contexts, including Judy Atkinson's landmark 1990 report on Violence in Aboriginal Australia, commissioned by the Federal Government. Here, Atkinson indicted history as a part of ongoing "myth-making" about Aboriginal people, and for its reproduction of "bad" anthropology, each underpinning the prevailing view that Aboriginal gender relations are naturally violent, and contributing both to continuing government inaction *and* to Aboriginal women's isolation from mainstream feminist critiques.[37]

Aboriginal women do not appear in Allen's work on domestic violence in the 1980s, including as part of the history of Australian "masculinism". Later, Saunders would reflect that while she and Allen concurred on the nature and ramifications of gendered inequalities of power, Allen located her analysis "entirely in a feminist discourse", while Saunders sought to

---

33 Vivien Johnson, "Love will tear us apart: Domestic violence and sexuality," in *National Conference on Domestic Violence*, 85–104.

34 Jocelynn Scutt, "'Still the same old story… ': Pornography and violence against women," in *National Conference on Domestic Violence*, 105–118.

35 Kate Gleeson, "From suck magazine to corporate paedophilia. Feminism and pornography—Remembering the Australian way," *Women's Studies International Forum* 38 (2013): 83–96.

36 Beverly Ridgeway, "Aboriginal women's viewpoint," in *National Conference on Domestic Violence*, 41–44.

37 See: Judy Atkinson, "Violence in Aboriginal Australia: colonisation and gender," *Aboriginal and Islander Health Worker Journal* 14, no. 2 (1990): 5–21; Evans and Saunders, ed. *Gender Relations in Australia*, 32.

locate "domestic violence within other forms of coercion".[38] Still, in 1984, this meant subsuming Aboriginal women into the general pattern of colonial and frontier violence, rather than as victims of gendered violence. In the frontier regions, noted Saunders, white women experienced precarious existences that made them more vulnerable to domestic violence. Identifying the various ways Aboriginal women were also vulnerable to gendered violence – including as domestic servants[39] – would be the work of future historians, as would proper attention to how colonialism and patriarchy together contributed to violence against Aboriginal women, from both European and Indigenous men.[40]

My intention here is not to undermine the major significance of these genuinely ground-breaking historical interventions. What is most striking re-reading work from this time is how emerging feminist knowledge about domestic violence coming from criminology and sociology was able to provide these intrepid historians with a more viable explanatory framework (and audience) than the discipline of history at that stage. Histories of the family were only beginning to emerge – Saunders cites Patricia Grimshaw and Graeme Willett's then-recent work on the colonial family as galvinising for her own research,[41] while Allen observed that the growing international field of family history allocated little or no space to domestic violence.[42] Feminist historian Linda Gordon's history of family violence in the US *Heroes of their Own Lives* would not emerge until 1988,[43] though each cited the survey on new scholarship on family violence by Gordon and Wini Breines published in *Signs* in 1983 – a survey which emphasised the dearth of properly historical work on family violence, a term they used

38 Saunders, *Pastiche*, 202.

39 See: Victoria Haskins, "On the doorstep: Aboriginal domestic service as a 'contact zone'," *Australian Feminist Studies* 16, no. 34 (2001): 13–25; Victoria Haskins, "'A better chance'? — sexual abuse and the apprenticeship of Aboriginal girls under the NSW Aborigines Protection Board," *Aboriginal History* 28 (2004): 33–58.

40 See: Evans, "A gun in the oven," 200; Larissa Behrendt, "Consent in a (neo)colonial society: Aboriginal women as sexual and legal 'other'," *Australian Feminist Studies* 15, no. 33 (2000): 353–367; Hannah Robert, "Disciplining the female Aboriginal body: inter-racial sex and the pretence of separation," *Australian Feminist Studies* 16, no. 34 (2001): 69–81.

41 Patricia Grimshaw and Graeme Willett, "Women's history and family history: An exploration of colonial family structure," in *Australian Women: Feminist Perspectives*, ed. Norma Grieve and Patricia Grimshaw (Melbourne: Oxford University Press, 1981).

42 See: Allen's first note for "The Invention of the Pathological Family," 23.

43 Linda Gordon, *Heroes of Their Own Lives: The History and Politics of Family Violence* (New York: Viking, 1988).

broadly to refer to child abuse, wife beating and incest.[44] The lack of suitable explanatory frameworks is reflected in Allen and Saunders' footnotes, which consist almost entirely of primary research, foregrounding how new this terrain was.

Two of the themes Allen and Saunders introduced as vital to comprehending domestic violence in the past and the present – the history of the family and the history of masculinism – would go on to become spirited topics of debate among Australian historians within a few years. Indeed, Allen was called in by *Historical Studies* in 1987 to adjudicate the Marilyn Lake and Chris McConville debate over the sexual and cultural politics of the 1890s and their alleged "masculinist" context. In what would become a much-cited historical debate, Lake argued that gender, "the sexual dynamic" and competing masculinities were at the heart of the contest over the nascent national culture in the 1890s, while McConville prioritised class struggle.[45] Allen concluded firmly in Lake's favour, partly on the basis that it was feminist historiography that raised the significance of historicising gender in the first place.[46] Meanwhile, Grimshaw had by 1986 begun to revise some of her earlier generally positive appraisals of family life, by noting the prevalence of marital violence in an article on the pioneering settlements of Castlemaine and Horsham.[47]

In 1992, Raymond Evans in the aforementioned chapter "Gun in the oven" from the edited collection *Gender Relations in Australia*, co-edited with Saunders, duly praised Allen and Saunders for their "preliminary work" on domestic violence and spouse murder, with some qualifications, particularly in regards to Allen's work which he read as propagating an undifferentiated assessment of masculinity across time and place, typical he thought of a branch of feminist history that had abandoned proper class analysis. As Evans saw it, so far historians of inter-personal violence had tended to concentrate on its effects, rather than probing its largely male-derived origins or the "plentitude" of masculinities. Nor had they properly reckoned with

---

44 Wini Breines and Linda Gordon, "The new scholarship on family violence," *Signs: Journal of Women in Culture and Society* 8, no. 3 (1983): 490–531.

45 Marilyn Lake, "Historical reconsiderations IV: The politics of respectability: Identifying the masculinist context," *Historical Studies* 22, no. 86 (1986): 116–131; Chris McConville, "Rough women, respectable men and social reform: A response to Lake's 'Masculinism'," *Historical Studies* 22, no. 88 (1987): 432–440.

46 Judith Allen, "'Mundane' men: Historians, masculinity and masculinism," *Historical Studies* 22, no. 89 (1987): 617–628.

47 Patricia Grimshaw, Charles Fahey, Susan Janson, and Tom Griffiths, "Families and selection in colonial Horsham, Victoria, Australia 1888," *Bulletin* 14 (1984): 27–59.

the statistical over-representation of working-class and Aboriginal men in any viable way: dismissing it under the auspices of the mantra that domestic violence is a cross-class, race and ethnicity phenomenon, he argued, was insufficient, inattentive to socialised processes and lacking in analysis of surveillance and policing. For Evans, the challenge remained to account for the "historical ubiquity of largely male-derived violence" without "making scapegoats of all men" and instead "directing social scrutiny towards the workings of patriarchy, capitalism, sexism and racism, of the hierarchical nuclear family and monopolistic heterosexuality".[48]

While it is hard to disagree with Evans about what the stakes are, it is perhaps not surprising that histories of domestic violence post-Allen and Saunders grew more modest in scope, at least temporarily and geographically, with a discernible move towards local case studies or more targeted research questions. A bibliographic note at the end of the 1994 re-publication of Saunders' essay in the collection *Pastiche* – a compilation of influential articles on nineteenth-century Australia – posited that "Historical analysis has not kept pace with the considerable analysis of domestic violence in its contemporary form".[49] In the mid-1990s this was certainly the case, but as this volume illustrates, historical scholarship on gendered violence has also grown in size, substance and sophistication since then, making it an opportune time to embark on a larger-scale history of domestic violence. The following and final section canvasses some more recent scholarship, continuing the central argument that a larger-scale feminist history of domestic violence is now both possible and timely.

What would a feminist history of domestic violence look like?

Any proposal to historicise and narrate domestic violence across a two hundred year-plus period would necessarily be a history that both synthesises existing historical work and generates new primary research. There are some models available for how to do this, such as Raelene Frances' 2007 history of prostitution,[50] and other histories of difficult themes in which women are primarily the victims and men the perpetrators, such as Joanna

48 Evans, "A gun in the oven," 215.

49 Saunders, *Pastiche*, 219.

50 Raelene Frances, *Selling Sex: A Hidden History of Prostitution* (Sydney: University of New South Wales Press, 2007).

Bourke's *Rape: A History from 1860 to the Present-Day.*[51] In addition to seeking out such models, previous historical scholarship on domestic violence in Australia has provided entry points and guidance, ranging from quite specific questions – for example, how concerned were first-wave feminists with the problem of male violence in the home,[52] – to larger ones, such as how did the aftermath of the First World War shape understandings of, and responses to, domestic violence.[53] The extent to which domestic violence is a primarily working-class phenomenon has also preoccupied historians, not to mention past and present contemporary observers. More generally, historians have been interested in the extent to which unique Australian conditions, such as a masculinist culture resulting from a demographic imbalance, could account for violence against women, including sexual assault[54] and wife desertion.[55] Still, Australia's history of domestic violence has hardly been so peculiar as to escape comparison. Carolyn Ramsey has argued, for example, that violent husbands in the American West and Australia were subject to sustained, though largely ineffectual, attempts to punish violence against women as part of a larger colonial project to civilise men at the turn of the nineteenth to twentieth century.[56] From another direction, as can be charted in the ongoing activism and scholarship of Judy Atkinson,[57] the much higher than average rates of violence against Indigenous women and children have been increasingly comprehended in a comparative settler colonial framework, including historically.

As when Saunders and Allen were first researching, the public space has opened up again in such a way that invites a feminist history of domestic violence, and this time there is also a massive archive of feminist knowledge production about domestic violence that demands both historicisation

51 Joanna Bourke, *Rape: A History from 1860 to the Present Day* (London: Virago, 2008).

52 Jo Aitken, "'The horrors of matrimony among the masses': Feminist representations of wife beating in England and Australia, 1870–1914," *Journal of Women's History* 19, no. 4 (2007): 107–131.

53 Elizabeth Nelson, "The First World War, returned soldiers and understandings of domestic violence in Australia," *Journal of Women's History* 19, no. 4 (2007), 83–106.

54 Kate Gleeson, "From centenary to the Olympics, gang rape in Sydney," *Current Issues in Criminal Justice* 16, no. 2 (2004): 183–201.

55 Christina Twomey, *Deserted and Destitute: Motherhood, Wife Desertion & Colonial Welfare* (Melbourne: Australian Scholarly Publishing, 2002).

56 Carolyn B. Ramsey, "Domestic violence and state intervention in the American West and Australia, 1860–1930," *Indiana Law Journal* 86 (2011): 185.

57 Judy Atkinson, "Intimate partner abuse and Indigenous peoples," in *Intimate partner abuse and health professionals: New approaches to domestic violence*, ed. Gwenneth Roberts, Kelsey Hegarty and Gene Feder (Edinburgh: Churchill Livingstone Elsevier, 2006), 197–212.

and historical intervention. Some of this work on the domestic violence services movement has already been done, particularly of refuges, and these are histories that have important and ongoing utility within a shifting and often dispiriting policy context that has seen feminist-run services reduced and compromised.[58] A wider history of domestic violence promises to situate and analyse these histories of specific feminist interventions, usually dated from the mid-1970s on, within a much broader narrative of activism, whether such responses were explicitly identified as "feminist" or not. A broader history, in turn, benefits from the rich empirical work already conducted, including oral history;[59] the ongoing analysis feminist scholars have offered of state responses to violence against women and children;[60] and from critiques of the feminist refuge movement, including from Indigenous and non-white women.[61]

Any feminist history of domestic violence embarked on in the contemporary moment, including from Australia, must engage with the emergence of intersectionality as a theoretical framework, an approach that has its origins both in black feminist thought and in a critique of domestic violence service provision.[62] In Australia, second-wave feminism in its various forms was roundly rejected or criticised by Indigenous women on a number of grounds, such as the perceived failure of white feminists to recognise the historic and ongoing impact of colonialism on Aboriginal families, including "attempts made over decades by welfare administrations to separate Aboriginal women and use them against their

58 For example, see: Suellen Murray, *More than refuge: Changing responses to domestic violence* (Perth: University of Western Australia Press, 2002); Jacqui Theobald, "Women's refuges and the state in Victoria, Australia: A campaign for secrecy of address," *Women's History Review* 23, no. 1 (2014): 60–81; Jacqui Theobald, Suellen Murray and Judith Smart, *From the Margins to the Mainstream: The Domestic Violence Services Movement, Victoria, 1974–2016* (Melbourne: Melbourne University Press, 2017).

59 Jacqui Theobald, "Feminist oral history and the Victorian domestic violence services movement," *Australian Feminist Studies* 28, no. 78 (2013): 364–374.

60 For example, see: Ruth Phillips, "Undoing an activist response: Feminism and the Australian government's domestic violence policy," *Critical Social Policy* 26, no. 1 (2006): 192–219; Anastasia Powell and Suellen Murray, "Children and domestic violence: Constructing a policy problem in Australia and New Zealand," *Social & Legal Studies* 17, no. 4 (2008): 453–473.

61 For example, see: Tikka Jan Wilson, "Feminism and institutionalized racism: Inclusion and exclusion at an Australian feminist refuge," *Feminist Review* 52, no. 1 (1996): 1–26.

62 Kimberlé Crenshaw, "Mapping the margins: Intersectionality, identity politics, and violence against women of color," *Stanford Law Review* 43, no. 6 (1991): 1241–1299.

families".[63] Part of this wide-ranging critique then included a rejection of mainstream feminist approaches to domestic violence and the development of alternatives to the women's-only feminist refuge and the criminal justice system.[64] Taking cues from scholarship and activism by Aboriginal women, any wide-ranging history of domestic violence in Australia would need to be mindful of the need to incorporate Aboriginal women into this general history without diluting the specificity of their experiences or their critiques of mainstream feminism. It would also require sustained attention to the ways violence against Indigenous women has been normalised within the discourses, institutions and practices of settler colonialism.[65]

More generally, a feminist history of domestic violence should set, acknowledge and work productively within its limitations. It may seem axiomatic that such a history would focus mainly on women, particularly given that women have been and continue to be the most likely victims of domestic violence.[66] Yet part of the history of domestic violence also includes increased recognition of different forms and relationships – the emergence of the term "intimate partner violence" addresses violence occurring in homosexual relationships and violence against men, while expanded definitions of domestic and/or family violence stress that its forms and effects are not exclusively physical and/or directly targeted, particularly given the ongoing impact on children who grew up in a violent household. When it comes to children in particular, feminism has been implicated in ongoing silence about or neglect of child victims and survivors. Arguably an equally strong case could be presented that violence by adults against children is a major social and historical issue deserving its own history *or* that children should sit at the centre of a feminist history of domestic violence. In contrast, it is easier to argue that men should primarily be addressed within a feminist history of domestic violence as perpetrators rather than victims as this reflects the demographic reality, while also speaking to one of the primary aims of an explicitly feminist history of the issue: to understand

---

63 Jackie Huggins, "A contemporary view of Aboriginal women's relationship to the white women's movement," in *Australian Women*, 70.

64 Heather Nancarrow, "In search of justice for domestic and family violence: Indigenous and non-Indigenous Australian women's perspectives," *Theoretical Criminology*, 10, no. 1 (2006): 87–106.

65 Behrendt, "Consent in a (neo)colonial society."

66 Peta Cox, *Violence Against Women: Additional analysis of the Australian Bureau of Statistics' personal safety survey, 2012*, Horizons Research Report, no. 1 (Sydney: ANROWs Horizons, 2015), 31. The 2012 personal safety survey, for instance, found that 16.8 per cent of Australian women have experienced violence at the hands of a former or current partner, compared to 5.1 per cent of men.

domestic violence in the context of historical and ongoing gender and other intersecting inequalities.

Finally, there is the question of evidence. Recent public discussions recognise the problem of secrecy, silence and shame at the heart of ongoing domestic violence. And while this is exacerbated by the absence of an overarching history, no history can definitively account for the prevalence and scale of what is paradigmatically a largely "behind closed doors" phenomenon. What feminist historians can do is raise questions about historical and ongoing silence and erasure, politicising both the past and the present in feminist terms. Saunders and Allen each recognised that the existing archive can only hint at the scale and nature of violence against women, and that historical amnesia about domestic violence – captured in the reiteration that it is a problem that is everywhere and nowhere, circuiting in and out of public view – should be traced and explained. Indeed, Allen influentially theorised back in 1986 that any historical practice that could not acknowledge and account for silence in the archive was not compatible with feminist aims, and that feminists seeking to engage with history continue to develop their own epistemologies.[67] Since then, there have been significant theoretical and empirical developments that have expanded the possibilities of a feminist history of domestic violence. Yet as Kathyrn M. Hunter cautioned recently, the challenges that Allen identified back in 1986 remain, perhaps even more so in an era of mass digitisation and "ultra-empiricism".[68] Thus both Allen and Saunders remain guiding lights, serving to remind feminist historians that our task is not only to preface contemporary discussions of domestic violence, but to transform them.

---

67 Judith Allen, "Evidence and silence: Feminism and the limits of history," in *Feminist Challenges: Social and Political Theory*, ed. Carole Pateman and Elizabeth Gross (Sydney: Allen & Unwin, 1986), 173–189.

68 Kathryn M. Hunter, "Silence in noisy archives: Reflections on Judith Allen's 'Evidence and silence – Feminism and the limits of history,' (1986) in the era of mass digitisation," *Australian Feminist Studies* 32, no. 91–92 (2017): 202–212, 204.

Chapter 2

DISCOVERING VIOLENCE IN THE FAMILY

Tanya Evans

In early 2016 a domestic violence survivor described family violence as a "silent tsunami" engulfing Australia,[1] its effects rippling out to overwhelm not just its immediate victims, but their wider networks of family and friends.[2] Many have difficulty admitting experiences of violence to their loved ones, let alone to the police or courts.[3] Meanwhile, those who observe violence from outside the family unit still often struggle to describe it to others.[4] Having worked on the history of the family for over two decades, I remain shocked by the many terrifying tales of domestic violence I unearth in my research on families in Britain and Australia from the eighteenth century to the present.

My collaborative research with Australian family historians continues to reveal the fascinating relationship between past and present, including

1 Rebecca Curtin, "Australian families suffering 'silent war' of domestic violence says advocate," *ABC News*, 18 May 2016, accessed 14 June 2018, http://www.abc.net.au/news/2016-05-18/australian-families-suffering-silent-war-of-domestic-violence/7422844.

2 Wendy O'Brien and Kate Fitz-Gibbon, "'Silent victims': Royal Commission recommends better protections for child victims of family violence," *The Conversation*, 1 April 2016, accessed 14 June 2018, http://theconversation.com/silent-victims-royal-commission-recommends-better-protections-for-child-victims-of-family-violence-56801.

3 "Hear them speak," *Guardian Labs*, n.d., accessed 19 December 2017, https://www.theguardian.com/nab-more-that-matters/ng-interactive/2017/dec/07/hear-them-speak-victims-of-domestic-violence-share-their-stories#/.

4 Sarah Wendt, "Why don't we speak up when we see signs of domestic violence?" *The Conversation*, 1 October 2014, accessed 14 June 2018, https://theconversation.com/why-dont-we-speak-up-when-we-see-signs-of-domestic-violence-32022.

the ways in which contemporary family historians are challenging the silences around women's lives in the past. I wonder how much the high-profile media and political campaign led by Rosie Batty since 2015 has heightened people's interest in the broader history of domestic violence? Batty, whose 11-year-old son Luke was murdered by his father in 2014, became Australian of the Year the following year. A prominent campaigner, she has played a crucial role in bringing domestic violence into the public eye. Many family historians I have communicated with note Batty's role in their understanding of domestic violence in contemporary Australia. The attention attracted by her campaign has fed their thirst for knowledge and reframed their understanding of partner violence, past and present. This chapter suggests that we need to recognise the opportunities for knowledge acquisition available to us in this historical moment, and then use it to acknowledge and document the long history of domestic violence in Australia – the structural circumstances that results in the ongoing perpetration of violence – to figure out how it can end. Might confronting family histories of violence in the past help us become more willing to begin conversations about violence in the present?

The accounts of domestic violence unearthed by family historians are often horrifically shocking. I am still particularly haunted by the episodes of one victim's life revealed to me by one of her descendants. A chapter of *Fractured Families: Life on the Margins in Colonial NSW* was structured around the life-story of Jane Kelly Digby, an Irish orphan famine girl.[5] Jane arrived in New South Wales with her sister at the age of 19 from Athlone Westmeath in 1849. She settled in Yass and worked as a domestic servant. Here, she courted, cohabited with and later married Thomas Digby, a man who became so violent towards her that she was hospitalised.

At a maintenance hearing in 1857, Jane claimed that their relationship soured when Thomas asked her to bring a charge of rape against one of his employees. She refused to do so. In response, he punished her by tying her to what she referred to in court as his "triangles". He had told her "they were used for punishment in the old times of the Colony". After tying her up, using a knife, he stripped her of her clothes and beat her with a whip that Jane claimed "he must have made for the purpose". Following a brutal and sustained attack, Jane left her five children with their father to seek urgent medical care.[6]

5 Tanya Evans, *Fractured Families: Life on the Margins in Colonial NSW* (Sydney: New South, 2015).

6 "Police reports," *Goulburn Herald and County of Argyle Advertiser*, 30 December 1857, 2.

She travelled twenty kilometres into Goulburn where the Church of England minister Reverend Sowerby helped her obtain admission to the local hospital. Her injuries required immediate surgery by Dr Hanford and she remained in hospital for three weeks. Following this violent assault, she told the local court that she was too afraid to return to live with Thomas. At the time of this ordeal she was six weeks pregnant.

The foetus survived the beating, and by the time the case came to court she had been delivered of the child. Jane claimed that she wanted to care for the infant and the five children she had borne by Thomas. However, he would not provide her with maintenance if she lived apart from him, and she could not afford to live independently of him. Forced to leave not only Thomas but also her children, as the lack of maternal rights was another factor that inhibited women from leaving abusive husbands, Jane began a cohabitational relationship with another man with whom she had another five children. He was not a good choice either. He eventually deserted her and she walked to Sydney from Yass with three of her children to seek relief. All became dependent upon The Benevolent Society for charity.[7]

Jane's life remained desperate following her assault and abandonment. She struggled with alcoholism and a feisty temper, slipping in and out of gaol and other asylums for the rest of her life. She eventually died of tuberculosis in St Vincent's Hospital at the young age of forty-two. Despite living a fraught life, it deserves to be remembered so that we understand the limited options she and thousands of poor women like her – with little education, skill and family support networks – had in a colony where there was no poor law and sparse charitable provision. Poor women's lives are still structured by similar constraints.[8] Jane's options were limited by poverty but also the societal silences around domestic violence. In spite of living a truly disadvantaged life, she still had the wherewithal to speak out against her husband's violence. Women today should have more capacity than Jane to publicly indict and leave abusive partners, but it is clear to contemporary researchers and campaigners that many still do not.

---

7 Ibid.; "Police reports," *Goulburn Herald and County of Argyle Advertiser,* 2 January 1858, 3.

8 Claire M. Renzetti and Vivian M. Larkin, "Economic stress and domestic violence," *National Online Resource Center on Violence Against Women*, September 2009, accessed 14 June 2018, https://vawnet.org/material/economic-stress-and-domestic-violence.

Domestic violence and family history

One of Jane's descendants – her great-great-granddaughter – Julie Poulter wrote to me after reading *Fractured Families* to tell me how much she appreciated the focus on the "failures" of colonial society. She had always enjoyed the stories her grandmother told her about their lives and relatives. When still a teenager she took detailed notes as they spoke. This laid the groundwork for her love of history. Julie acknowledges her family history research as a feminist project:

> Perhaps why I have become so attached to Jane's story is informed by my own mother's family history. ... On my maternal side I come from a long line of strong independent women. Starting from me. I guess it is something each of us has seen our mother do and it was a normal thing to have a mother both work before and after marriage... I am the beneficiary of those who have come before me and fought for equal rights... researching history and genealogy gives me a more rounded view of how marriage/motherhood/fatherhood has changed over time and allows me to advocate for a fairer system all round for fathers, mothers and most importantly, the children.[9]

Julie works full-time in medical administration but studies history part-time at the University of New England. She hopes to become a professional historian one day. She began her research using the support of her local historical society in Dubbo. She wrote up her family history after many years of research and travel, both nationally and internationally. "Family history research is almost my favourite thing in the world to do!" Julie claims. "I have decided to not have children, and as a result have much more time to devote to the family history cause! This will be my legacy." Julie feels like she "owes" her female ancestors the benefit of her research skills and the time it takes to reveal their life stories.

It is due to the diligence and detective work of an army of family historians like Julie that we can learn about Jane Kelly's life and the lives of women like her. Women like Jane Kelly left their mark on the historical record because of the extent of their desperation and the deprivation caused by domestic violence. Family history has allowed people like Julie to craft stories about the past in order to help them understand how their own lives and the lives of others in the present are shaped by the past. Julie is giving voice to these women in the present, when past societies tried to silence

9 Julie Poulter email correspondence, September 2014.

them and normalise domestic violence by marginalising women's voices and lives. Julie wants our collaborative research to show that someone cares about these individuals in contemporary Australia – that they mean something, not just to her, but also to others. Family historians like Julie are also enabling contemporary Australians to problematise domestic violence in the past by calling out violence as violence – as deviant behavior in colonial Australia as well as now.

Revealing stories like these can teach us valuable lessons about history and humanity, but not all family historians agree that this is the case. Graeme Landsown, another descendant of Jane and Thomas Digby's who is also a practicing family historian, wrote to me recently claiming to be offended by the way in which I revealed this story of domestic violence. He told me that:

> While I do not condone Thomas' actions, they need to be placed in the context of the social expectations of the day and not in the morality and social values expected in today's society. This needs to be a point made in your future discussions about both Jane's and Thomas' circumstances.
>
> They were both not perfect in their behaviour and actions.[10]

Unlike Julie, it seems to me that Graeme wants to normalise the incidence of domestic violence towards women in colonial Australia even though media reports at the time were deeply critical of Thomas' actions. As a feminist historian it is important for me to challenge this assumption. This is why I continue to collaborate with family historians and to ask them about the impact of discovering domestic violence in their family histories.

Challenging the silences around domestic violence

Recent researchers and popular writers, keen to shift our focus from histories of prominent men to learning more about the women in their lives, are also unearthing domestic violence in well-to-do colonial Australian families. For example, Kerrie Davies asks readers to think about why generations of biographers have glossed over Henry Lawson's violence towards his wife after their secret marriage in 1896.[11] Lawson's publisher

10 Graeme Lansdowne, email communication, 2 December 2017.

11 Kerrie Davies, *A Wife's Heart: The Untold Story of Bertha and Henry Lawson* (St Lucia: University of Queensland Press, 2017).

had tried to intervene to prevent Henry's marriage to Bertha, knowing how prone Henry was to excess drinking, a vile temper and violence. Their Divorce Court files detail the ways in which he hid money to pay to feed his alcoholism and numerous terrible examples of violence as their marriage broke down after 7 years:

> My husband has during three years and upwards been a habitual drunkard and habitually been guilty of cruelty towards me. My affidavit consists of the acts and matters following. That my husband during the last three years struck me in the face and about the body and blacked my eye and hit me with a bottle and attempted to stab me and pulled me out of bed when I was ill and purposely made a noise in my room when I was ill and pulled my hair and repeatedly used abusive and insulting language to me and was guilty of divers [sic] other acts of cruelty to me whereby my health and safety are endangered.

The couple eventually opted for judicial separation and, in return for maintenance, Bertha agreed to drop the domestic violence charges. What choice did she have? Friends were mostly unwilling to support her; while she cared for the couple's two children, she struggled to work. She needed the famous poet's money to survive. Few women were able to escape the consequences of domestic violence in colonial Australian families because they did not have the resources or confidence to do so.

The phenomenally popular family history television program *Who Do You Think You Are?* (*WDYTYA?*), I have argued, brings social history and the history of women to an audience of millions of viewers around the world.[12] It has also contributed to knowledge production about domestic violence in the past. My role in relation to media productions of history stems from my historical expertise in family relations, with a focus on illegitimacy. This subject has provided fertile ground, especially in Britain, for television productions over the past few years. I helped to make *Jamelia: Shame about Single Mums* (2011) the British Broadcasting Corporation (BBC), and I assisted Wall to Wall television with the British production of *Who Do You Think You Are?* (*WDYTYA?*), a production company which also makes *Secrets of the Workhouse* (2013–) and *Long Lost Family* (2011–). These programmes – like my own historical research – are designed to destroy myths about

12 Tanya Evans, "Who do you think you are? Historical television consultancy," *Australian Historical Studies* 46, no. 3 (2015): 454–467; Evans, *Fractured Families*, 250.

the so-called "traditional family" and questions "authoritative" accounts of family life in the past. Television is superbly placed to do this.

Television, like family history, can facilitate the democratisation of historical knowledge, in both its production and consumption.[13] While there are clearly limits to the format of *WDYTYA?*, its strength lies in the way it demonstrates the complicated, ambiguous, messy details of family life in many celebrities' pasts as well as their present lives. The programme encourages a critical understanding of the past. We learn that there was no "golden age" of the family in any national context. It does not present an unequivocal, authoritative, "easy" or "soft" history, a charge some historians have laid at the feet of other examples of history on television.[14] One of the most important messages of *WDYTYA?* is that fractured, complicated, messy families were as common in the past as they are now. It makes clear the provisionality of our knowledge and how history, people and documents have the capacity to tell many lies. One of its real strengths is the diverse ways in which the history of women, especially marginalised women, is represented. It also reveals a hidden history of domestic violence to millions of viewers.

For example, famous Australian journalist Ray Martin, whose mother escaped violence at the hands of his father when he was eleven, has been one subject of *WDYTYA?*. Ray continues to involve himself in hard-hitting programmes about domestic violence in contemporary Australia in tandem with Rosie Batty.[15] After his parents' split, Ray never saw his father again and thought of him as dead for the rest of his life. He grew up knowing very little about his paternal side of the family, and as a self-confessed "history nut" was excited to follow the research undertaken by the *WDYTYA?* team as they constructed their narrative using aspects of his and his family's life story.[16] Other subjects of *WDYTYA?*, such as Delta Goodrem, have confronted unknown histories of family violence that have been unearthed.[17] Programs like these encourage viewers to question the

---

13 Paul Ashton and Paula Hamilton, *Australians at the Crossroads: Australians and the Past* (Halstead: Sydney, 2013).

14 Ruth Balint, "Where are the historians?" *Inside Story*, 30 July 2009, accessed 14 June 2018, http://insidestory.org.au/where-are-the-historians/; Tristram Hunt, "Time bandits," *Guardian*, 10 September 2007, accessed 14 June 2018, https://www.theguardian.com/media/2007/sep/10/mondaymediasection.television1.

15 *Dark Secrets: Australia's Hidden Shame*. News production special on domestic violence. Prime7, 28 May 2017.

16 *Who Do You Think You Are?* Episode 8, Season 7. SBS, 22 September 2015.

17 *Who Do You Think You Are?* Episode 3, Season 8. SBS, 9 September 2016.

past and realise the limits of our historical knowledge. Family history has a similar radical potential to disrupt our certainties about the past as it allows individuals to use new knowledge about the past to reframe our understanding of the present.

History and gender

When family historians learn about the incidence and prevalence of domestic violence in the past through their own family histories, it transforms their understandings of domestic violence in the present. We need to better understand family historians as historical subjects and how historical research has transformed their lives. If academic historians revalue family history then we can continue to subvert the gendered structure of the discipline of history, as well as the gendered social order. We need to embrace the positive political consequences of an emotional engagement with people's historical subjects and the broader social impact that engagement can produce.

My research has revealed the symbiotic relationship between family history, social history and women's history. Family historians are passionate about the lives of "ordinary" people in the past and they revel in their emotional attachment to their subjects. They feel like family history "speaks to them" in a way that other forms of history fail to do. In their eyes, "national history" tends to be "male and political" and does not engage them in the ways that social history – with its focus on women, the ordinary and the everyday – does. They want national history to become "personal" so that they can connect to it. This means they will learn more and engage with the past more passionately.[18] As Jeanette Tsoulos, an active member of the Australian Jewish historical community in Sydney and past president of the Australian Jewish Genealogical Society, told me: "[T]he written history of the nation or globe takes no account of family history unless it's that of kings and queens. It's invisible, like women's lives." When women's lives are marginalised in these ways, gender-based violence is much more easily perpetrated.[19]

Family history is understood as bringing women's lives to the fore when other forms of history marginalise them. Many of the family historians I have worked with, like Julie Poulter, are self-consciously informed by feminist beliefs. In response to my question: "Has your research challenged

18 Barbara Barclay, survey response, 2016.

19 Jeanette Tsolus, survey response, 2016.

the way that you think about the history of the family or national history more broadly?" Maria stated:

> For sure. I have become more aware of the role of women, especially in relation to their work. I think national history emphasises women's roles in history as mothers and wives. ... My family history research has challenged my previous views of women in national history.[20]

Many family historians in contemporary Australia (and around the world) undertake genealogical research for similar reasons. They "despair at how hard it is to find ancestral women in my family."[21] The microhistories they produce have become significant for their present lives and the lives of women more broadly.

Gay Horsbrugh was born in 1958 and became a family historian in the early 2000s. She works as a health planner within a local health district in NSW. In her family history research, she has "mainly been interested in... the female side of the family as usually existing trees focussed on men." When the wife of one of her ancestors left him, this precipitated acts of domestic violence:

> He pursued her through the local press, denigrated her and then burnt down his father-in-law's house. He then spent years justifying these acts by saying that his wife deserved it. This form of domestic violence and justification continues to resonate with the current world. This behaviour is inconsistent with the values I hold.[22]

Family historians like Gay have come much closer to understanding the impact of legislative reform on individual lives in the past and present through their family history research. Gay's parents divorced before Prime Minister Gough Whitlam introduced the Family Law Act in 1975 and she relished the opportunity to read her parent's divorce papers as part of her research:

> I realised how unfair those laws were for the individuals concerned – in revealing their lives and in having to do "illegal acts" to get a divorce; and the value of more progressive legislation.

20 Maria Northcote, survey response, 2016.

21 Anne Cavenagh, survey response, 2016.

22 Gay Horsbrugh, survey response, 2016.

Family historians are often criticised for seeking out the past lives of their forebears for nostalgic reasons. However, many researchers love discovering the secrets and lies their research reveals and the lessons they learn about past and present lives, as well as the impact of legislative change on individual lives, on their journeys.

My current research is focused on the practice and meanings of family history in Australia, England and Canada. Using survey data and oral histories with family historians, my research is detailing the motivations for undertaking family history research and the emotional impact of discoveries. What secrets and lies are contemporary family historians revealing and how have the meanings of those secrets and lies changed over time?[23] I am struck by how many contemporary family historians in Australia have described the shock and shame of discovering ancestors who have been violent towards their spouses. I think responses to domestic violence have changed dramatically in recent years. Yet if people have difficulties confronting the realities of domestic violence in the past, how much more difficult must it be to acknowledge its presence in the present?[24]

The impact of discovering domestic violence in family trees

The reach of the Internet has opened up archives and the potential of historical research to anyone with a computer. The lines between the production and consumption of history have become increasingly blurred as local and family historians share methods and data with researchers around the world. Popular historical programs and resources, such as *WDYTYA?* (UK 2004–; Aus 2008–; US 2013–) and Ancestry.com (est. 1983) continue to spawn global franchises in response to an apparently insatiable popular historical appetite as people learn more about the past lives of their forbears. Family history has become one of the world's most popular leisure pursuits, understood by sociologists to be a form of "serious leisure", a means of both

23 Ashley Barnwell, "Convict shame to convict chic: Intergenerational memory and family histories," *Memory Studies* (published online first 24 May 2017): 1–14. DOI: 10.1177/1750698017709870

24 NSW Government, "Focus topic: Under-reporting of domestic violence assaults," in *Women in NSW 2013* (Sydney: Family & Community Services, Women NSW, 2013); "Fact file: Domestic violence in Australia," *ABC News* 15 April 2016, accessed 14 June 2018, http://www.abc.net.au/news/2016-04-06/fact-file-domestic-violence-statistics/7147938.

enjoyment and education.[25] This significant educative function among lifelong learners, at all stages of the life-cycle, is often unappreciated and can have an enormously positive impact on people in the present day.[26]

These "ordinary" researchers around the world are linking the past to the present in powerful ways, transforming their understanding of themselves and the wider world. But there has been little appreciation of the broader impact of their work. As I have argued, we need to trouble the academic disdain targeted at family and local historians and recognise the power of history at a familial and local level to transform people's historical consciousness and present politicisation.[27]

Research on family history provides insight into how history is undertaken, imagined and discussed and gives us understanding into the potential social and political uses of history. Global national surveys like Ashton and Hamilton's in Australia, but also those undertaken in Canada and elsewhere, have revealed the extent of "popular history-making" and the primacy of family history, confirming that the personal and familial remain "ordinary' people's 'principal focus for connection with the past'".[28] These historians have shown that family history enables people to construct a sense of community belonging and it can have a political purpose. For many groups — such as immigrants and Indigenous peoples, for example, in Australia, Canada and the United States — family histories have existed as counter narratives to dominant national histories from which they have frequently been excluded. In the process, they are challenging our understandings of "history" and "the nation" – and reimagining our communities as a result. Family historians are also using their research to challenge the

25 Robert A. Stebbins, *Serious Leisure: A Perspective for our Time* (New Brunswick: Transaction, 2007). See also: *The Serious Leisure Perspectives*, n.d., accessed 14 June 2018, http://www.seriousleisure.net/concepts.html.

26 Wendy Bottero, "Practising family history: 'Identity' as a category of social practice," *British Journal of Sociology* 66, no. 3 (2015): 534–556; Wendy Bottero, "Who do you think they were? How family historians make sense of social position and inequality in the past," *British Journal of Sociology* 63, no. 1 (2012): 54–74.

27 Tanya Evans, "Love thy neighbour: Local and community history," in *What is Public History Globally?* ed. Paul Ashton and Alex Trapeznik (London: Bloomsbury, 2018).

28 Paul Ashton and Paula Hamilton, *History at the Crossroads: Australians and the Past* (Ultimo, NSW: Halstead Press, 2010); Margaret Conrad, Kadriye Ercikan, Gerald Friesen, Jocelyn Létourneau, Delphin Muise, David Northrup, and Peter Seixas, *Canadians and their Pasts: The Pasts Collective* (Toronto: University of Toronto Press, 2013); Tanya Evans and Anna Clark, "Family history and transnational historical consciousness," in *Transnationalism, Nationalism and Australian History*, ed. Anna Clark, Anne Rees and Alecia Simmonds (Singapore: Palgrave Macmillan, 2017), 167–178.

gendering of history and the omission of women from the history they have been taught.

There was a time when genealogists were coded in particular ways – middle-aged, bespectacled, middle-class and usually female. They often still are. As a feminist historian I want to explore why family history is gendered in particular ways. Why are family historians understood to be women when we frequently rely on anecdote rather than sound empirical evidence to make our case? I think family history has been much derided by professional historians and others because it is mostly undertaken by women of a certain age, and at a local and familial rather than national and global, micro rather than macro level. My work is focused on revaluing the work of family historians and continuing to question the easy division some people make between academic and amateur, objective and emotional, micro and macro histories.

Caryn Patterson was born in Moree but she has spent most of her life living in Sydney where she became a family historian in 1985. She has had powerful emotional reactions to her research. It's "made me cry to learn just how hard the lives of some of my ancestors were (for example, my 3 times great grandmother was subjected to abuse from a very violent alcoholic husband … and he was jailed numerous times for it)." This has shocked her; because some of her ancestors, "were subjected to some awful treatment," she reflects, "I think I've learned to be much more aware of the way people live and their right to live the way they chose."[29] My research has revealed that many family historians like Caryn have become increasingly sensitive and empathetic to cases of domestic violence since discovering its existence in her own family tree.

Another passionate family historian who works in education, Margaret Nelly,[30] was born in Darlinghurst, Sydney in 1963 and began working on her family history in the 1990s. Through a growing interest in social history and the history of "ordinary"/commoners like her ancestors, she felt herself becoming more "connected" to her ancestors. She feels that this personal connection enables her to understand the past, and especially domestic violence in the past, better:

> I have found so many heart-wrenching, sad stories that have increased my empathy for my ancestors. Sometimes I also get annoyed and feel

---

29 Caryn Paterson, survey response, 2016.

30 Nelly is one of the few participants who has asked to be anonymised.

> shameful when I find out an ancestor beat up his wife so badly that she was expected to die.[31]

Shame as a response to research revelations was particularly strong with respect to examples of domestic violence. Australian family historians are, for the most part, no longer ashamed about discovering convict ancestry, illegitimacy and mixed raced relationships in their families' past, but they are embarrassed about discovering domestic violence. Karin Davis grew up in Victoria and she became a family historian when she was 14 years of age in 1970. She was desperate to learn more details about her father's side of the family but all her relatives were "so close mouthed". She:

> Wanted to make them understand that ANYTHING and EVERYTHING is ok by my standards and not to feel shame or fear – I failed.

In response to my question – "Do you think emotional responses to family history have changed over time?" – she replied:

> Yes, whilst we no longer stigmatise illegitimacy, we do as a society however have a far less tolerant attitude to family violence. This may have been more accepted in the past (a husband's right and all that) but now I am sure a woman may well feel the object of ridicule in some ways for not leaving an abusive partner. After all, it is "easy to leave" people think...[32]

She claims that her work as a family historian has enabled her to become more empathetic, "it has made me much more understanding of what is sometimes termed people's 'shortcomings'". She is not alone among my cohort of family historians who believe passionately that their research has made them more empathetic generally.

Les De Belin likes discovering the skeletons in his family's closet but he doesn't understand why people get so emotional about these sorts of discoveries. He's unearthed Aboriginal ancestry:

> love affairs resulting in divorces, illegitimate children, criminal offences, and even my 2 x great grandfather attempting to murder my x great grandmother by cutting her throat. That was something nobody in the family knew of until I found it in an old newspaper.

31 Margaret Nelly (anonymised), survey response, 2016.

32 Karin Davis, survey response, 2016.

While he disputed people's emotional responses to family history discoveries he cannot understand why more people don't undertake their family history in order to learn more about the world.[33] He agrees that it remains a significant conduit to historical knowledge and understanding about the world in the present.

"Ordinary" family historians and "professional" feminist academic scholars are working in tandem to reveal many of these troubling stories of historical domestic violence. This is one of the many legacies of the women's liberation movement, when campaigners finally listened to the "quiet screaming" occurring behind closed doors during the 1970s. More and more research has revealed how these quiet screams have a long history and can be found among families of all classes, nations and races. Zora Simic's chapter reveals how her current research project on the history of domestic violence, shared with Ann Curthoys and Catherine Kevin, has a political and methodological purpose. She shows how the knowledge production spurred on by feminist academic historians in the 1980s was a vital phase in helping to label and generate campaigns for the rights of domestic violence victims. Let's use the knowledge production among celebrities, "ordinary", everyday people and millions of family historians across the globe, which has been perhaps partly created by the high-profile campaign against domestic violence led by Batty, to demand change for women and their children now and in the future.

---

33 Les De Belin, survey response, 2016.

Chapter 3

UNDERSTANDING ECONOMIC ABUSE AS DOMESTIC VIOLENCE

Alana Piper

In April 1890, Michael Barry was tried at the Rockhampton sittings of the Queensland Supreme Court for the murder of his wife Mary. Barry's lawyer called no witnesses during the trial.[1] The basic facts of the case were not in dispute. In February Barry had committed a violent attack on his wife that lasted several hours. Their eldest child, twelve-year-old Johanna, had tried to intervene and consequently was also assaulted by her father. Neighbours heard Mary's screams but had not interfered. Such disturbances were common in the Barry household.[2] When Barry emerged later that day a neighbour did ask him why the children were crying. He told her, "They will have something more to cry for before long. I gave her a beating last night and kicked her, and she is dead."[3] He then went to the police station and made a full confession of the events leading up to his wife's death.

Despite the clear evidence in the case, the jury ended up taking seventeen hours to reach a verdict. This would have been an unusually long deliberation even in a more ambiguous case; at the time, most juries were discharged if they failed to return a verdict within six hours. In the end, the judge practically ordered the jury to find the defendant guilty of murder, declaring that any attempt to acquit, or find him guilty of the lesser charge of manslaughter, would be an infamous betrayal of their oaths.[4] What excuse had Barry

---

1 "The West-street murder," *Morning Bulletin*, 25 April 1890, 4.

2 "Dreadful murder in Rockhampton," *Queensland Times, Ipswich Herald and General Advertiser*, 27 February 1890, 2.

3 R v Michael Barry, 24 April 1890, Item ID 3530, Queensland State Archives (hereafter QSA).

4 "The West-street murder," 4.

offered for his violence to prolong the jury deliberations? He asserted that his wife had stolen a money-purse containing £5 from him.

The circumstances of Barry's violence were disclosed in detail in his daughter Johanna's testimony. Johanna revealed that the night before Mary's death her mother had sent her to collect her father, who was lying drunk on the roadside. After Johanna got him home in a cab, he sent her younger sister to the hotel for more liquor. A short time later he complained that his purse was missing, and started to beat her mother. Johanna and Mary both fled the house to spend part of the night in a neighbour's yard, sneaking back inside during the early hours. When her father woke up, he began beating Mary again. The violence lasted some time, with Barry pausing occasionally to search for the purse or have a smoke. His contention during the trial was that his wife was a drunkard who had likely taken the money to buy beer. In colonial Queensland, female drunkenness was widely accepted by judges and juries as a justification for violence, even murder; similar clemency was also shown on the rarer occasions where women murdered drunken husbands.[5] Michael Barry, however, was an exception to this trend. Found guilty of murder, Barry was executed on 2 June 1890.

It was not unreasonable for Barry to presume that his case would receive a degree of leniency, if not exoneration by an all-male jury, similar as it was to many others (Figure 1). An almost identical incident would occur at Charters Towers in 1904, when August Voght was charged with beating his wife to death after discovering she had taken some coins from his purse. The jury took only fifteen minutes to reach a verdict of guilty of manslaughter with a recommendation to mercy on the grounds of the wife's alleged drunken habits.[6] The judge discharged Voght without sentence, leaving him free to marry again; in 1909 he was convicted of beating his new wife with a rope with an iron ring attached.[7] That Barry did not enjoy the same leniency as Voght was probably due to Johanna's staunch assertion that her mother had not taken the purse, or she would have produced it during the attack; while she confirmed that Mary at one point during the violence admitted taking the purse, Johanna stated that this was a ruse to try to stop the assault. Whatever the truth, the purse was found lying outside by a neighbour shortly after the murder.

5 Ruth McConnell and Steve Mullins, "'We had both been drinking since Christmas': Battered wives and dead abusive husbands in early colonial Rockhampton," *Journal of Australian Colonial History* 5 (2004): 100–119.

6 "Circuit court," *Northern Miner*, 3 October 1904, 6.

7 "Police court," *Evening Telegraph*, 12 January 1909, 5.

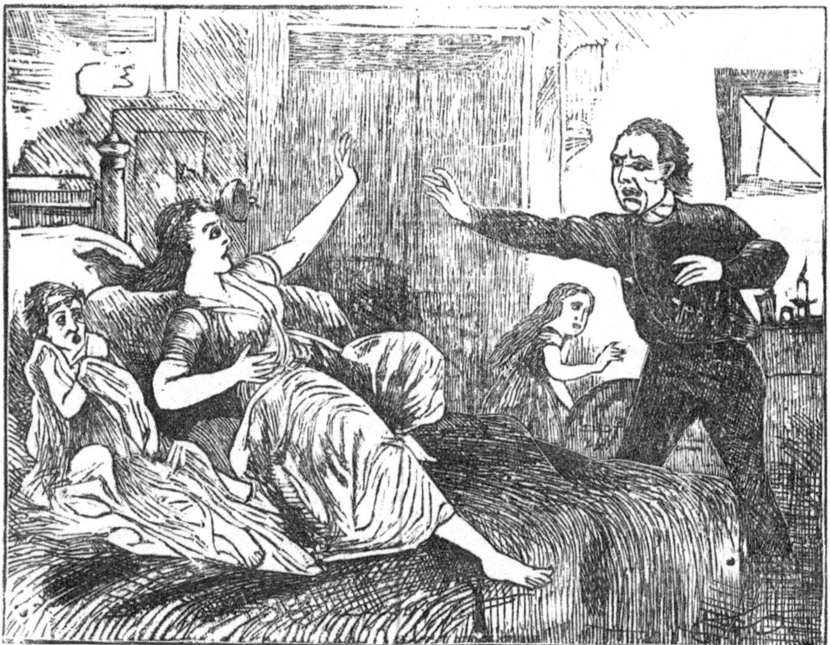

Figure 1. Drunken husband attacks wife while children watch.
Cartoon published in *Police News*, 29 April 1876, 1.
Image courtesy of the State Library of Victoria.

Today it is to be hoped that Barry's allegation would be seen not as a justification for his crime, but as an example of the type of unequal power relations – especially in matters of finance – that facilitate domestic violence. Over the last twenty-five years, economic abuse has increasingly been recognised as a form of domestic violence encompassing a variety of behaviours, including: preventing a partner's access to shared financial resources; controlling their acquisition of independent resources; and refusing to contribute to household expenses or child-rearing costs. Such abuse undercuts victims' security and independence, often with the intention of keeping them within the abusive relationship. But while research indicates economic abuse is widespread, it tends to be poorly understood and hard to recognise, even by those who experience it.[8]

Empirical research on economic abuse also remains limited, meaning the variety of behaviours that might be understood under this rubric are still

8 Emma Smallwood, *Stepping Stones: Legal Barriers to Economic Equality After Family Violence* (Melbourne: Women's Legal Service Victoria, 2015), 6.

evolving.[9] Beginning by outlining how economic inequality underpinned marriages in colonial society, this chapter contributes to this developing discussion by examining the different forms of economic abuse evident in cases heard by the Brisbane Court of Petty Sessions during the 1890s, a tumultuous period for both Australia's economy and gender relations. Such analysis underscores the important role that economic abuse has historically played in enabling domestic violence, and the ways in which such violence is facilitated by the attitudes towards women perpetuated by traditional understandings of what might be referred to as the "marriage bargain".

Female dependence and the marriage bargain

Historically, economic abuse was built into household gender relations. Men, as the traditional breadwinners, were seen as entitled to direct the household finances as they wished. Under the legal principle of *coverture*, their control extended to any property or earnings of their wife. It was only at the end of the nineteenth century that this condition was ameliorated to allow married women to own and control property in their own right. Queensland passed the *Married Women's Property Act* in 1890, just months after Mary Barry's murder. The other Australian colonies all passed similar legislation between 1870 and 1892.[10]

This legislation did little to change the perception and status of most women as financial dependents, although their dependence on male providers was seldom absolute. As early as 1890, about one-third of Australian women were working outside the home.[11] A considerable "informal" economy also existed that enabled married women to earn money from home by selling their services in everything from washing and sewing to teaching music and providing lodgings.[12] Nevertheless, most women's work was poorly remunerated, partly under the fallacious justification that women, supported by their fathers or husbands, did not need to rely on their own wages to keep themselves or their families.

---

9 Judy L. Postmus, Sara-Beth Plummer, Sarah McMahon, N. Shaanta Murshid, and Mi Sung Kim, "Understanding economic abuse in the lives of survivors," *Journal of Interpersonal Violence* 27, no. 3 (2012): 411.

10 *Married Women's Property Act* 1870 (VIC); 1879 (NSW); 1883 (TAS); 1884 (SA); 1892 (WA).

11 Beverley Kingston, *My Wife, My Daughter and Poor Mary Ann: Women and Work in Australia* (Melbourne: Thomas Nelson Australia, 1980), 7.

12 Raelene Frances, "Shifting barriers: Twentieth century women's labour patterns," in *Gender Relations in Australia: Domination and Negotiation*, ed. Kay Saunders and Raymond Evans (Marrickville: Harcourt Brace Jovanovich, 1992), 251.

While the ideal of companionate marriage became more dominant in this period, marriage was still understood in society and at law as a bargain in which men provided financial support in exchange for their wives' domestic and sexual services. Historian Katie Spearritt suggests that Queensland men took a particularly utilitarian view towards a wife's worth, regarding it as a means to forego the cost of servants and otherwise save in matters of household economy.[13] In 1882, Queensland newspaper *The Week* thus published a column advising men to marry on the grounds that wives' domestic labour could double their salary.[14] A woman who wrote to the weekly periodical *Queensland Figaro and Punch* three years later deemed the marriage bargain less beneficial to women; under a husband's control, she was denied the material comforts she enjoyed even while working as a lowly-paid teacher. Why, she queried, should girls "struggle to become the slave of a husband and children, and tie themselves to a man when they might be free and happy?"[15]

Public sensitivities to the gendered inequalities of marriage increased during the late colonial and early federation period, driven by transnational feminist rhetoric that equated marriage with economic and sexual slavery.[16] In 1904, this analogy was even drawn on by an Australian judge, who claimed the abuse and desertion of wives was becoming "a national crime", with men – in the name of marriage – treating women as they would not treat an African slave.[17] While men had achieved an eight-hour working day, *The Queenslander* complained, their wives laboured from dawn to dusk in onerous domestic duties.[18] Ignored in such rhetoric was the exploitation of the economic and sexual labour of non-white women in Australia, discussed elsewhere in this collection by Liz Conor and Rae Frances.

Albeit focused hegemonically on white experiences, the late colonial period saw a growing critique of women's economic position within marriage, partly driven by temperance organisations that blamed drink for male

---

13 Katie Spearritt, "The sexual economics of colonial marriage," in *On the Edge: Women's Experiences of Queensland*, ed. Gail Reekie (St Lucia: University of Queensland Press, 1994), 73.

14 "Advice to a young man," *Week*, 18 November 1882, 19.

15 "Some matrimonial advice," *Queensland Figaro and Punch*, 1 August 1885, 37.

16 "Should wives be penniless? A plea for pocket-money," *Brisbane Courier*, 17 December 1890, 7. For the comparison between marriage and slavery, see: Ana Stevenson, *The Woman as Slave in Nineteenth-Century American Social Movements* (Palgrave Macmillan, *forthcoming*).

17 "Dissolute husbands," *Darling Downs Gazette*, 18 November 1904, 3.

18 "Are wives 'supported'?" *Queenslander*, 5 March 1904, 6; "A strike of housewives," *Queenslander*, 30 June 1906, 4.

fiscal irresponsibility and domestic violence. A newspaper report on the murder of Mary Barry alluded to the wider role of economic relations in gender violence:

> There have been other cases in Rockhampton, in which the wife beater has been begged off by the woman who is dependent upon his wages for her living. The Rockhampton people are so accustomed to this sort of thing, that they look upon a man who is beating his wife as one specially licensed by the judges and magistrates to do as he pleases with his own property, provided he stops short at quenching the last vital spark.[19]

Female dependence thus encouraged a sense of entitlement among abusers who viewed wives as property, and inhibited the ability of wives to resist such treatment.

The economic difficulties faced by women wishing to escape marriages to violent men were given limited means of redress. Under the colonial legal system, legislation enabled deserted wives to sue errant husbands for maintenance. In 1858, New South Wales passed an amendment that meant a wife "compelled" to leave her home through violence might also be considered deserted. Queensland inherited these laws when it became a separate colony the following year. Yet as jurist Marcia Neave has observed, maintenance legislation was not only hard to enforce, but "entrenched women's dependency", thereby supporting conceptualisations of marital dynamics that underpinned men's abusive and controlling behaviours.[20]

Identifying economic abuse

Contemporary studies suggest that the vast majority of victims of intimate partner violence also experience economic abuse as part of a more general pattern of coercive control.[21] Quantifying historical levels of economic abuse and its overlap with other forms of domestic violence is difficult: not only did assaults routinely go unreported, but the details surrounding the crimes have often been lost even in cases that were brought to court. While depositions and newspaper reports preserve the stories of the most serious cases like the Barry murder, the majority of assaults were heard in the

19 "Vita sine literis mors est," *Western Champion*, 4 March 1890, 2.

20 Marcia Neave, "From difference to sameness: Law and women's work," *Melbourne University Law Review* 18 (1992): 773.

21 Postmus et al., "Understanding economic abuse in the lives of survivors," 411.

lower courts, which generally were not subject to extensive record-keeping or reporting. One exception was the Brisbane Court of Petty Sessions, for which detailed minute books from the 1890s remain extant. Even in these, witness statements about domestic assaults seldom offer insights into marital relations beyond the specific incident; the way such violence existed within a wider context of marital power relations was not of immediate interest to the courts. However, cases of wife desertion exposed more general marital troubles, including both physical and economic abuse.

Of 226 wife desertion cases brought before the Brisbane Petty Sessions between 1890 and 1899, witness depositions were preserved for 101 cases. In many of the others, prosecution was either withdrawn by the complainant or discontinued after their non-appearance in court (Table 1). Notably, in cases where testimonies were heard, many women had been compelled to leave their husbands rather than being deserted by them. Allegations of husbands committing physical violence were made in 41 of the cases where witness depositions survive. Intimations of economic abuse were also common, appearing in 47 cases. This figure likely points to a much higher experience of economic abuse within the community, given the prevailing acceptance of husbands' control over household finances. In women's recounting of the histories of their marriages, four types of abusive behaviour related to control of property or finances became apparent: failure to support during marriage (31 cases); financial or labour exploitation (7); economically-motivated violence (9); and post-separation economic abuse (12). A number of women were subject to more than one type of behaviour.

Table 1. Outcomes of wife desertion cases heard Brisbane Court of Petty Sessions, 1890–1899.

Outcome	No. of cases
Order of maintenance made	84
Withdrawn by complainant or dismissed on complainant's non-appearance	81
Dismissed on complainant accepting offer of reconciliation	5
Dismissal – other/unknown cause	38
Abandoned following adjournment of case	10
Non-appearance of defendant (warrant issued)	8
Total number of cases	**226**

Failure to support

The failure of husbands to provide material support to their wives and children during marriage was the most common economic abuse complained of in wife desertion. Some women alleged such abuse without citing physical violence. When Frances Slee brought her deserting husband to court in 1890 to seek support for her two children, for instance, she testified that he had ill-treated her during the marriage by keeping her without food.[22] In most cases however, women who alleged that their husbands had denied them access to money, food or other goods during their marriage also reported spousal assaults. Allegations of drunkenness frequently joined these; wives (as well as courts, temperance advocates and the media) blamed liquor as the root of most physical and economic mistreatment (figure 1). The narrative Kate Reid told the court when suing for maintenance seems typical: her husband spent his money on drink and became violent when drunk. Even before their separation, he had not provided for her in two years, during which time she relied on her sewing and teenage son for support.[23]

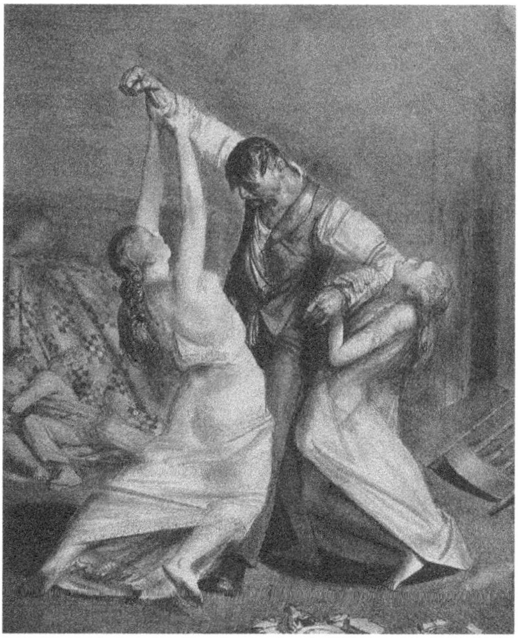

Figure 2. *The Drunk*. Lithograph by George Bellows, circa 1923.
Image courtesy of the US Library of Congress.

22 Frances Slee v James Slee, 20 March 1890, Item ID 518893, QSA.

23 Kate Reid v George Reid, 21 April 1890, Item ID 518893, QSA.

Possibly some men were simply incapable of feeding or clothing their families. The 1890s were a disastrous period for Queensland that saw strikes, economic depression and the worst flood in Brisbane's history. Many husbands claimed that their work was irregular or ill-paying, but this was likely also a tactic to lessen the amount of maintenance they would be required to pay if the magistrate decided against them. (As Queenslanders were not subject to income tax prior to the introduction of the federal tax in 1915, independent evidence to verify the pay men received was lacking.) In most cases the issue appears less one of income than a desire to exert control by dictating women's consumption and spending habits.

Some men countered allegations that they had refused to provide for their wives by claims that the women were financially irresponsible. It was not just misuse of household funds on drink that was considered objectionable when it came to female spending: any indulgence – from theatre visits to clothing purchases – potentially warranted husbandly interference. Mary Ann Sully's husband met claims that he had tried to cut his wife's throat with a razor, by cross-examining her about whether she had not pawned some clothes to buy a hat without his permission.[24] Mary Ann admitted this, but pointed out that she only needed to do so because her husband had torn up all her other hats in a fit of rage and refused to give her money for a new one.

Some women brought charges of wife desertion against husbands with whom they were still living in an effort to compel them to provide support. Rose Summer summoned her husband for desertion in 1893 because he had only given her four shillings over the last two months. A butcher by trade, Joseph Summer would also bring home meat from the shop, but had allegedly told his wife that she ought to earn her own living for anything else she needed for herself and their three-year-old child, as he intended to keep his money for his own use.[25] As separation was necessary to prove desertion, her application was dismissed, as were similar others.

Exploitation

Class was no protection against economic abuse.[26] Women with their own means risked financial exploitation by their husbands. In applying for maintenance in 1892, Margaret Cope revealed that £200 she received

---

24 Mary Ann Sully v William James Sully, 3 November 1890, Item ID 518895, QSA.

25 Rose Summer v Joseph Summer, 15 June 1893, Item ID 518901, QSA.

26 Judith Allen, "The invention of the pathological family: A historical study of family violence in NSW," in *Family Violence in Australia*, ed. Carol O'Donnell and Jan

upon marriage from her family had disappeared into her husband's hands.[27] She related how he had taken subsequent smaller sums given to her by her parents, meanwhile ruining his business through alcoholism. Following numerous acts of violence – so many she had taken to sleeping in her clothes in case she needed to flee at night – Margaret eventually left him when he arrived home drunk one morning and began to abuse her, telling her to get out and work for herself or get someone else to keep her and the children.

Educated women or those of independent means were actually at a disadvantage in wife desertion cases, as they had to prove the necessity of their husband's support. During the late 1880s, Maria Stamp's attempts to have her husband, a prosperous farmer, ordered to pay maintenance were thwarted by the assertion that she was in a position to support herself.[28] She eventually succeeded in 1890 when she revealed that her husband had used physical violence to intimidate her into selling two houses she owned and giving him the proceeds. Maria had since maintained herself by teaching, but could no longer continue as her eyesight had started to fail.

Women who lacked financial means could still be exploited for their domestic labour. Some men seemingly viewed women as little more than interchangeable commodities. When Eliza Brickerdike was unable to cook and clean after just coming out of the hospital, her husband told her if she could not keep house for him he would find another woman.[29] He was not the only husband who did not regard exhaustion or illness as an excuse for women's dereliction of their end of the marriage bargain (that is the provision of domestic labour in exchange for financial support). Rosalie Magdolinski's husband made her get up the day after her confinement to do the housework.[30] Similarly, when Catherine Kann sued her husband Henry for wife desertion in 1890, he pointed out that she had been "delicate for ten or twelve years" and consequently often left housework unperformed. Catherine countered that for a three-year period it had been she who brought in wages while her husband could not get work.[31]

Craney (Melbourne: Longman Cheshire, 1982), 19; Kay Saunders, "The study of domestic violence in colonial Queensland: Sources and problems," *Historical Studies* 21, no. 82 (1984): 74.

27 Margaret Ann Cope v John Cope, 15 February 1892, Item ID 518898, QSA.

28 Maria Stamp v Jacob Leopold Stamp, 14 April 1890, Item ID 518893, QSA.

29 Eliza Brickerdike v Thomas Brickerdike, 3 March 1892, Item ID 518898, QSA.

30 Rosalie Magdolinski v Carl Magdolinski, 13 January 1890, Item ID 518893, QSA.

31 Catherine Kann v Henry Kann, 20 October 1890, Item ID 518895, QSA.

Newspaper reports also expose instances of economic exploitation, from men living off their partners' prostitution to husbands' supporting their liquor habits through their wives' laundry-work.[32] Only one case appears in the sample where a husband exploited his wife's economic labour, but it points to the more general risk to which women were exposed. Mary Betar worked as a waitress at her husband's restaurant prior to their marriage in 1896.[33] Within a week of the wedding, Nicholas Betar discharged the other waitress, compelling his wife to take on the work of waiting on an average of fifty people a day over a ten-hour period. A few months later, Mary, now pregnant, found herself unable to cope, often retching at the smell of food and collapsing during the washing up. When she asked her husband to hire another woman to help her, he laughed and said that the laws of his country (Greece) let men shoot women. (This episode possibly points to a wider story about cultural expectations of marriage varying among different migrant groups, which may have exacerbated tensions in inter-marriages like the Betars.) Eventually Mary fainted during a visit from her father, who convinced her to leave her husband.

Nicholas was unrepentant at the subsequent hearing, with his lawyer arguing that many women worked during pregnancy. The probity of his conduct ultimately seems to have rested on whether such work fell within the domestic duties to which husbands were entitled by the marriage bargain. The doctor who attended Mary during her convalescence stated that he did not consider waiting on fifty people "ordinary household work", and as such was not something that could be reasonably expected of Mary while pregnant and in poor health. An order of maintenance was made, yet the circumstances of the case reveal the extreme power husbands were understood to exert in directing household resources, including their wives' labour.

Economically-motivated violence

Male authority in household economic relations frequently provided an excuse for physical abuse. Attempts to subvert male control by taking money or pawning goods – even to buy food or pay rent – could elicit violence. More passive forms of resistance also led to actual or threatened violence. Johanna Ennis told the court how one day she had gone to her aunt's to get herself and her child food because her husband refused to provide her with

---

32 "Guarantee for wives," *Evening Telegraph*, 5 August 1902, 2.

33 Mary Betar v Nicholas George Betar, 11 February 1897, Item ID 518909, QSA.

money. When she came home, her husband locked her out and threatened to shoot her if she came inside.[34]

Questioning men's financial management was a dangerous business. Mary McGrath's husband, despite well-remunerated employment as a gas-fitter, was allegedly tight-fisted with his earnings. Mary received a severe beating when her husband criticised the meagre dinner she had prepared, and she responded that she would need more money to provide a better meal.[35] Albert Kaminski, after his wife complained that there was no food in the house and she had not eaten at all that day, responded by telling her "to clear to buggery with your baby. There are plenty more women about Queen Street".[36] In a previous violent episode, Albert had taunted her economic dependence, throwing her bodily into the street while yelling "Now you can go and see what you can do".

While the marital bargain had evident disadvantages for women, historian Judith Allen observes that it also created resentment among men whose violence could be ignited by the perception of their wives as "parasitic dependants".[37] This perception at times extended to men's children, who often suffered the same economic abuse as their mothers. Women who accepted ill-treatment themselves were sometimes moved to protest unfair treatment of their children. Conflict erupted between Eliza Fordham and her frequently violent husband Henry in 1890 when he ordered their eldest daughter to leave the house the next day, declaring that their second-born daughter was now old enough to assist Eliza with the housework. When Eliza announced that if her daughter left, she would go too, Henry responded with another beating, one that finally convinced Eliza to leave him.[38]

Historian Pamela Haag suggests that domestic violence in nineteenth-century New York often revealed fundamentally different conceptions of economic relations for men and women.[39] While men were conditioned to regard themselves as the independent and ultimate authority in financial matters, women understood their economic relations as a series of dependencies, not only on their husbands, but others in the community to whom

34 Johanna Ennis v Thomas Henry Ennis, 19 May 1892, Item ID 518899, QSA.

35 Mary McGrath v Edmund McGrath, 18 February 1895, Item ID 518905, QSA.

36 Mary Ann Kaminski v Albert Kaminski, 2 March 1896, Item ID 518907, QSA.

37 Allen, "The invention of the pathological family," 18.

38 Eliza Fordham v Henry Fordham, 16 October 1890, Item ID 51889R, QSA.

39 Pamela Haag, "The 'ill-use of a wife': Patterns of working-class violence in domestic and public New York City, 1860–1880," *Journal of Social History* 25, no. 3 (1992): 470.

they might appeal in times of hardship. Seeking to maintain such relations could bring women into conflict with their husbands' conceptions. In 1890 Brisbane woman Wilhelmina Duhrer summoned her husband for assault after he strangled her so hard that blood came from her mouth following the discovery that she had leant an old coat of his to a neighbour.[40] While Wilhelmina probably considered this act – common among working-class "borrowing networks" of the period – as a type of investment to ensure they would receive neighbourly help in the future,[41] to her husband it evidently represented a contravention of his authority that merited violence.

Post-separation economic abuse

Just as household economics could offer an excuse for physical abuse, resisting such violence could prompt episodes of economic abuse. John Reynolds thus responded to his wife's success in getting an order made against him to keep the peace towards her by packing up all the household goods and moving out that same night.[42] There were 12 instances in the sample of husbands enacting some form of financial revenge against their wives at the termination of their relationship, either by selling, destroying or otherwise depriving them of property. Bridget McAllen's husband jealously guarded his property rights even though it was he that insisted she take their child and leave the house: when he discovered she had taken some bedding to stay on a neighbour's floor, he broke in during the night, awakening his sleeping wife and child to retrieve his property.[43] Male property rights provided other opportunities for vengeance. Police gazettes regularly contained warrants for the arrest of women charged with stealing jewellery or household items from their husbands upon departing their homes,[44] or, in cases of adultery, warrants for the arrest of men with whom the women had absconded.[45]

Although not defined as such for the purposes of this analysis, wife desertion itself can be construed as a form of economic abuse. A commonality throughout such cases was male indifference to what became of their

40 Wilhelmina Duhrer v Francis Duhrer, 28 January 1890, Item ID 518893, QSA.

41 Haag, "The ill-use of a wife'," 470.

42 Mary Reynolds v John William Reynolds, 3 June 1897, Item ID 518910, QSA.

43 Bridget McAllen v James William McAllen, 26 June 1890, Item ID 518894, QSA.

44 *Queensland Police Gazette*, 1 October 1894, 276; *Queensland Police Gazette*, 29 June 1896, 208.

45 *Queensland Police Gazette*, 13 January 1886, 46; *Queensland Police Gazette*, 17 August 1896, 260.

wives – and often their children – post separation. When Mary O'Brien asked her husband Frank for support after he had thrown her bodily from their house (breaking her arm), he told her that he did not plan to work anymore and that the Government could support her and the children.[46] Even when ordered by courts to pay maintenance towards their wives' support, many husbands either failed to do so or stopped as soon as the orders (limited to a twelve month period) expired, compelling their wives to return to court again and again.[47] Ultimately, the number of cases in the sample where women withdrew their prosecution suggests that many felt that reunion with husbands – even violent ones – was preferable to the economic uncertainties of relying on the legal system and their own limited resources.[48]

Conclusion

Over a hundred years later, and despite Australian women's rising workforce participation, the lived experience of family power dynamics over finances remains unchanged for many women. A 2004 report on financial decision-making found that while women often *managed* household finances in terms of allocating available funds to daily needs, *control* of the finances in terms of access and major spending decisions still rested with the male partner in the majority of Australian families.[49] In both historical and contemporary contexts, women's individual experiences of financial agency undoubtedly vary. Nevertheless, it is easy to see how the traditional societal conception that women ought to defer to their husbands in financial matters might elide into subtle forms of economic abuse.

Of the billions of dollars that domestic violence costs Australia annually, the greatest proportion of costs are borne by victims.[50] Several Australian jurisdictions, including Queensland,[51] now expressly include economic

46 Mary Jane O'Brien v Frank O'Brien, 15 June 1896, Item ID 518908, QSA.

47 Eliza Keane v Patrick Michael Keane, 2 July 1891, Item ID 518897, QSA; Eliza Keane v Patrick Michael Keane, 11 August 1892, Item ID 518899, QSA.

48 Christina Twomey, *Deserted and Destitute: Motherhood, Wife Desertion and Colonial Welfare* (Kew: Australian Scholarly Press, 2002), 19.

49 Saba Waseem, *Policy Research Paper no. 23: Household Monies and Decision-making*, Australian Government Department of Family and Community Services (Sydney: Social Policy Research Centre, University of New South Wales, 2004).

50 Access Economics, *The Cost of Domestic Violence to the Australian Economy: Part I* (Australian Government Office for the Status of Women, Commonwealth of Australia, 2004).

51 *Domestic and Family Violence Protection Act* 2012 (Qld), section 12.

abuse as a specific form of violence in their legislation. The effectiveness of such legislation has been questioned, however, due to its narrow application to spousal relationships and because of the high threshold required for proving a "coercive" or "intimadatory" intention behind such behaviours in court.[52] This has led to discussion of the potential benefits of introducing a specific domestic violence criminal offence that focuses not on a single event but a course of conduct indicative of "controlling or coercive behaviour".[53] Tasmania introduced specific offences covering economic and emotional abuse back in 2004 but uncertain statutory construction suggests their practical implementation remains limited.[54]

Yet while the legal system struggles with how to deal with economic abuse, the historical literature makes clear that this is far from a new – or even newly recognised – issue. Analysis of the socio-historic contexts of economic abuse emphasises the inter-relationship between domestic violence and the economic status of women more generally, suggesting what is needed is also a wider cultural shift in gendered economic and social relations. Expansion of the legal definition of domestic violence must be accompanied by expanded understandings at the societal level of the multitude of pernicious actions and attitudes that accompany and facilitate such gender violence.

---

52 Smallwood, *Stepping Stones*, 7.

53 Heather Douglas, "Do we need a specific domestic violence offence?" *Melbourne University Law Review* 39, no. 2 (2015): 434–571.

54 *Family Violence Act 2004* (Tas). Marilyn McMahon and Paul McGorrery, "Criminalising emotional abuse, intimidation and economic abuse in the context of family violence: The Tasmanian experience," *University of Tasmania Law Review* 35, no. 2 (2016): 1–22.

Chapter 4

"YOUR TROUBLES ARE OVER, MUMMY"

Prosecuting children who kill violent men

Lisa Durnian

On 29 March 1949, sixteen-year-old James Murray stood trial for the murder of his father.[1] His mother testified to longstanding violence against her and her children, including the defendant. On the day of his death, the victim chased her with an axe and later tried to strangle her. James physically intervened after the man threatened to kill the entire family. She fled the house when he turned on James with a knife.[2] James told the court he stayed home from work that day, fearing for his mother's life. At some point he retrieved a shotgun from a neighbour's home, hiding it close to the kitchen. James testified that he was "hysterical" when his father attacked him, waving a gun around to frighten his father away, but it accidentally discharged. He had no intention of shooting his father. The all-male jury believed him, retiring briefly before acquitting him of both murder and manslaughter.[3]

Previous research suggests that men prosecuted for domestic homicide in colonial and early-twentieth-century Australia received a "domestic discount". All male juries and judges extended men who killed intimate

1 Title quotation: "Boy charged with killing father," *National Advocate,* 30 March 1949, 3.

2 Defendant's name is a pseudonym, see: "Patricide charge against youth," *Morning Bulletin,* 1 March 1949, 4.

3 "Patricide charge: Youth acquitted in Melbourne," *West Australian,* 31 March 1949, 5.

partners and children more lenient treatment when compared with case outcomes for men who killed strangers.[4] Some research argues that this discount extended to women prosecuted for murdering abusive husbands.[5] The outcome in James Murray's case suggests the domestic discount may have also extended to juvenile and adult children who killed abusive fathers and step-fathers. To date, no research examines the prosecution of patricide – the homicide of a father or step-father – in Australian courts.

This chapter provides the first international socio-legal research examining case outcomes of historical patricides committed in the context of family violence. The first section discusses contemporary patricide research, and the limited data on the prosecutions of patricide specifically associated with family violence. Next, I outline current knowledge about the historical incidence of patricides alongside prosecutions of other forms of domestic homicide in the Australian context. This provides a framework for analysis of the historical prosecutions of thirty children who killed abusive men while protecting their mothers. The judicial system's responses to these defendants are examined – including the coroner's inquiry, the trial outcome, and sentencing – to detect any evidence of the "domestic discount" phenomenon. The evidence suggests that children who killed violent men historically received greater leniency than might currently be the case.

Contemporary research

Domestic homicides of parents are relatively rare events in Australia. About thirteen homicide events annually involve children killing a parent or step-parent.[6] Children typically kill their parents because of extreme mental illness, inherent sociopathy, or in response to severe abuse.[7] Abused children who kill abusive parents are sometimes described as suffering "battered children syndrome". They experience similar dynamics and patterns

---

4 Amanda Kaladelfos, "The dark side of the family: paternal child homicide in Australia," *Journal of Australian Studies* 37, no. 3 (2013): 333–348; Carolyn Strange, "Masculinities, intimate femicide and the death penalty in Australia, 1890–1920," *British Journal of Criminology* 43, no. 2 (2003): 310–339.

5 Ruth McConnell and Steve Mullins, "'We had both been drinking since Christmas': Battered wives and dead abusive husbands in early colonial Rockhampton," *Journal of Australian Colonial History* 5 (2004): 100–119.

6 Jenny Mouzos and Catherine Rushforth, "Family homicide in Australia," *Trends & Issues in Crime and Criminal Justice*, no. 255 (Canberra: Australian Institute of Criminology, 2003), 4.

7 Kathleen M. Heide, *Understanding Parricide: When Sons and Daughters Kill Parents* (Oxford: Oxford University Press, 2013), 8.

in abuse that courts now recognise as "battered women's syndrome", including hypervigilance and increased sensitisation to behaviours that signal a potential attack.[8] Witnessing family violence can thus be as psychologically damaging for children as direct abuse.[9] It is unsurprising that children sometimes kill parents in the context of family violence, to protect themselves or other family members.[10]

Homicide scholarship typically investigates "parricides" because of the low rates of these offences, combining both patricide offences (killing of fathers) with matricide offences (killing of mothers). Most parricide research relies on large-scale homicide data sourced from the Supplementary Homicide Report in the United States.[11] Australian homicide research relies on data from the National Homicide Monitoring Program.[12] Most Australian parricide offenders are adults (89 per cent), and male (80 per cent). Victims are more likely to be fathers or step-fathers than mothers or step-mothers. Critically, almost one fifth (18 per cent) of parricide deaths occurred in a context of family violence.[13]

It is difficult to know how contemporary courts respond to family homicides perpetrated by children, particularly in the context of family violence. Neither Australian or American data reports prosecution outcomes for homicide offences. Britain's Home Office Homicide Index, however, does

---

8 Kurt M. Bumby, "Psycholegal considerations in abuse-motivated parricides: Children who kill their abusive parents," *The Journal of Psychiatry & Law*, 22 (1994): 60–62.

9 Cindy Sousa, Todd I. Herrenkohl, Carrie A. Moylan, Emiko A. Tajima, J. Bart Klika, Roy C. Herrenkohl, and M. Jean Russo, "Longitudinal study on the effects of child abuse and children's exposure to domestic violence, parent-child attachments, and antisocial behavior in adolescence," *Journal of Interpersonal Violence* 26, no. 1 (2011): 111–136.

10 Christine E. Newhill, "Parricide," *Journal of Family Violence* 6, no. 4 (1991): 376.

11 Kathleen M. Heide, "Parents who get killed and the children who kill them," *Journal of Interpersonal Violence* 8, no. 4 (1993): 531–544; Kathleen M. Heide and Thomas A. Petee, "Parricide: An empirical analysis of 24 years of U.S. data," *Journal of Interpersonal Violence* 22, no. 11 (2007): 1382–1399; Jeffrey A. Walsh, Jessie L. Krienert and Danielle Crowder, "Innocence lost: A gender-based study of parricide offender, victim, and incident characteristics in a national sample, 1976–2003," *Journal of Aggression, Maltreatment & Trauma* 16, no. 2 (2008): 202–227.

12 Paul Mazerolle, Li Eriksson, Richard Wortley and Holly Johnson, "Homicide in Australia and New Zealand: Precursors and prevention," in *The Handbook of Homicide*, ed. Fiona Brookman, Edward R. Maguire and Mike Maguire (Chichester, UK: John Wiley & Sons, 2017), 413.

13 Family violence is indicated when "there may have included a current or former protection order between the victim and offender". Tracy Cussen and Willow Bryant, "Domestic/family homicide in Australia," *Research in Practice* no. 38 (Australian Institute of Criminology, 2015), 6.

include both incident characteristics and prosecution information.[14] Recent research shows there are high conviction rates for parricide prosecutions: between 1996 and 2012, 80 per cent of 335 such prosecutions ended in a conviction.[15] There does appear to be some degree of leniency in sentencing. Defendants were less likely to receive an imprisonment sentence than other homicide offenders (44 per cent against 94 per cent).[16] Like studies from the United States and Australia, prosecutions for patricide and matricide are conflated. It is difficult to assess any variation in case outcome dependent on the gender of either the victim or the defendant.

Some limited case study research from the United States notes the difficulties for parricide defendants facing prosecution. Self-defence is difficult to argue, so acquittals are rare.[17] Self-defence requires that the defendant can prove that they reasonably believed they were in "imminent danger of death or substantial bodily injury" when they committed the offence.[18] Traditionally, the law defines self-defence "in terms of an adult male, rather than in taking into account the unique characteristics of a crime committed by a child or a female".[19] Feminist scholars criticise the law's failure to encompass the experience of female offenders who kill abusive partners, arguing that self-defence and provocation do not provide an adequate defence.[20]

Recent legislative reforms aimed to provide protections to abused women who killed violent men. Yet 'discounts' extended by the Victorian offence of defensive homicide, or modifications to provocation and self-defence are often employed to benefit violent men. The 'defensive homicide' offence

14 Amanda Holt, "Parricide in England and Wales (1977–2012): An exploration of offenders, victims, incidents and outcomes," *Criminology & Criminal Justice* 17, no. 5 (2017): 4.

15 Ibid., 11.

16 Ibid., 12.

17 Jessica L. Hart and Jeffrey L. Helms, "Factors of parricide: Allowance of the use of battered child syndrome as a defense," *Aggression and Violent Behaviour* 8, no. 6 (2003): 671–683.

18 Paul Mones, "When the innocent strike back: Abused children who kill their parents," *Journal of Interpersonal Violence* 8, no. 2 (1993): 298.

19 Marc Hillbrand, Jason W. Alexandre, John L. Young, and Reuben T. Spitz, "Parricides: Characteristics of offenders and victims, legal factors, and treatment issues," *Aggression and Violent Behaviour* 4, no. 2 (1999): 179–190.

20 Rebecca Bradfield, "Domestic homicide and the defence of provocation: A Tasmanian perspective on the jealous husband and the battered wife," *University of Tasmanian Law Review*, 19, no.1 (2000): 5–37; Mandy Burton, "Sentencing domestic homicide upon provocation: Still getting away with murder," *Feminist Legal Studies* 11, no. 3 (2003): 279–289.

was intended to provide a 'safety net' to battered women who killed violent men in situations where women could not meet the self-defence test to prove reasonable grounds for their belief that the killing was necessary.[21] Yet between 2005 and 2010, thirteen convictions of defensive homicide all involved male defendants.[22] Furthermore, the modification of the requirement of suddenness in provocation extended the defence to men who killed their partners sometime after discovering an adulterous affair, but not to women who killed violent partners while the men were sleeping following a violent attack the same day.[23]

It is difficult for women who cannot provide sufficient evidence of their abuse history to defend themselves successfully against homicide charges.[24] Some literature suggests it is even more difficult for battered children to argue self-defence, even in jurisdictions where "battered women syndrome" is accepted. In the United States, for example, judges have failed to recognise the qualitatively different nature of adult violence perpetrated against children and resisted the introduction of expert testimony in battered-children cases.[25] Furthermore, courts are not provided with "comprehensive assessments" of the defendants, including histories of abuse or exposure to family violence.[26]

Histories of patricide, men's violence, and the 'domestic discount'

Patricide has a long history across time and place, with strong patriarchal, mythological and religious connotations. By the early modern period, patricide was considered treason against a father's religious and legal power

21 Elizabeth Sheehy, Julie Stubbs, and Julia Tolmie, "Defences to homicide battered women: A comparative analysis of laws in Australia, Canada and New Zealand," *Sydney Law Review* 34 (2012): 478

22 Charlotte King, Lorana Bartels, Patricia Easteal, and Anthony Hopkins, "Did defensive homicide in Victoria provide a safety net for battered women who kill: A case study analysis," *Monash University Law Review* 42 (2016): 144. Defensive homicide was abolished in 2014.

23 Bradfield, "Domestic homicide," 15.

24 Danielle Tyson, Deborah Kirkwood, and Mandy McKenzie, "Family violence in domestic homicides: A case study of women who killed intimate partners post-legislative reform in Victoria, Australia," *Violence Against Women* 23, no. 5 (2017): 576.

25 Mones, "When the innocent strike back," 297–299.

26 Kathleen M. Heide and Jessica McCurdy, "Juvenile parricide offenders sentenced to death," *Victims & Offenders* 5, no. 1 (2009): 94–95.

over his family; as such, it was the "blackest of crimes".[27] Yet patricide is an under-researched area in historical gender and violence studies.[28]

An emerging literature investigates parricide events across historical contexts and time periods. These include England and Wales between 1600 and 1760; Russia between 1600 and 1800; Scotland between 1700 and 1850; and the United States, between 1851 and 1899.[29] Most historical parricide studies focus on the offender, victim, and incident characteristics, ignoring criminal justice responses to the phenomenon. Like contemporary findings, most parricide offenders were male,[30] and most victims were fathers.[31] Although incidents were generally precipitated by alcohol and domestic arguments,[32] there was little evidence of children killing in response to domestic violence or abuse.[33]

Few studies investigate the prosecution of parricide. Anne-Marie Kilday's analyses of nine prosecutions in the Scottish Judiciary Court between 1700 and 1850 focuses on offence characteristics rather than judicial attitudes.[34] Most defendants were convicted, however, and sentences were severe: prisoners were executed and publicly dissected. Carolyn Strange's case study of "respectable" patricide offender Frank Walworth is unique in patricide research.[35] Despite his mother's testimony that her divorced husband

27 Garthine Walker, "Imagining the unimaginable: Parricide in early modern England and Wales, C. 1600–C. 1760," *Journal of Family History* 41, no. 3 (2016): 271–293.

28 Walsh, Krienert and Crowder, "Innocence lost," 203.

29 Walker, "Imagining the unimaginable," 202–227; Marianna Muravyeva and Raisa Maria Toivo, "'Honor thy father and thy mother': A History of violence against parents," *Journal of Family History* 41, no. 3 (2016): 231–235; Anne-Marie Kilday, "'Sugar and Spice and All Things Nice?': Violence against parents in Scotland, 1700–1850," *Journal of Family History* 41, no. 3 (2016): 318–335; Phillip C. Shon and Michael A. Roberts, "Post-offence Characteristics of 19th-Century American Parricides: An Archival Exploration," *Journal of Investigative Psychology and Offender Profiling* 5, no. 3 (2008): 147–169; Phillip C. Shon and Shannon M. Barton-Bellessa, "Pre-offense characteristics of nineteenth-century American parricide offenders: An archival exploration," *Journal of Criminal Psychology* 2, no. 1 (2012): 51–66; Phillip C. Shon and Christopher R. Williams, "An archival exploration of 19th-century American adult female offender parricides," *OMEGA – Journal of Death and Dying* 67, no. 3 (2013): 247–268; Carolyn Strange, "The unwritten law of executive justice: Pardoning patricide in reconstruction-era New York," *Law and History Review* 28, no. 4 (2010): 891–930.

30 Shon and Williams, "An archival exploration," 256.

31 Kilday, "Sugar and spice and all things nice?," 324; Shon and Roberts, "Post-offence characteristics," 154.

32 Ibid, 327.

33 Walker, "Imagining the unimaginable," 280.

34 Kilday, "Sugar and spice and all things nice?," 325.

35 Strange, "The unwritten law," 891–930.

repeatedly threatened to kill her and her sons, Walworth was convicted of second-degree murder, but was subsequently pardoned.[36]

Historically, male violence, including homicide, was often condoned by all-male juries and judges if committed in a range of circumstances involving masculine honour.[37] However, men who killed wives and children received a special degree of leniency. Men who killed their partners were more likely to have death sentences commuted to life imprisonment than men sentenced for the murders of strangers or acquaintances.[38] Violent fathers who killed their children were more likely to avoid execution than men who killed other people's children.[39]

By the early twentieth century, social and judicial attitudes had changed markedly and become more attuned to family violence than earlier colonial attitudes.[40] Men were expected to protect women, rather than use violence to control them.[41] This raises questions about social and judicial responses to the killing of violent fathers and male guardians who failed in their duty to provide a safe home for their families. Did all-male juries and judges extend leniency to juvenile and adult children who killed violent men when they protected their mothers and siblings? The following section tests the hypothesis that the "domestic discount" also functioned in prosecutions of patricide.

Prosecuting patricide, 1905–1954: Methodology and offence characteristics

These analyses draw on historical newspaper reports of 30 patricides prosecuted between 1905 and 1954 in Australian Supreme Courts. Reports were sourced through the National Library of Australia's Trove database of digitised newspapers. News reports provide a nuanced perspective of infrequent

36 Ibid, 896, 929.

37 Jeffrey S. Adler, "'It is his first offense. We might as well let him go': Homicide and criminal justice in Chicago, 1875–1920," *Journal of Social History* 40, no. 1 (2006): 10–11.

38 Judith Allen, "Desperately seeking solutions: Changing battered women's options Since 1880," in *National Conference on Domestic Violence: Proceedings*, Vol. 1, ed. Suzanne E. Hatty (Canberra: Australian Institute of Criminology, 1986), 130.

39 Kaladelfos, "The dark side of the family," 338.

40 Carolyn B. Ramsey, "Domestic violence and state intervention in the American West and Australia, 1860–1930," *Indiana Law Journal* 86, no. 1 (2011): 198.

41 Allen, "Desperately seeking solutions," 119–136.

homicide offences that may not be available using official data.[42] There are some limitations with this method of data collection. As Trove has fewer digitised newspaper titles from the 1950s onwards, this analysis focuses on patricide cases prosecuted in the early twentieth century period. Reporting of events is reliant on editorial decision-making, so it is likely that more sensational stories were reported, and some overlooked.[43] The sample is selective rather than random, so the findings are not wholly representative of early twentieth century prosecution practices.[44]

Search terms "patricide", "protected mother", and "killed father" identified newspaper articles about deaths occurring in the context of family violence. Further searches on defendants' names sourced articles reporting case outcomes at different stages of the prosecution process. Data was collected on offender and incident characteristics (including defendant's gender and age; weapon used) and prosecution variables (including coroner's findings; verdict; and sentence).

Most reported prosecutions occurred in Victoria (12), New South Wales (8), and Queensland (6). There were two South Australian prosecutions, and one reported in Western Australia and Tasmania respectively. Defendants included 13 juveniles (aged 15 to 17), and 17 adults (aged 18 to 27). Seven defendants were daughters. Most victims were fathers (22) but five victims were step-fathers, and three were mothers' boyfriends (Table 1).

Table 1. Patricide characteristics.

Variable	Characteristic	Male defendants	Female defendants
Victim relationship	Fathers	16	6
	Stepfathers	4	1
	Boyfriends	3	–
Weapon used	Gun	16	7
	Knife/axe	4	–
	Blunt object	3	–

In most cases, the primary cause of death was due to gunshot wounds. All female and most male defendants used guns. These weapons arguably provided defendants with a physical advantage when confronting violent

42 Denise Paquette Boots and Kathleen M. Heide, "Parricides in the media: A content analysis of available reports across cultures," *International Journal of Offender Therapy and Comparative Criminology* 50, no. 4 (2006): 418–445.

43 Ibid., 419.

44 Shon and Williams, "An archival exploration," 254.

men. (Contemporary research finds that women generally use a weapon in domestic homicides whereas men use their hands.[45]) Many of the guns used by children were ex-service weapons, perhaps reflecting the ineffectiveness of gun control legislation during the inter-war period. Despite concerns about ex-military firearms entering the wider population at the end of both World Wars, more than 45,000 surplus rifles were sold to civilians by 1948.[46] For example, one nineteen-year-old married daughter shot her father in 1946 with a pistol given to her by an American soldier.[47]

Sons availed themselves of whatever weapons were close at hand. When one sixteen-year-old boy's mother was attacked in her front yard in 1931, her son threw a large garden stone, felling the boyfriend.[48] He later died from a head injury sustained in the fall. One defendant killed his father with a kitchen chair, when his father rushed at him with a knife. Another son used a carving knife when his step-father had his mother by her throat.[49] In many cases, children used the same weapons victims had earlier threatened to use against their mothers.

Mothers, as well as defendants and their siblings, testified about their experiences of victimisation at the hands of the deceased. Some women had been hospitalised on previous occasions; many had been threatened with murder. One 15-year-old daughter described how her father had beaten her "with a whip, a belt, stick and his fists".[50] These men's deaths arguably led to a better outcome for the family, at least in terms of personal safety. Case outcomes suggest that juries and judges thought similarly and acted accordingly.

Coroners and committals

The coroner's role involved investigating the relevant factors associated with the death. The inquest was inquisitorial rather than adversarial: it focused on collating all information relating to the physical description of the body,

45 Tyson, Kirkwood and McKenzie, "Family in domestic homicides," 561.

46 Mark Finnane, "Guns and massacres: The politics of firearms control in Australia," in *Australian Violence: Crime, Criminal Justice and Beyond* ed. Julie Stubbs and Stephen Tomsen (Sydney: The Federation Press, 2016), 36–37.

47 "Woman shoots father," *Maryborough Chronicle*, 11 January 1946, 3.

48 "In mother's defence," *National Advocate*, 15 January 1931, 3.

49 "A charge of murder," *Advertiser*, 3 June 1925, 11.

50 "Shellharbor tragedy," *Daily Advertiser*, 7 June 1913, 4.

how it was found, and by whom.[51] In some patricide cases, the coroner's findings ended the prosecution process. In 1920, a coroner ruled the death a justifiable homicide, when a boy threw a rock at his mother's boyfriend.[52] Another coroner ruled the father's death a "misadventure".[53] In total, six of the sample – four sons and two daughters – were never prosecuted.

Most coroners did find a case against the child. In James Murray's case, the coroner did not believe the gun had accidentally discharged yet managed to shoot the father in the back of the head.[54] In 1948, a nineteen-year-old youth killed his stepfather with a German army rifle after earlier being knocked unconscious when he tried to intervene in the violence against his mother. Although the Coroner acknowledged that the son's actions were "laudable", he committed him for trial because he questioned whether he was justified in "taking the final step".[55] This was typical even when defendants argued they intervened to save their mothers in situations where there was an immediate threat to her life. Most of the children were ultimately charged with murder (25) or manslaughter (3).

Trials, verdicts, and sentence

In total, 24 defendants were committed to the relevant Supreme Courts (Table 2). Few defendants faced multiple offences, although one defendant was charged with three homicide-related charges.[56] Fourteen defendants were found "not guilty" and acquitted. All five female defendants were acquitted, perhaps reflecting the historically lower conviction rates for females than males.[57] Outright convictions were rare. Only one male defendant was found guilty of murder, and a further two were found guilty of a lesser offence (manslaughter). Not all cases proceeded to trial, however. Three defendants, who initially pleaded "not guilty" to murder at their committal hearings, subsequently entered guilty pleas to the lesser offence of manslaughter. Some cases were withdrawn from the prosecution process entirely.

51 Lee Karen Butterworth, "What good is a coroner?: The transformation of the Queensland office of Coroner 1859–1959" (PhD diss., Griffith University, 2012), 210.

52 "In mother's defence," 3.

53 "Saving his mother," *Riverine Herald*, 17 April 1920, 2.

54 "Patricide charge against youth," 4.

55 "Strong plea for youth on murder charge," *Barrier Daily Truth*, 20 April 1948, 1.

56 "The charge against Hilary Broderick," *Evening News*, 9 November 1911, 7.

57 Kathy Laster, "Arbitrary chivalry: Women and capital punishment in Victoria, Australia 1842–1967," *Women & Criminal Justice* 6, no. 1 (1994). 67–95.

Table 2. Prosecution outcomes.

Charge	No.	Acquitted	Convicted	Convicted of lesser offence	Guilty plea	Case withdrawn
Murder	22	13	1	2	3	3
Unlawful killing	1	–	–	–	–	1
Manslaughter	1	1	–	–	–	–
Totals	24	14	1	2	3	4

Crown Prosecutors withdrew four cases through either a "no true bill" (not presenting an indictment to the Court), or a "*nolle prosequi*", a rate comparable to that found in other historical Australian homicide research.[58] Sometimes the evidence could not sustain the charge. For example, in 1911 a coroner ruled that the patricide was "justifiable homicide"; however, the defendant had been "committed to his court wrongly, and he had no power to discharge him... it would be a matter for the magistrates' Court".[59] The magistrate committed him for trial despite the coroner's finding, and the NSW Attorney-General subsequently disposed of the case by *nolle prosequi*. The cases were all withdrawn prior to 1935, suggesting a possible willingness to withdraw patricide cases earlier in this period.

Most defendants (14 of 17) who were tried were subsequently acquitted. Newspaper reports did not usually refer to the specific defence raised by defendants' lawyers. The facts in some cases suggested a defence of accidental death. In 1934, for example, the judge told the jury that if they believed "the evidence showed that there had been a tragic accident they could acquit without waiting to hear the counsel's [final] addresses".[60] They retired directly, returning a "not guilty" verdict 20 minutes later.

Most defendants probably argued the homicide was justified as self-defence. If the necessary requirements were met, self-defence provided defendants with a complete defence (guaranteeing acquittal). The degree of force used should be reasonable, and necessary to repel an attack.[61] Lethal force was only justified if the defendant reasonably believed the attack

58 Mark Finnane and Andy Kaladelfos. "Race and justice in an Australian Court: Prosecuting homicide in Western Australia, 1830–1954," *Australian Historical Studies* 47, no. 3 (2016): 454.

59 "Justifiable homicide," *Daily Telegraph*, 9 November 1911, 7.

60 "Final act in Cadell drama," *Recorder*, 27 June 1934, 1.

61 Eric Colvin, Suzie Linden, and John McKechnie, *Criminal Law in Queensland and Western Australia*, 4th ed. (Chatswood, NSW: LexisNexis Butterworths, 2005), 262.

would cause death or grievous bodily harm.[62] Further, a child could kill to defend a parent "if there is good reason to believe the parent is in danger from this other".[63] In most cases victims made threats to kill just prior to their death; some threats included strangulation or severe violence against the mother. The all-male juries were clearly swayed by any self-defence argument, even where the evidence suggested that the defendant might not have been in immediate danger at the time of the killing. Newspapers referred to these as "sympathetic verdicts".[64]

Further evidence of a "domestic discount" in patricide trials was the speed with which juries decided these verdicts. Deliberations were sometimes very quick: five minutes in one case, ten minutes in another.[65] When the case closed in the 1926 trial of a seventeen-year-old that shot his father while the man physically assaulted his mother and seven-year-old brother, the jury returned their verdict "without leaving the box".[66]

Previous research notes the reticence of historical juries to convict in death penalty cases.[67] This reticence might explain some juries' attitudes in failing to convict patricide defendants charged with murder. Sympathetic verdicts were arguably motivated by a reluctance to expose young defendants to a death sentence; if so, we might expect to see alternative verdicts of manslaughter. Yet all-male juries in this sample rarely returned a manslaughter verdict. In 1931, the jury ignored the judge's comment that "a judge might think she [the sixteen-year-old defendant] deserves no punishment at all, but she might still be guilty of manslaughter".[68] She was subsequently acquitted. Juries were also less likely to convict defendants for a lesser offence than the one charged. For example, under statutory provisions and common law principles, juries were authorised to convict defendants "of a lesser offence which is an element of the offence charged".[69] Yet only two defendants in this sample were found guilty of a lesser offence. This suggests that juries were extending a domestic discount to patricide defendants.

The low conviction rate for children who killed fathers and step-fathers is in stark contrast to historical conviction rates of fathers who killed children. Andy Kaladelfos found no evidence of a domestic discount in 26

62 Ibid., 264.

63 "When killing is not murder," *Truth*, 18 January 1931, 18.

64 "In defence of his mother," *West Australian*, 17 March 1920, 7.

65 "Stepson acquitted of murder charge," *Truth*, 30 May 1948, 8.

66 "Gahan acquitted," *Daily Advertiser*, 16 January 1926, 5.

67 Adler, "It is his first offence," 11.

68 "Girl admits she shot father," *Weekly Times*, 17 June 1931, 9.

69 Colvin, Linden, and McKechnie, "*Criminal Law,*" 709.

prosecutions of paternal filicide between 1855 and 1954.[70] The high rate of patricide acquittals provides further evidence that masculine empathy was evoked in cases where fathers breached their duty to protect.[71] This empathy extended to providing a discount in sentencing. Although only six of the thirty offenders were convicted, their sentencing outcomes show that patricide defendants also received a discount. Sentences ranged between probation to five years imprisonment. The most severe sentences were for the two defendants sentenced for murder, a conviction that carried a death penalty for most of the twentieth century, although in most cases the Executive would commute that sentence to a term of imprisonment.[72]

The first sampled case involving a murder conviction related to a 24-year-old defendant who alleged he was trying to frighten his father into leaving his step-mother alone, and did not know the gun was loaded. But although his brother testified to their father's violent temper, their step-mother denied it.[73] The jury strongly recommended him to mercy, and his death sentence was commuted to 15 years imprisonment.[74] The second case involved a 15-year-old boy who pleaded guilty to murdering his father with an axe. Perhaps the evidence did not support self-defence: he confessed to police that he intended to kill him; the father was sleeping, so the boy was not in immediate danger; and the mother did not live in the same house. However, she had recently instigated maintenance proceedings, seeking economic support from her ex-husband. The father told his son he would "do her in" if she was successful. The defendant believed him, because his father had once shot his mother.[75] In light of the evidence presented here, a jury might conceivably have extended him the "domestic discount" and convicted him on a lesser charge. It is unclear why he pleaded guilty. However, the judge did take a lenient view at sentencing, possibly after consultation with the Solicitor-General.[76] Noting the boy's tragic life, he sentenced him to indefinite detention; while sounding harsh, this ironically meant that authorities could end his detention much earlier than if they commuted the death sentence to a specified prison term.

---

70 Kaladelfos, "The dark side of the family," 338.

71 Strange, "Masculinities, intimate femicide and the death penalty in Australia," 312.

72 Mark Finnane, *Punishment in Australian Society* (Melbourne: Oxford University Press, 1997), 129.

73 "Sailor for trial on murder charge," *Age*, 21 November 1952, 4; "Death sentence," *Truth*, 22 February 1953, 40.

74 "Hector gets reprieve," *Argus*, 21 April 1953, 3.

75 "Boy Sentenced for murdering father with axe," *Mercury*, 7 October 1953, 22.

76 Ibid.

Conclusion

In the contemporary criminal justice system, victims of family violence who kill their abuser rarely avoid a conviction. Abused women prosecuted for domestic homicide, for example, often plead guilty to manslaughter because of the "significant possibility" they will receive a non-custodial or suspended sentence.[77] Further, recent reforms of defensive homicide fail to provide women (and presumably children) with a full defence when prosecuted for killing violent men.

Yet the early twentieth century prosecutions in this chapter provide strong evidence of a more reflective criminal justice system. As this chapter – the first empirically based study of patricide prosecutions in Australian courts – shows, the "domestic discount" was evident in decisions to prosecute, acquit, and sentence children and young people who killed their fathers. Juries were not as strictly constrained by the legal requirements of specific defences and even acquitted children who were legally guilty of manslaughter. This perhaps indicates a greater understanding of the dynamics of family violence than contemporary juries appear to hold. Historically, there was a higher degree of social tolerance for domestic homicides involving male victims who contravened expected social and gender norms by engaging in family violence. The typical view appeared to be that these men were "not worthy to bear the name of father, husband, or man".[78]

---

77 Julie Stubbs and Julia Tolmie, "Battered woman syndrome in Australia: A challenge to gender bias in the law?," in *Women, Male Violence and the Law*, ed. Julie Stubbs (Sydney: The Institute of Criminology, 1994), 203.

78 "Son slays father," *World*, 17 April 1920, 5.

Chapter 5

UNCOVERING A HIDDEN OFFENCE

Social and legal histories of familial sexual abuse[1]

Andy Kaladelfos

In July 1903, husband and wife, James and Maria Horne appeared in the dock at their joint Perth trial. James was accused of raping his step-daughter, 15-year-old Florence Squires, and Maria of a rare crime, the aiding and abetting of James' offences on her daughter. Squires testified that James Horne raped her at regular intervals for four years and used a range of coercions to facilitate his abuse, including threats against her life. At the conclusion of the trial, however, the jury returned an ambiguous verdict, finding him guilty of "carnally knowing the girl" but holding "doubt" as to whether the offence was "with or without her consent".[2] The jury's verdict was referred to the Full Court for a ruling on how it should be interpreted, a referral that sparked a lengthy series of judgements that illuminate how the criminal law treated long-term familial abuse.

Using the case-study of *R v Horne* (1903) as a window into the challenges of familial sexual abuse prosecutions, this chapter investigates trends and patterns in the historical treatment of familial sexual abuse at law. First, the chapter explores the legal treatment and social experience of long-term

1 This project was supported by ARC Laureate Fellowship FL130100050 and ARC Discovery Project DP150101798. I thank my colleagues on our collaborative research team, The Prosecution Project, for their role in constructing the datasets drawn upon in the paper.

2 *The Prosecution Project*, Griffith University, 2014–2018, accessed 14 June 2018, https://prosecutionproject.griffith.edu.au/prosecutions/, Trial ID #3606 and 3607, Western Australian Supreme Court, James Horn and Maria Ann Horn, 1903. R v Horne, Western Australia, *Law Report*, 56, 1903. I have used the spelling 'Horne' as per the official law report.

abuse in the case of *Horne*. Historically, as today, familial sexual abuse often occurred in combination with violent, domineering and coercive relationships between male and female members of the family that had developed over many years, even decades; legal conceptualisations of coercion, violence, and consent were thus fundamental to familial abuse prosecutions. The chapter then takes a macro view of longitudinal patterns in incest prosecutions and their outcomes. It analyses the legal frameworks that facilitated their prosecution, how Australian supreme courts dealt with these cases, and the nature of the allegations that led to prosecutions. In doing so it provides the first Australian national-level historical analysis of prosecutions of incest and familial sexual offences.[3]

Rex v Horne (1903)

At the opening of the Hornes' trial on 7 July 1903, the Crown Prosecutor explained that Florence Squires had been raped by her step-father for a number of years, the first instance occurring when she was 11 years old. In her testimony, Squires told the jury that the abuse began while her mother had been absent from the family home, a common circumstance in cases of familial sexual abuse. She testified that her step-father had beaten and threatened to kill her to force her compliance. She explained that her mother had known about the abuse and had "frequently forced her to go into Horn's room for the purpose".[4] Defence counsel objected to the Crown presenting evidence of instances of rape that occurred before the matter in question, that is, before the particular act of rape named on the indictment as occurring on 20 January 1903. This objection, overruled at the time, would later become important to legal appeals.

Squires explained that the abuse continued for many years until January 1903, when she went to stay with her grandmother. After she left, her mother promised the abuse would not reoccur, and Florence returned home only to have her step-father rape her again. She then told her mother that she wanted to live permanently with the Salvation Army. Her mother

3 For previous Australian historical studies, see: Penelope Hetherington, *Incest and the Community: Australian Perspectives* (Perth: Centre for Western Australian History at the University of Western Australia, 1991); Jill Bavin-Mizzi, *Ravished: Sexual Violence in Victoria Australia* (Sydney: University of New South Wales Press, 1995); Yorick Smaal, "'Keeping it in the family': Prosecuting incest in colonial Queensland," *Journal of Australian Studies*, 37, no. 3 (2013): 316–332; Lisa Featherstone and Amanda Kaladelfos, "Hierarchies of harm and violence," *Australian Feminist Studies* 29, no. 81 (2014): 306–324.

4 "Criminal court," *West Australian*, 8 July 1903, 2.

agreed, telling her not to reveal the abuse to anyone. A month later at the Salvation Army Squires disclosed the abuse to a female officer, who was central to bringing the case to police. At trial, Adjutant Sawtell, the organiser of the Women's Rescue branch of the Salvation Army, testified that when she confronted James and Maria Horne they had admitted the offences. The Hornes later denied all previous admissions to involvement in the abuse.

At the conclusion of the Hornes' trial, the jury returned a "special verdict", meaning a verdict with a qualifier attached. They found James Horne guilty of "carnally knowing the girl" but added the rider that "whether [the offence was] with or without her consent, we are in doubt". Their rider, which doubted the elements of consent, clouded their already problematic finding of "carnal knowledge", which was not a possible alternate charge to rape. They were further unable to agree on the aiding and abetting charge against Maria.[5] At this stage the prosecution of the Hornes looked in jeopardy, with Commissioner Roe referring the jury's verdict to the Western Australian Full Court for a ruling on how it should be interpreted.

The Crown then took an unusual step. Without waiting for the ruling of the Full Court, the Crown indicted James and Maria on another offence on Florence Squires, alleged to have been committed on 18 January, not 20 January, the date of the original indictment. At the committal hearing on the second indictment, the Hornes' defence counsel responded by putting forward a special plea: *autrefois acquit*. James Horne submitted that he had already been acquitted on an identical matter at a previous trial (invoking the double jeopardy principle). A jury was empanelled to rule on whether Horne's plea was valid. Horne's defence counsel argued that the offence on 18 January was identical to that of 20 January, of which the accused had been "virtually acquitted". The offence on 18 January, the defence argued, was part of a series of actions that "really constituted one continuous offence, and that the alleged act on the 18th January was part of that 'system'".[6] In other words, the defence counsel argued that Horne's actions were one long instance of abuse, not multiple individual actions. In contrast, the Crown asserted that each instance of rape was a distinct offence.

Justice Parker, presiding over the hearing, directed the jury to find in Horne's favour. But the jury did not take his advice. They ruled that the accused had not been acquitted on the previous charge and should stand trial. Parker sent the verdict to the Full Court on appeal, but before the

5 "Criminal court," *West Australian*, 10 July 1903, 3.

6 "The Leederville case," *West Australian*, 21 July 1903, 3.

appeal took place the Crown proceeded with the second charge against the Hornes. At the second trial, a jury was empanelled to hear the evidence of the offence alleged on 18 January. Presided over by the same Justice Parker, the second jury convicted both James and Maria of the offence, giving a strong recommendation to mercy in the case of Maria. The Hornes' sentencing was withheld until the appeal had proceeded through to the Full Court.

A month later the case finally arrived at the Full Court, who handed down their important ruling. Presided over by Chief Justice Onslow, Justice McMillan and Justice Parker, the court held that the two offences on the girl were not a "continuous offence" as had been alleged by Horne's defence counsel. They were two separate offences and thus that Horne had been properly indicted and convicted on the second.[7] Their findings rested upon the purpose of the Crown's presentation of evidence about the long-term abuse of Squires. The Chief Justice and Justice McMillan found that the evidence had been admitted for the purpose of establishing the victim's consent. Specifically, they found that the evidence of long-term abuse was admitted to show the "reign of terror" that the accused exercised in the family home. This evidence was pursuant to the purpose of establishing Section 323 of the criminal code, which noted that consent under threats of violence was not consent at all.[8]

This section codified the nineteenth-century legal acknowledgement of the role of coercion in sexual consent, first established in English judgements in family violence cases. In the leading decision on coercion, *R v Jones* (1861), the defendant had repeatedly raped his fourteen-year-old daughter, who testified to submitting under death threats and physical violence. It was held that this showed a "reign of terror" in the home and the consequence of such "terror and dread" was that the daughter consented to her father's advances.[9] The jury in *Jones* was told that her father could be convicted of rape if they found that consent only occurred due to threats. The Western Australian Full Court cited *Jones*, and even used the very same words and sentiments, in their judgement in *Horne*.

After the Full Court's ruling, James Horne was sentenced to 10 years' imprisonment with hard labour, being spared a death sentence by the recent removal of capital punishment for rape in 1902. Maria Horne was sentenced to six months' imprisonment with hard labour. Even in the face

7 R v Horne, Western Australia, *Law Report*, 56, 1903.

8 *Criminal Code Act* 1902 (WA).

9 Rex v Jones, North Wales Circuit, *The Law Times* (LT), 13 April 1861.

of their convictions, their defence counsel still sought to minimise the sentence against James Horne by arguing that the offence "barely came within the region of rape". In the case of Maria, he asked the court not to impose a custodial sentence stating that the "woman was more or less under the influence of her husband".[10] The Horne's defence counsel thus simultaneously recognised the coercive behaviour of James Horne in his plea for Maria, while still attempting to mitigate James' actions. At sentencing, Justice Parker stated that it was a grievous offence, but thought that James Horne had not "resorted to violent measures" with his daughter and thus took a "somewhat merciful" view of the case. In sentencing Maria, Parker acknowledged that she had been under the influence of her husband in committing the offence.[11]

These lengthy proceedings against James and Maria Horne offer insights into a number of prevalent patterns in family violence. First, the case is representative of the dynamics in many cases of prolonged abuse. Squires' home was clearly one where the threat of physical violence had been present for many years, with well-established coercive emotional, physical, and sexual dynamics pervading the relationships between all family members. Abuse of this type often involved the entire family in emotional manipulation and threats, and sometimes in facilitation and cover-ups, with families often dependent upon abusers for financial and social security. These dynamics created strained and traumatic relationships between all members of the family.[12] These circumstances of family violence make such cases altogether different from single instances of sexual abuse outside the home that did not involve emotional or financial dependence or manipulation of witnesses in the way familial sexual violence did. And, as the prosecution of the Hornes showed, the circumstances of long-term familial abuse gave rise to range of evidentiary and procedural issues as the law attempted to grapple with these cases.

From one perspective, the Horne case could be testament to the law's success at dealing with long-term abuse. Horne was prosecuted, resulting in a lengthy custodial sentence. The law recognised that sexual intercourse under threat of coercion was not consent, and it allowed Squires to testify to the full extent of her abuse. But the case of *Horne* also revealed loopholes in the law's approach to violence in the home. For example, the criminal

10 "Criminal court," *West Australian*, 7 October 1903, 2.

11 "The Leederville horror," *Daily News*, 7 October 1903, 7.

12 Michael Salter, "Grace's story: Prologued incestuous abuse from childhood into adulthood," *Violence Against Women* 19, no. 2 (2013): 146–165.

law facilitated the prosecution of Maria despite an acknowledgement of her husband's coercive influence. In other words, the law could still punish others in the home acting under the coercion of abusive fathers. Further, the verdict of the first jury—that they could not decide on the issue of consent—and the defence's contention that the father's actions were one continuous offence, reveal contested understandings of the dynamics of family violence in the home. These understandings were especially prevalent in instances where dependence, threats and physical violence limited the ability to report the offence to anyone outside the family—thus it is not coincidental that it was only when Florence left the family home that she was safe to speak out.

Finally, and perhaps most importantly, Horne's prosecution revealed holes in the available statutory apparatus to deal with familial sexual abuse cases. At the time of Horne's prosecution Western Australia had legislation criminalising "incest". The crime had been introduced through criminal law amendments in 1892 that created the offence "incest" in addition to a range of other offences against women and girls. Like rape, incest clauses contained the provision that consent was not a defence to the charge, and further acknowledged the "coercion" involved in the offence by providing it as a defence for a woman above the age of 18 being charged reciprocally with the offence.[13] But the crime of "incest" applied only to lineal descendants—not step-fathers. The preclusion of step-fathers from the charge "incest" meant that there was no other option than to charge Horne with rape. In doing so the consent of the complainant became the central issue at trial, making his prosecution harder than it would have been for a biological father.

Further, had the offence occurred in another Australian state, the general carnal knowledge provision would have been available to prosecute Horne. However, this could not be applied in Western Australia as an indictment for "carnal knowledge" had to be filed within three months of the offence. In England at the time of *Horne*, this same problem with the statute of limitations was an argument put forward for the introduction of incest provisions.[14] The statute of limitations was a problem for family violence prosecutions precisely because of the fact that coercive dynamics and manipulation limited the ability to immediately report offences. Many family violence cases were only discovered once the victim was pregnant as a

13 *Criminal Law Amendment Act* 1892 (WA), section 18.

14 Victor Bailey and Sheila Blackburn, "The punishment of Incest Act 1908: A case study of law creation," *Criminal Law Review* (1979): 711–712.

result of the abuse, or once a third party became aware of the offences. Thus, the Horne's prosecution offers a window into the many legal challenges presented by long-term abuse. The legal concepts of coercion, violence, and consent were fundamental to successful prosecutions: in *Horne* they worked in favour of conviction, but the case also shows how easily the rulings could have gone the other way.

Prosecuting incest

How representative was the Horne case of prosecutions in Australia's past? The second part of this chapter addresses this question through a macro view of long-term trends in the prosecution of familial sexual assault cases in Australian courts. Historically, there were two legal approaches to prosecuting familial sexual offences. The first were relational offences, a type of "carnal knowledge" charge. These charges removed the element of consent in sexual offences for those under a certain age. The age of consent and maximum penalty provided for relational offences was higher than other carnal knowledge offences. For example, in New South Wales the age of consent for familial offences was 16 when the general age of consent was 14, and then later 17 when the general age of consent was 16. Carnal knowledge provisions were distinctive for allowing step-fathers to be prosecuted under the higher age of consent (in New South Wales and Victoria). The other legal approach to familial crimes was the provision for "incest" offences, which was an offence defined as sexual relations between lineal — or "bloodline" — relatives (either direct descendants or siblings). Incest provisions had two elements: the provision for offences on children under a particular age (18 in most states) and further provisions for adult male and female relatives in which both parties could be held liable for the offence.

Taken together, Australian criminal law's approach to sexual relations between family members were two-fold: first, the law recognised the power differentials and removed the element of consent for crimes against female relatives under certain ages; and second, it criminalised sexual relations in the "bloodline". Examining the application of the law reveals that the first purpose was more important than the latter. In general, prosecutors and judges were far less concerned with "bloodline" cases than they were with prosecuting abusive sexual relations within the family, evident from the types of cases that proceeded throughout the court system.

Using Australian supreme court data from The Prosecution Project database, a flagship historical project on the Australian criminal trial, all prosecutions where the indictment stated that the case was one of familial sexual abuse have been identified.[15] Aggregate level prosecutorial data shows that defendants indicted for incest and familial carnal knowledge offences were a little less than five per cent of all those indicted for sexual offences in Australian supreme courts. Between 1869 and 1954, no less than 631 defendants came before Australian supreme courts indicted for familial sexual offences.[16]

These 631 defendants were certainly not the only family members charged with sexual assault. Most criminal charges did not distinguish the relation between the defendant and complainant—charges of rape, sodomy, indecent assault, and general carnal knowledge offences could be laid against anyone whether they were in a familial relation or not. Offences listed as familial sexual abuse were limited by statutory definitions (applying only to fathers, step-fathers, grandfathers, and brothers) and the type of sexual offence (penetrative only) that could be charged under familial provisions. Taking these factors into account, it can safely be assumed that the real number of those charged with familial sexual abuse was much higher than five per cent of cases. Case-level studies from Queensland and New South Wales found that familial abuse comprised as little as six to as many as twenty-seven per cent of all sexual offences charges at different times.[17] Today victim survey data finds that 45 per cent of abuse before the age of 15 is committed by family members, and 14 per cent by fathers.[18]

Notwithstanding these limitations, within its remit the criminal law provided a range of avenues for successful prosecution. Historical prosecutorial data shows that when the criminal law encountered familial abuse cases it took them very seriously. Examining outcomes as a whole, conviction and sentencing data shows that familial sexual abuse was not generally tolerated

15 *The Prosecution Project* (v. 1. downloaded 20 September 2017). The charges examined were incest, carnal knowledge of daughter, and one charge containing the wording "rape upon daughter".

16 The year 1869 was the first entry that identified an offence committed upon a daughter. The raw number of identified prosecutions is expected to increase as The Prosecution Project data is finalised, but not by a large amount. Prosecutorial data is near complete for the supreme courts of Western Australia, New South Wales, South Australia, Tasmania, the Northern Territory, with only small sections of Victorian and Queensland data to finalise.

17 Smaal, "Keeping it in the family," 326; Featherstone and Kaladelfos, "Hierarchies of harm and violence," 310.

18 Australian Bureau of Statistics, *Personal Safety Survey, 2005* (2006), 42.

by the criminal law.[19] Acquittal rates were low for familial sexual offences: just 20 per cent of defendants were acquitted outright, with more than two thirds of cases gaining convictions (Table 1). This conviction rate was higher than the overall conviction rate for child sexual offences. Furthermore, 86 per cent of defendants convicted of familial sexual offences received custodial sentences (Table 2), with the average length of imprisonment at 4.68 years.[20]

Judges' sentencing remarks regularly expressed their disdain for the offence, and its implications for social order and family life. For example, in handing down a life sentence against one defendant for the abuse of his daughter, Justice Draper stated that this father had "destroyed the sanctity of his own home, and ruined his daughter", noting that "a life sentence was necessary to protect the accused's own family, and the general public".[21] The use of non-custodial sentence was sparing in most states, but Queensland and Tasmania had higher rates of non-custodial sentences than others, with close to 20 per cent of sentences, most handed down to youthful men convicted of sibling abuse. On a macro level, the application of the criminal law to cases of familial sexual offences was thus a high number of convictions and imprisonments from the late nineteenth to the mid-twentieth century.

What kinds of cases comprised these prosecutions? To establish the finer details of such trials, the following sections analyse case characteristics of every prosecuted case of the criminal offence "incest" in two jurisdictions, examining eighty-five cases in Western Australia (1892–1954) and sixty-three cases in Tasmania (1899–1954). In both jurisdictions, the most prevalent group indicted for the offences was fathers accused of committing offences upon their daughters. In Western Australia, fathers were 64 per cent of those indicted, and in Tasmania they were 44 per cent—the largest group in both jurisdictions (Figure 1). In terms of victimisation, the largest proportion of complainants in these cases were children: 55 per cent of the cases of prosecuted of male defendants in Western Australia and 40 per cent of prosecuted cases of male defendants in Tasmania were for the abuse of girls under the age of eighteen, with the average age of girls being 14 years of age in both states (Figure 2). Historically, the types of cases that

---

19 There is increasing evidence that this approach of the law occurred in a number of jurisdictions including England. Kim Stevenson, "'These are cases which it is inadvisable to drag into the light of day': Disinterring the crime in incest in early twentieth-century England," *Crime, History and Societies*, 20, no. 2 (2016): 6–28.

20 These figures include a small number of suspended sentences.

21 "The Balingup horror," *South Western Times*, 6 September 1924, 6.

Table 1: Outcomes, Familial Sexual Offences: All Australian Supreme Courts.

			Outcome, Per Defendant			Total
			Not guilty	Guilty	Withdrawn	
Supreme Court Jurisdiction	NSW	Count	11	16	0	27
		Percent	41%	59%	0%	100%
	NT	Count	1	0	0	1
		Percent	100%	0%	0%	100%
	QLD	Count	25	95	37	157
		Percent	16%	61%	24%	101%*
	SA	Count	17	65	9	91
		Percent	19%	71%	10%	100%
	TAS	Count	12	35	13	60
		Percent	20%	58%	22%	100%
	VIC	Count	32	132	4	168
		Percent	19%	79%	2%	100%
	WA	Count	17	62	7	86
		Percent	20%	72%	8%	100%
Total		Count	115	405	70	590
		Percent	20%	69%	12%	101%*

* rounding error

Table 2: Sentences, Familial Sexual Offences: All Australian Supreme Courts.

			Sentences, Per Convicted Defendant			Total
			Custodial	Non-custodial	Other custody	
Supreme Court Jurisdiction	NSW	Count	16	0	0	16
		Percent	100%	0%	0%	100%
	QLD	Count	76	18	1	95
		Percent	80%	19%	1%	100%
	SA	Count	58	7	0	65
		Percent	89%	11%	0%	100%
	TAS	Count	22	8	5	35
		Percent	63%	23%	14%	100%
	VIC	Count	123	8	1	132
		Percent	93%	6%	1%	100%
	WA	Count	54	6	2	62
		Percent	87%	10%	3%	100%
Total		Count	349	47	9	405
		Percent	86%	12%	2%	100%

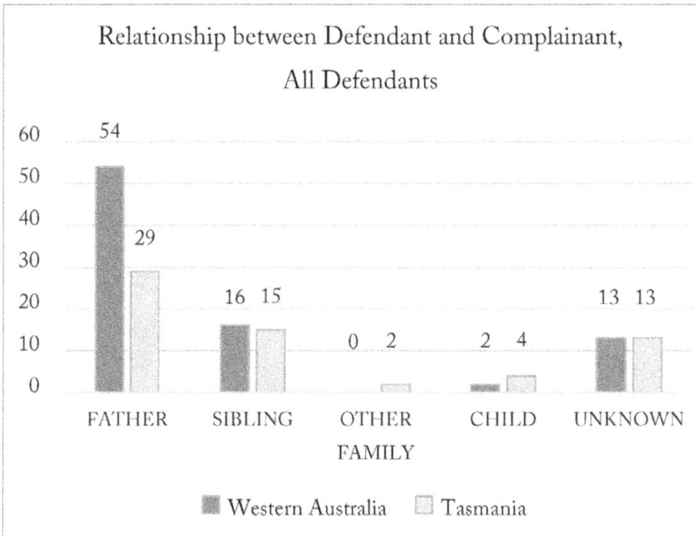

Figure 1: Count of Incest Prosecutions: Western Australia and Tasmania.

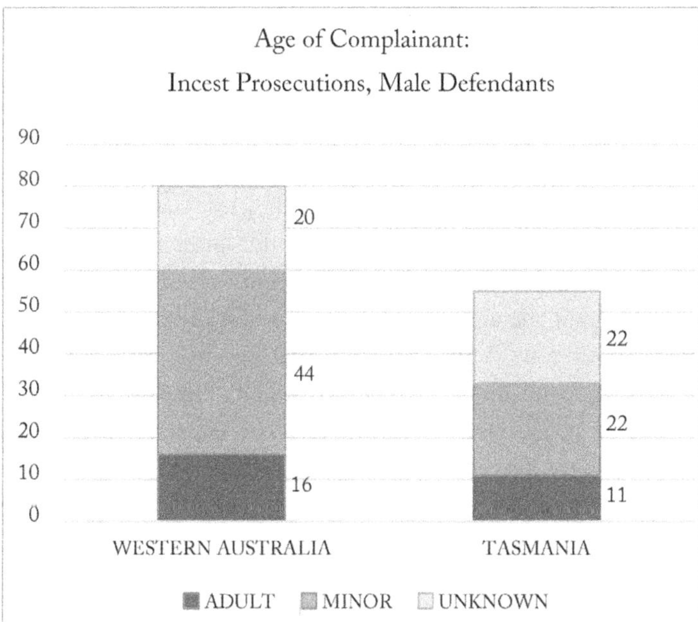

Figure 2: Count of Incest Prosecutions: Western Australia and Tasmania.

came before the courts were not cases that involved taboo relations between related adults. Rather they were most commonly abusive relations between fathers and daughters. Examining the application of historical incest laws shows that in practice the offence was used to prosecute cases that would be understood today as familial child sexual abuse.

Fathers' abuse of their daughters was similar across prosecuted cases. One common factor was the absence of the mother from the home due to work, illness, or following her death. For example, in one case of a father's incest against his sixteen-year-old daughter, she told the court that she had lived with her parents and three siblings, with all the children sleeping in the same room. But one night, when her mother was out caring for someone who was ill, her father called for his daughter to come into his room. She testified that she was scared he would beat her, and told the court that later her father sexually assaulted her in the bed she shared with her sister.[22] In a social and legal system where rape in marriage was not an offence and where patriarchal models of the family dominated social norms, some fathers viewed their daughters as a type of "sexual substitute" for an absent wife, a belief explicitly articulated by fathers into the mid-twentieth century.[23]

Daughters' relationships with their fathers came under scrutiny, with the dynamics of the family taking centre stage in building the defence's case. For example, George Simpson's daughter gave testimony that her father had been abusing her for four years. In 1910, the daughter was arrested on the charge of being a neglected child, whereupon she disclosed the abuse of her father to the arresting constable. Under cross-examination, the defence counsel questioned the girl about her public presentation of her relationship with her father, putting forward that in a letter to the girl's aunt she had spoken affectionately about him.[24] The implication was that the daughter was lying about the abuse, otherwise she would not have written about her father in this way. After the committal hearing, the Crown declined to proceed with Simpson's case. The example of Simpson illustrates social expectations of sexual abuse victims: first, the expectation for victims to immediately report offences; and second, for victims to act in particular ways towards abusive men. As scholars have noted, these dynamics within family violence cases work against victims: emotionally manipulative relations

22 "Alleged incest," *Coolgardie Miner*, 29 January 1897, 3.

23 Featherstone and Kaladelfos, "Hierarchies of harm and violence," 317.

24 "A daughter's charge," *Daily News*, 20 January 1910, 3.

between family members, together with shame and financial dependence, seriously limit the victim's abilities to report offences.[25]

Another incest prosecution revealed the impediments of controlling family dynamics to successful prosecutions. In 1903, father Charles Martin was charged with incest with his 16-year-old daughter who had recently given birth. At the committal hearing, two female witnesses testified that Martin's daughter told them the child was her father's and that Martin had himself confessed. But when his daughter was called to the stand she was declared a hostile witness. She rebutted the women's allegations and testified that her father was not responsible for her pregnancy.[26] Martin's defence counsel put forward that the *prima facie* case had not been made out, but the Resident Magistrate overruled his contention and Martin was committed to trial. At trial, the Crown proceeded with the case without the daughter's testimony, instead relying upon the testimony of the two female witnesses about their previous admissions. Without the daughter's testimony, the defence counsel went to town with assertions about the two female witnesses. "Everyone knows how women loved a dish of scandal", said the defence, claiming that the women were lying about the confessions. In the face of this conflicting evidence, the jury could not agree on Martin's guilt.[27] Later the Crown issued a *nolle prosequi* in the case, electing not to take the matter further. Martin's case further illustrates the difficulties that could arise from prosecuting offences where complainant and defendant have long-term bonds and dependent relationships, including witnesses retracting their statements.

Like fathers, prosecutions of brothers often involved testimony and actions from multiple members of the same family. These dynamics are illustrated by a 1947 Tasmanian prosecution. In this case, a father and his son were indicted for incest offences committed upon the nineteen and sixteen-year-old daughter of the father, and the thirteen-year-old sister of the brother (himself aged 17). The father was sentenced to three years' imprisonment with the Chief Justice stating there were no extenuating factors in his favour.[28] By contrast, the son was given a good behaviour bond on the condition that he maintained employment. Of the ten children living in their home, the abusive relations involved at least four siblings, and two

25 Anne Morris, "Gendered dynamics of abuse and violence in families: Considering the abusive household gender regime," *Child Abuse Review* 18 (2009): 414–427.

26 "Alleged incest," *Northam Advertiser*, 31 January 1903, 3.

27 "Alleged incest," *Northam Advertiser*, 7 March 1903, 3.

28 "Charges of incest admitted," *Mercury*, 8 March 1947, 20.

of the daughters were now pregnant from their father's abuse. The circumstances of this prosecution show how cases of family violence intersected throughout households, encompassing acts of abusive and coercive familial relations.

Women charged with incest fell under the legal remit of "permitting" an offence upon themselves. In most states, the law provided that only women over 18 could be charged with "permitting" offences, recognising the power relations that occurred in fathers' and brothers' relations with young female family members. However, Tasmania was an outlier. In 1924, Tasmania introduced 16 as the age at which women could be charged with "permitting" offences. But prior to this introduction, Tasmanian incest legislation (1899) did not provide any age-based barrier in the prosecution of the offence. That is, a female of any age could be charged with "permitting" offences. Fortunately, the provision was sparingly used while in operation, with Supreme Court data revealing only one example of the charge. This example was from 1904 when a father and his 15-year-old daughter appeared as co-accused in an incest prosecution.[29] Newspaper reports of this case indicate that the daughter had given birth to a child born from the sexual abuse of her father. But no further documentation exists of the outcome of this prosecution, leading to the assumption that it was discontinued before trial.

In Tasmania, half of the women prosecuted for incest in Tasmania were accused of offences with brothers, while the other four were accused of offences with fathers. Two of the female defendants related to one very unusual case from a rural area outside Launceston where four adult members of the same family were indicted on incest charges: a father and his adult daughter, and an adult son and his adult sister. Both daughters, aged 25 and 26, had recently given birth to children born of the relations with their male family members.[30] All members of the family pled guilty to the offences, but only the father eventually received a custodial sentence. This can be seen as evidence that the court saw the father as the most responsible for the sexual behaviours of the family.

---

29 Trial ID #62088 and #62087, Tasmanian Supreme Court, Martha Mansson and Sven Mansson, 1904; "St Helens," *Examiner*, 30 November 1904, 3.

30 "Four persons charged with incest," *Mercury*, 5 March 1949, 8.

Conclusion

The dynamics of family violence were underscored by the unequal and gendered power relationships between husband and wife, parents and children, and between siblings. Within families, these relationships developed over years, even decades, making the circumstances of abuse within the family fundamentally different in character and prosecution to singular instances of violence between acquaintances or strangers. Family violence cases were characterised by a number of elements of control: financial dependence, the closed nature of the family, and the social expectations of the family unit, including sexual expectations of female family members. All these roles and relationships were governed by patriarchal models of male power within the household that saw threats, violence, and control over many aspects of family life.

The criminal law itself recognised these power relations by stipulating that sexual consent was immaterial to the charge of incest for girls under the age of 18. When the law was called upon to act, it was robust enough to see a very low acquittal rate of these cases in comparison to other types of sexual offences and a high imposition of custodial sentences. Examining the practical application of the law shows that the prosecution of incest did not involve, by and large, policing consensual sex between related adults. Historical prosecutions were far more concerned with a father's (often prolonged) sexual abuse of their young daughters and, in rarer instances, with a brother's abuse of their younger sisters. Historically, the criminal law was used primarily to deal with cases that involved the abuse of trust and responsibility within the family, a recognition of the potential for violence within the family. But because of the nature of the dynamics of the home and the power relationships between complainant and defendant, these cases walked a fine line between successful prosecution and serious evidentiary problems that could easily stymie prosecution.

Chapter 6

CRIMINALISING THE HUSBAND AND THE HOME

Marital rape law reform, 1976–1994[1]

Lisa Featherstone

From 1976 to 1994, Australian states and territories introduced various reforms to sexual assault laws, expanding the definition of sexual assault and reconsidering the treatment of victims in the courtroom.[2] The legislative changes were driven by the broader social and sexual shifts surrounding feminism and the sexual revolution, including changing ideas about women's roles, morality and sexual practice. Most changes to rape legislation, seen as reflective of women's shifting status in a modernising society, were welcomed. Just one reform caused prolonged, even virulent, controversy: rape in marriage law reform. Prior to the feminist legal interventions of the late 1970s and 1980s, marital rape was not criminalised at all: a husband had immunity from prosecution for the rape of his wife. Though rape in marriage was ultimately criminalised in all Australian jurisdictions, there was much opposition to the idea that it should be a criminal offence for a husband to sexually assault his wife.[3]

---

1 This chapter is a version of a longer article, first published in *Gender and History*. With thanks to the editors of *Gender and History* and Wiley publishers for permission to republish this work.

2 Gail Mason, "Reforming the Law of Rape: incursions into the masculinist sanctum," in *Sex, Power and Justice*, ed. Diane Kirby (Melbourne: Oxford University Press, 1995), 50–69.

3 The state and territory-based legislation includes *Crimes (Sexual Assault) Amendment Act* 1981 (NSW); *Crimes (Amendment) Act* 1985 (Vic); *Criminal Code Amendment (Sexual Offences) Act* 1987 (Tas); *Acts Amendment (Sexual Assaults) Act* 1985 (WA);

This chapter will explore the heterogeneous opposition to rape in marriage law reform to illuminate the profound and lingering tensions between legislative change and diverse, complex public opinions towards intimate partner violence. I argue that the criminalisation of marital rape was disturbing for many because it crossed the boundaries of private and public spaces. In an attempt to ensure women's physical, emotional and sexual safety, reformers demanded state intervention into the private world of the home and family. Yet for those who opposed the concept of marital rape, this was a boundary that should not be traversed: the marriage bed ought, in their opinion, to remain untouched by the state.

Further, this chapter explores the ways the rapist had to be redefined to include the husband. Suggesting that rape in marriage was both possible and reasonably common demanded rethinking the category of "rapist": far from being a monstrous stranger in a dark alley, he might now be a partner and thus indistinguishable from other men. He might be in any – or indeed every – home. Criminalising rape within marriage offered a fundamental challenge to how both masculine and familial authority were conceptualised, established and policed. Rape in marriage legislation was confronting precisely because it questioned the relationship between protection, the state and the family. These tensions rendered rape law reform complex and highly contested.

Marital rape and the law

A husband's immunity from rape prosecution had a long historical tradition in British law, established by the eminent judge and jurist Sir Matthew Hale in 1736:

> A husband cannot be guilty of rape upon his wife for by their mutual matrimonial consent and contract the wife hath given up herself in this kind to her husband which she cannot retract.[4]

Crimes (Amendment) Ordinance (No 5) 1985 (ACT); *Criminal Code, Evidence Act and Other Acts Amendment Act* 1989 (Qld); *Criminal Code Amendment Act (No 3)* 1994 (NT). In South Australia, *Criminal Law Consolidation Act Amendment Act* 1976 (SA) was a partial criminalisation of marital rape; full criminalisation took place under *Criminal Law Consolidation (Rape) Amendment Act* 1992 (SA). In Common Law, R v L, *Commonwealth Law Report* 174 (1991): 379, the High Court held that if a wife giving irrevocable consent was ever part of the common law in Australia, it was no longer so.

4 Sir Matthew Hale, in David Lanham, "Hale, misogyny and rape," *Criminal Law Journal* 7 (1983): 148.

Marriage was understood, in and of itself, as consent to sex between spouses at any time: a woman could not deny her husband sexual access to her body, granting a husband immunity from prosecution for the rape of his wife. Hale's authority was established through a series of common law rulings in Britain, and Australia followed suit.

The long-held legal truism of a husband's immunity only began to unravel in the twentieth century, beginning in cases of separated spouses. At what point of a separation would a wife no longer be legally committed to her sexual duties? By the mid-twentieth-century in Britain, case law suggested that a husband could expect sex from a wife even after divorce proceedings had begun, but not after a *decree nisi* had been granted.[5] While some rulings chipped away at a husband's right to sex after separation, more broadly, the sanctity of a husband's immunity remained.[6]

It was not until the social and sexual revolutions of the 1960s and 1970s that there was a profound challenge to the idea that a man had full and unquestionable sexual access to his wife. Second-wave feminism brought gender inequality to the fore of public consciousness in many western nations.[7] Feminist arguments began to permeate society; what had once been a specifically feminist agenda was debated increasingly openly in the press. Many emerging discussions centred on the lack of "logic" in the law: it was illogical that a woman could prosecute for rape before marriage and after a marriage, but not within a marriage.[8] Most of the arguments that supported legislative change relied heavily on these common-sense

---

5 Criminal Law and Penal Methods Reform Committee of South Australia, *Special Report* (1976), 13. On the South Australian situation, see: Lisa Featherstone and Alexander George Winn, "Marital rape and the marital rapist: The 1976 South Australian rape law reforms," *Feminist Legal Studies* (2018): 1–22. DOI:10.1007/s10691-018-9382-3. For a short study of some cases from Victoria in the mid 1970s, which attempted to define "separation" in cases of rape within marriage, see: Christopher Corns, "Liability of husbands for rape-in-marriage – the Victorian position," *Criminal Law Journal* 7 (1983): 104–106.

6 Joanna Bourke, *Rape: A History from 1860 to the Present Day* (London: Virago, 2007), 318–319.

7 For second-wave feminism in Australia, see: Marilyn Lake, *Getting Equal: The History of Australian Feminism* (St Leonards: Allen & Unwin, 1999), 231–252; Gisele Kaplan, *The Meagre Harvest: the Australian Women's Movement 1950s-1990* (St. Leonards: Allen & Unwin, 1996); Ann Curthoys, "Doing it for themselves: The women's movement since 1970," in *Gender Relations in Australia: Domination and Negotiation*, ed. Kay Saunders and Raymond Evans (Sydney: Harcourt Brace Jovanovich,1992), 425–447.

8 Jacqueline Rees, "Researching the hidden crime of family violence," *Australian Women's Weekly (AWW)*, 13 December 1978, 21.

propositions, especially the idea that married and unmarried women should have the same rights.[9]

Yet arguments in favour of criminalisation dug deeper than a simple call for equality. The core of the debate, feminists asserted, was that women needed to be understood as autonomous agents who had the right to reject sex at any time.[10] Delving into ideas of violence and patriarchy, feminists argued that the law was nonsensical in attempting to define what forms of violence were acceptable in the home. The Women's Advisory Council of New South Wales noted that it was illegal for a husband to physically assault his wife, steal her property, kidnap or forcibly detain her. Yet it was not illegal for him to rape her.[11] Feminists showed that if a woman refused to have sex with her husband, and he beat her, theoretically he could be charged with physical, but not sexual, assault. These incongruities were often contextualised by broader substantive feminist demands to collapse the divide between the private and public: feminist lawyer Jocelynne Scutt in particular spoke out against the legal and policing cultures that turned a blind eye to the 'private' assaults of domestic violence and marital rape. Her work, which was published widely in both mainstream and feminist media, condemned the idea that marriage and family had to be protected at a cost to the sexual autonomy and physical safety of the wife.[12]

Philosophical and legal appeals to autonomy, equality and women's rights were backed by the stories of individual women who stepped forward to tell of their experiences in violent marriages. Influenced by the feminist assertion that the personal was political, even mainstream media began to give voice to women who had been sexually assaulted by their husbands. Media outlets published quite raw interviews, often with graphic content.[13] The shock of these individual stories disrupted the idea that the family home was a safe haven from violence and sexual abuse. The publication of first-hand accounts of marital rape, other forms of physical and sexual violence, and explicit detailing of sexual humiliations, offered a window into the

9 Marie Fisher, Crimes (Sexual Assault) Amendment Bill, *NSW Parliamentary Debates* 1980–1981, 160, 8 April 1981, 5487; "Law and Rape," *Sydney Morning Herald*, 18 October 1977, 6.

10 Michele Howell-Price, "Concept on rape gets blessings," *Adelaide Advertiser*, 11 August 1976.

11 "Both men and women should enjoy the full protection of the law," *AWW*, 13 August 1980, 15.

12 Rees, "Researching the hidden crime of family violence," 21.

13 For example, see: Stewart Cockburn, "Women tell of rape within marriage," *Adelaide Advertiser*, 25 September 1976. This newspaper article was mentioned in parliamentary debates on a number of occasions.

sexually abusive household and made it difficult to argue that such violence was not a scourge on Australian society.

This new knowledge was further heightened by community unease over horrific local and international cases that demonstrated the protection the law offered husbands who sexually assaulted their wives.[14] While a number of shocking high-profile cases occurred in Britain,[15] controversial were also cases reported from local jurisdictions. One such trial occurred in Victoria in 1985, known as *Re C*. In Victoria, legislation criminalising rape in marriage after a separation had occurred had been introduced in 1980.[16] *Re C* involved a woman, now living with her mother, who had left her husband after a violent physical assault. Two days after the assault, she had returned to the marital home to pack her belongings. Her husband then sexually attacked her – anally raping her three times, forcing her to perform fellatio and vaginally raping her. In court, the Judge ruled that the separation was not fully established, and thus the man would have immunity from prosecution. There was widespread outcry. Feminist graffiti sprung up in Melbourne: "Marriage is not a licence to rape." Even the conservative newspaper *The Age* expressed shock at the judgement.[17] Public pressure was effective in forcing governments to act – in Victoria, a husband's immunity was removed in 1985, not long after the *Re C* case. The same pressures were also brought to bear in other states, producing change in all jurisdictions, sometimes quickly, sometimes more slowly.[18] But despite the ultimate success of campaigners, there was much opposition from a range of sectors to the removal of a husband's immunity.

Defining rape

For many of those who opposed marital rape law reform, the problem was an inability to reconcile the concept of sexual assault and the public image of the rapist as a masked stranger, with actions by intimate partners.

---

14 Joelle Chenoweth, "Rape, and nothing else: Sex, violence and law reform in NSW," *Antithesis* 6 (1993): 34–38; Deidre O'Connor, "Rape law reform – The Australian experience Part 1," *Criminal Law Journal* 1 (1977): 305. For a detailed examination of pertinent case law prior to law reform, see: Jocelynne Scutt, "Consent in rape: The problem of the marriage contract," *Monash University Law Review* 3 (1977): 255–288.

15 For example, see the British case: *Morgan v DPP* (1975).

16 Corns, "Liability for Husbands," 104–06.

17 Jocelynn Scutt, "Judgements of right thinking men: Marriage, rape and law reform," *Scarlet Woman* 21 (1986): 23.

18 Mason, "Reforming the law".

Marital rape was thus not always recognised as criminal behaviour, either in the courtroom or in the broader culture. Professor Duncan Chappell, who interviewed workers and clients of women's shelters while heading a Law Reform Commission, suggested that women did not necessarily see sexual violence as rape. Rather, women saw it as "merely one part of the general violence they had to put up with".[19] Similarly, Annette Wilcox of the Naomi women's shelter revealed that women who came to the refuge rarely identified their partners as rapists. When asked, women replied that they had not ever been raped. But when the staff interrogated further about unwanted sex, they replied, "Oh yes, that happens all the time". Instead of recognising this as an assault, Wilcox claimed the women felt this was simply a part of their married life.[20] Men, too, did not recognise forced sex within marriage as rape. As one caller to a talkback radio show claimed in 1980, it was simply not possible for a man to rape his wife. The radio jock agreed, adding, "I think a lot of men may feel this way".[21]

There was a great deal of slippage in mainstream Australia between concepts of rape and ideas of unwanted sex during marriage. The boundaries were unclear for many. This ambivalence was highlighted in 1980, when the *Australian Women's Weekly* (*AWW*) held a major survey of over 30,000 local women. It was not a survey specifically about rape, but it was one of the largest, most in-depth surveys on women's issues in Australia, and it drew on a broad sample.[22] When questioned on the right of a man to rape his wife, over two thirds of women agreed that a husband should be prosecuted. On the surface, it would appear that by 1980, a significant majority of mainstream Australian women believed that husbands should no longer be immune from prosecution for marital rape.

Yet, there was still a notable level of ambivalence. In addition to the statistical analysis of the survey, the *AWW* invited women to attach letters, and some 10,000 Australian women did so. From these letters, the *AWW* printed three quite divergent views on rape in marriage. The first, from "A Melbourne Woman," showed an ingrained belief in the right of a man to sexual access during marriage: "I cannot see how a husband could rape his wife (unless they were separated). If they are together, then sex is part of

19 Cited in "An investigation into the myths of domestic violence," *AWW*, 17 September 1980, 60.

20 Interview conducted by female researcher for Peter Sallmann and Duncan Chappell, *Rape Law Reform: A Study of the South Australian Experience* (Adelaide: Australian Criminology Research Council, 1977), 31.

21 "Pam on 2GB," *WEL* 97, December 1980, 2–4.

22 "Women talk about rape," *AWW*, 23 July 1980, 30.

marriage".[23] It was a definitive response. A second letter from a "Hobart Woman" accepted the overly amorous husband within the "normal" relationship, but not the separated husband. She suggested that an "over-romantic or drunk husband, who has normal sexual relations with his wife, is hardly a rapist and should not be prosecuted". She noted that marital sex was complicated, and she pondered, "where does one draw the line?"

Only one of the three published comments suggested women should be autonomous within marriage, though even this did not necessarily discuss concepts of consent. "A Sydney woman" drew instead on older notions of chivalry, suggesting: "Husbands should be taught to respect their wives wishes, and the same with men and their girlfriends. Respect is important".[24] Thus even after almost a decade of second-wave feminism, traditional ideas about marriage, masculinity and female autonomy were still prominent, and many were ambivalent about what constituted rape. Beyond this, however, there remained a number of core groups who openly and determinedly opposed marital rape law reform.

The 'destruction' of marriage itself

The most powerful argument put forth by critics of marital rape law reform was both simple and emotive: it was a direct challenge to paternal authority and to the sanctity of marriage and the family. The narrative of familial destruction depended on two imaginings. First, it required a neat split between the public and private worlds – where the former had little impact on the latter, and where the state had no jurisdiction within the family home. Second, it required rape in marriage law to be seen as a concerted attack on this "right" to home authority: a woman's physical safety had to be subsumed to the greater good of the family itself. And it is surprising just how common and pervasive this discussion was.

The perceived attack on "the family" was often explained in impassioned, even sensationalised terms. In South Australia in 1976, the conservative Women's Council of the Liberal Party suggested the legal changes were "divisive, an attack on the family, and a ridiculous piece of legislation".[25] Similarly, in New South Wales, Senator O'Dowd of the Liberal Party suggested that his Party opposed rape in marriage legislation because

---

23 "Should husbands be prosecuted for rape?" *AWW,* 23 July 1980, 35.

24 Ibid.

25 *The National Times,* 27 September-20 October 1976, cited in Sallmann and Chappell, *Rape Law Reform.*

"the law should not come between husband and wife and thereby harm marriage".[26] His compatriot Mr Cameron went one step further, claiming the proposed laws "touched directly on the traditional standing of marriage as the foundation of our community".[27]

In a period of social and sexual change, conservatives imagined marriage as a "frail institution" that needed constant bolstering.[28] Keeping the family intact was key, even in cases of violence. As one member of Parliament suggested, "even after such an appalling event as rape in marriage, some marriages can be saved. However imperfect the institution of marriage may be, it is far too important to society for it to be endangered".[29] This argument did not deny that rape could and did occur within marriage. Instead, it suggested that violence should not necessarily end a marriage, and it was argued that once the heat of the moment had passed, reconciliation might be possible.[30]

This seeming deference to the concept of the family was profoundly troubling, as it wrote out issues of consent and autonomy for women. Those who opposed rape law reform were suggesting that sex was not a negotiation between partners, but a right triggered by the act of marriage. Many saw this as unproblematic. One commentator suggested that "a husband should not walk in the shadow of the law of rape in trying to regulate his sexual relationships with his wife".[31] In this way, marriage was constructed as a "special relationship", with specific rights and responsibilities.[32] This included the right to demand sex, and some argued that women did not often actively oppose or reject sex, but they were sometimes indifferent.[33] In these cases, a man had the right to insist. Refusing sex was "ill–conceived", noted one politician.[34] Still others rejected the idea that a wife could or would consent to individual acts of sex: as one politician noted, marriage itself entailed access to a spouse's body. Clearly, he remained unswayed by

---

26 Mr O'Dowd, Crimes (Sexual Assault) Amendment Bill, *NSW Parliamentary Debates* 1980–81, 60, 25 March 1981, 5197.

27 Mr Cameron, Crimes (Sexual Assault) Amendment Bill, 5215.

28 Mr O'Dowd, Crimes (Sexual Assault) Amendment Bill, 5382.

29 Mr O'Dowd, Crimes (Sexual Assault) Amendment Bill, 5387.

30 Mr JA Clough, Crimes (Sexual Assault) Amendment Bill, 5386.

31 Colin Howard, *Australian Criminal Law*, Melbourne, 1970, cited in Cameron, Crimes (Sexual Assault) Amendment Bill, 5216.

32 "Rape within Marriage," *Light*, November 1976, 6. See also: "Women Reject NSW Rape in Marriage Proposal," *Light*, February 1981, 6.

33 O'Dowd, Crimes (Sexual Assault) Amendment Bill, 5387.

34 Ibid.

the feminist agenda, claiming that "no one would disagree with that".[35] Even some female politicians argued that a wife should "submit" to sex as a marital obligation, even if intercourse was undesired.[36]

Alongside arguments over how consent might be defined, the debate also centred on the spatial politics of the home.[37] Opponents argued that the new legislation aimed to "knock down the bedroom door and invade the sanctum for the express purpose of bringing a prosecution against a husband".[38] Comments such as this revealed what might be termed a domestification of violence, where violence was sanctioned within certain domestic spaces, namely the marital bed. This attempted rearticulation of the divide between the public and private spheres – where the bedroom was the most private space of all – was also an assertion of the role of the state within the home. As one New South Wales parliamentarian noted, it was unimaginable that police should be asked to deal with marital rape. He claimed that police already avoided domestic disputes unless the neighbours were being disturbed. It would be an "intolerable burden", he claimed, to ask law enforcement to step into the sanctity of the home to police sexual violence between married couples.[39]

Debates in parliament indicate that conservative views on marriage and rape were not solely based on religious views, and many religious groups did not necessarily publicly comment on the new legislations. Some, however, were vocal opponents to the criminalising of marital rape. Most notable was the Festival of Light, a non-denominational, conservative Christian organisation led by Fred Nile. The Festival of Light claimed the new legislation dealt marriage a "crushing blow".[40] According to the group, it would mean that couples would not attempt to "repair a crack in the marriage", but instead women would use the law "like a sledge hammer on a wedge".[41] Most notably, the Festival of Light were alarmed that, under the new laws, a husband who raped his wife would be seen "as guilty of rape as the teenage lout who waylays a young girl crossing the park".[42] The Festival of Light were reasonably unconcerned about the consent of women

35 NM Orr, Crimes (Sexual Assault) Amendment Bill, 5479.

36 Mrs Foot, Crimes (Sexual Assault) Amendment Bill, 5204.

37 For the politics of sexual geographies and public/private spaces, see: Phil Hubbard, "Sex zones: Intimacy, citizenship and public space," *Sexualities* 4 (2001): 57–71.

38 Mr Hatton, Crimes (Sexual Assault) Amendment Bill, 5384.

39 Mr Hatton, Crimes (Sexual Assault) Amendment Bill, 5384.

40 "Rape within marriage," 6.

41 Ibid.

42 Ibid.

to sex within marriage. As members of the Church noted in their official magazine, "Most husbands and wives are habituated to sexual intercourse and it must be obvious that this will sometimes happen against the protests of the wife".[43] Even women in the movement promoted radical ideas about sex and marriage. Prominent Festival of Light barrister Miss Janet Coombs suggested that if a woman did not want to have children, and her husband did, it was part of his "marriage right" to expect sex even on her most fertile days.[44] Within this framework for thinking about marital rights and obligations, a wife's consent did not matter at all.

The concept of the "vindictive wife"

In some ways, the wife was – ironically – a shadowy figure in discussions about marital rape.[45] While the media had opened up to offer her a small voice in public debate, within conservative discourses she was once again silenced. Instead, she stood as a proxy for marital privilege; her body was her husband's, to do as he pleased. She was therefore both present and absent in arguments from those who opposed criminalising marital rape. The only time she became truly visible was in discussions about the "vindictive wife." Fears over the vindictive wife were regularly expressed, and she became a stock figure representing anxieties over the misuse of power within the marital relationship. Today, we would read the husband who demanded sex as the troubling spouse. But for those who opposed marital rape law reform, the so-called vindictive wife was the problem, for she could and would raise false accusations against hapless or innocent men.

The discourse of the vindictive wife was incredibly powerful. In New South Wales parliamentary debates, her spectre was raised over and over again. The conservative Opposition were concerned women would be "malicious" or "bitchy".[46] There were concerns that the legislation would be misused to solve other marital complaints, including broader domestic violence.[47] Opponents to the law reform often made light of the difficulties women had in negotiating consensual sex. As one member of Parliament

43 Ibid.

44 Cited by Mr Bretton, Crimes (Sexual Assault) Amendment Bill, 5228.

45 For a wider discussion on the ways individual women stood outside narratives of domestic violence, even while they were supposedly at the centre, see: Ann Genovese, "The battered body," *Australian Feminist Studies* 12, no. 25 (1997): 91–103.

46 NM Orr, Crimes (Sexual Assault) Amendment Bill, 5480; Mr JA Clough, Crimes (Sexual Assault) Amendment Bill, 5386.

47 Mr Moore, Crimes (Sexual Assault) Amendment Bill, 5391.

noted, it offered avenues for women who had "a headache" to charge her husband with sexual assault. He added that the husband who dared stop his wife taking money out of the bank might be in for "a real bother".[48] The trivialising of women's sexual autonomy was common in these debates.

Others were concerned not with women, but with men, and more specifically with the rights of men. As one parliamentarian argued, it was men who "should be protected".[49] But like women (other than the fictional vindictive wife), men figured very little in public discourses around rape in general. This absence is telling, and reflected a wide public unease about men's role in sexual assault. This tension had a substantial historical tradition across twentieth-century Australia, where violence was discursively displaced from the home to the street.[50] Criminalising marital rape destabilised these ideas, indicating that the home was not necessarily a place of sanctity, and the rapist was not always a psychopath or social deviant. Instead, he might be a "normal" male, in a seemingly average home.[51] Indeed, one of the key challenges of rape law reform was that it established everyman as a potential rapist, and every home as the potential site of sexual assault.

The crime that would be 'impossible' to prove

The final counter to criminalising marital rape was simple: it would be simply impossible to prove rape within marriage. This idea was surprisingly prevalent, across a significant array of interest groups.[52] Amongst conservatives, the issue of practicalities may simply have been an excuse to cover ideological opposition. But the Left also raised concerns. Sociologist and libertarian Paul Wilson firmly supported the criminalisation of marital rape, suggesting it was essential to sexual autonomy and the rights of women. He was concerned, however, that legislative change would have

48 LA Solomons, Crimes (Sexual Assault) Amendment Bill, 5462.

49 NM Orr, Crimes (Sexual Assault) Amendment Bill, 5481.

50 Lisa Featherstone and Amanda Kaladelfos, "Hierarchies of harm and violence: Historicising familial sexual violence in Australia," *Australian Feminist Studies* 29, no. 81 (2014): 306–324; Amanda Kaladelfos, "The dark side of the family: Paternal child homicide in Australia," *Journal of Australian Studies* 37, no. 3 (2013): 333–348; Yorick Smaal, "Keeping it in the family: Incest in colonial Australia," *Journal of Australian Studies* 37, no. 3 (2013): 316–332.

51 On defining "normal", see: "Stop rape, an observation," *Sydney Women's Liberation Newsletter* (*SWLN*), July 1977, 7; "Canberra rape crisis centre, an observation," *SWLN*, February 1983, 7.

52 "Law and rape," 6.

little impact. Few men would be prosecuted, and even fewer found guilty, because the prejudices of the judicial system remained largely intact. In particular, Wilson was concerned by the impossibility of corroboration: how would rape in marriage be proven?[53]

Similarly, some feminists, including radical feminists, challenged the concept of marital rape reform. This stemmed from broad misgivings about the state's ability to deal with women's issues. Feminists – already concerned about the high rates at which women were raped, the low rates of prosecution of offenders, and the treatment of women victims in the courtroom – advised that rape in marriage laws would never be effective under the conditions of a patriarchal culture. They feared that any legislative change would do little, as the traditions of the patriarchal family (including a man's right to sex) were supported by the Church, the broader culture, and, in reality, the courts.[54] Feminists recognised that the raft of laws designed to "protect" women were not functional. Existing laws did not protect women from domestic violence; when it did occur, policing and legal frameworks took little action. Similarly, there were strong penalties for rape and indecent assault, but these did not prevent sexual assault in the wider community.[55] As one anarchist-feminist group argued, this "reform does nothing but attempt to placate married women into a feeling of security (a false security)".[56]

Marital rape law reform, it was felt, would not change this dual problem of violence and misogyny.[57] Those feminists who had already witnessed law reform in some states suggested that earlier legislative changes had not altered the policing or prosecution of rape in marriage:

> There hasn't been a prosecution in NSW and there probably won't be one if the woman is still living with her husband or hasn't a divorce. Even if a miracle did happen and a woman did get it as far as the courthouse, court procedures were such that it is still the word of a woman against a man.[58]

---

53 Paul Wilson, *The Other Side of Rape* (St. Lucia: University of Queensland Press, 1978), 105.

54 "Women and violence conference, 15–16 March 1980," *SWLN*, April 1980, 1; "Violence in marriage and the law," *SWLN*, November-December 1976, 5.

55 Coonan, "Rape law reform," 43.

56 "Laws rape," *Everything: Anarchist-Feminist Magazine* 3 (n.d., circa early 1980s), 7.

57 Coonan, "Rape law reform," 43.

58 "Marital rape week," *SWLN*, November 1981, 7.

Thus while the women's liberation movement had in many ways conceptualised and driven marital rape law reform, there were nonetheless deep ambivalences within the broader feminist movement about the role of the state and the gendered institution of the law. Many feminists remained unconvinced that the law was an effective tool to protect women from violence.

Conclusions: Marital rape, gender, family

Removing marital immunity through rape law reform was, on the surface, about offering wives protection via the criminal law code. It aimed to be educative (and hence preventative), but also punitive if and when required. But it was never as simple as that. This chapter has offered a detailed genealogy of the opposition to marital rape law reform in Australia in the 1970s and 1980s, and explores the ambivalences, ambiguities and occasional downright hostility towards criminalising marital rape. It reveals that many felt that the intrusion of the state into homes and bedrooms could undermine the traditions of marriage, and similarly, could break down paternalistic authority within the home. Some argued that such violence did not exist; sex remained a right and obligation within marriage, whether or not the wife consented. Other forces of opposition focused on the "vindictive wife", and the additional power such legislation would allegedly grant to vicious women. Finally, many agreed that the laws simply would not work, for it was impossible to prosecute sex within the marital bed.

Read together, these voices reveal much about how sexual violence was understood in a period of substantial social and political change. The forces of opposition were wide and varied, but all argued stridently that legislative reform could not solve the problem of violence against women in the home. Underlying these debates was a deeply felt crisis over gender and the relationship between men, women and the state. Legislating marital rape challenged the sovereignty of the family itself by questioning the split between the public and private. Further, it challenged the ideas about what kinds of men could and would be a rapist – moving the idea of a rapist from a man in a dark alley, to incorporate everyman, potentially in every neighbourhood.

All of these cultural challenges ensured there was substantial opposition to rape law reform around marital rape, and that legislation did not, and could not, entirely solve the problem of violence against women within the home. The legacies of these debates remain with us today. Intimate partner sexual violence continues to be difficult for victims to define and report, and for authorities to police and prosecute. Though the law does now acknowledge the potential for intimate partner sexual assault, there are a range of cultural and legal prohibitions preventing reporting and successful prosecution. Rape within marriage may not always be considered "real rape", with criminological and sociological studies consistently proving that the closer the relationship between victim and offender, the less likely that forced sex is defined as "rape".[59] Intimate partner violence is also invisibilised through the idea that the family home is a privileged space, and marriage a private relationship, where the law has little impact.[60] Assumptions of "wifely duties" and sexual obligations, as well as confusion when a victim continues to live with the offender after the assault, all serve to make marital rape difficult to prosecute. The situation is further complicated in cases of physical, emotional or financial abuse (where the victim may not be safe to report the crime or may withdraw the complaint), or in instances where evidence of non-consent may be lacking, leading police to decline prosecution. Despite significant legislative change, and a wider social acknowledgement that rape in marriage is possible, cultural and legal constructions of family, marriage and gendered sexual autonomy mean that we have not yet solved the issue of sexual violence within intimate relationships.

---

59 Jennifer A. Bennice and Patricia A. Resick, "Marital rape: History, research, and practice," *Trauma, Violence and Abuse* 4, no. 3 (2003): 231–234.

60 T.K. Logan, Robert Walker and Jennifer Cole, "Silenced Suffering: The Need for a Better Understanding of Partner Sexual Violence," *Trauma, Violence and Abuse* 16, no. 2 (2015): 111–135.

Section II

Gender Violence in the Community

Chapter 7

THE "DROVER'S BOY" AND INDIGENOUS WOMEN'S UNTHINKABLE CONSENT

Liz Conor

A 1990 song by Australian folk musician Ted Egan narrates the burial of a Drover's Boy and the stockmen's confusion about the Drover's grief:

> And he told of the massacre in the west
> Barest details guess the rest
> Shoot the bucks, grab a gin, cut her hair,
> Break her in, call her a boy. The Drover's Boy.[1]

Urging us never to forget the Drover's Boy, Egan sings of how she was a "faithful wife but never a bride". A 1997 picture book illustrated by Robert Ingpen (Figure 1 and Figure 2) set the lyrics against drawings ostensibly taken from historical photographs and official forms replicated from the Northern Territory Aboriginals Department. This included a 1911 ordinance which proposed specific sartorial codes aimed at curtailing the exploitation of young Aboriginal women, but actually governed the employment of women stockworkers on the pastoral frontier. "Should an Aboriginal or half-caste woman be found "in male attire and in the company of any male person other than an Aboriginal or half-caste'", the ordinance proclaimed, "both were guilty of an offence."[2] Effectively,

1 Ted Egan, "The drover's boy," on Ted Egan and Nerys Evans, *The Drover's Boy: A Celebration of Australian Women* (Alice Springs: Ted Egan Enterprises, 1993), CD.

2 Quoted in C.D. Rowley, *The Destruction of Aboriginal Society* (Harmondsworth: Penguin, 1974), 219.

this provision outlawed the "Drover's Boy" – a cross-dressing racialised typecast at the intersections of gender, sexuality, race and class. It effaced the immense contribution of women's labour in the pastoral industry. Quite literally disguised, women were not even recorded in station employment or protectorate records.[3] But something else was equally effaced through the Northern Territory ordinance and the racialised type of the Drover's Boy, namely Aboriginal women's capacity for consent.

In his illustrated book (Figure 2), Egan wants 'these pioneering women of northern Australia' to be remembered for their contribution to the pastoral industry. He notes they were dressed as men to circumvent laws forbidding their employment. Disturbingly, he says the girls were mostly the spoils of reprisal raids, becoming "virtual slaves", and yet "genuine love" sometimes developed between Drover's Boys and their "bosses" because of their "mutual dependence" in harsh circumstances. Egan himself worked as a patrol officer and reserve superintendent for the Department of Aboriginal Affairs from the early 1950s to 1974. In an unusual stance for the era, he decried the ban on interracial marriages and said their mixed-race children testified to their love.[4]

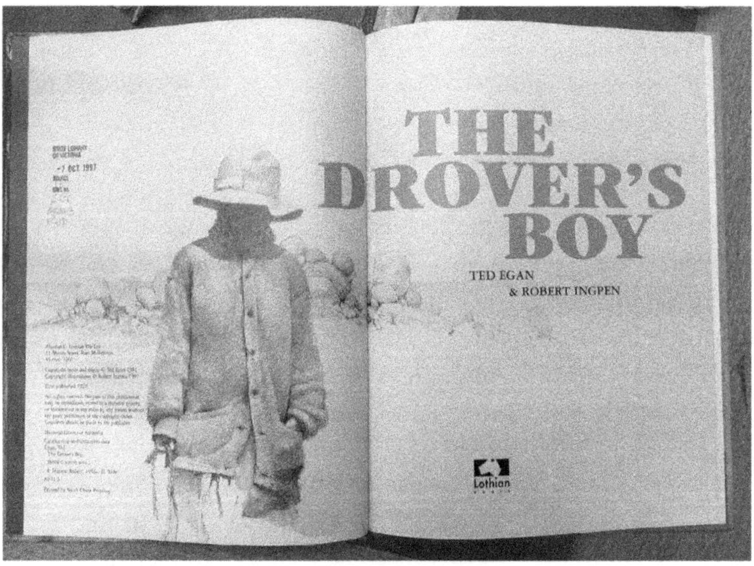

Figure 1. *The Drover's Boy*, 1997, illustrations Robert Ingpen.
Photograph by Liz Conor. Courtesy of the author, Ted Egan.

3 Tauri Simone, "Aboriginal stockwomen: Their legacy in the Australian pastoral industry" (Doctor of Philosophy, Deakin University, 2016).

4 "About the drover's boy," in Ted Egan and Robert Ingpen, *The Drover's Boy* (Port Melbourne: Lothian, 1997), unpaginated.

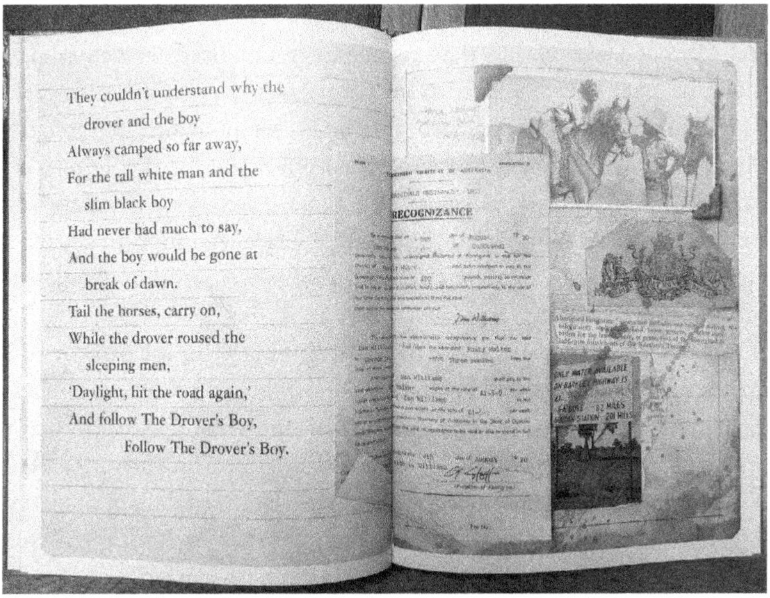

Figure 2. *The Drover's Boy*, 1997, illustrations Robert Ingpen.
Photograph by Liz Conor. Courtesy of the author, Ted Egan.

However, in the promotional blurb for a 2014 short film based on Egan's song, a focus on mutual love has all but drowned out his original exposure of the abduction and rape of Aboriginal girls and women, chillingly euphemised as "breaking in" on the northern pastoral frontier.[5] Sexual violence is entirely absented in this short film, and Egan's song becomes "a retelling of forbidden love":

> The story is set in the 1920s in outback Australia, and evokes a time when it was illegal for white Australians and Aboriginal people to marry. It was not uncommon for a drover and his Aboriginal wife to pass off their relationship under the guise of her being 'a drover's boy'. In subterfuge, she had to bind her breasts, cut her hair and change her name to disguise herself as an Aboriginal boy.[6]

The picture that forms around this colonial type – much like other types, such as the "Spinifex Fairy" or the "Stud", about Aboriginal women with

---

5 *The Drover's Boy*. Film proposal. Margaret McHugh (Australia: 2015). See the trailer for the unmade film: "Drover's boy short," *Vimeo*, 2015, https://vimeo.com/117983200.

6 "Drover's boy," *Ronin Films*, 2018, accessed 2 July 2018, https://www.roninfilms.com.au/feature/14176/drovers-boy.html.

whom white stockmen had sexual relations – is one of deeply equivocal sexual consent.[7] The notion that abducted, traumatised women who were "broken in" after being plucked from the carnage of reprisal raids came to feel attachment and love for their assailants is repugnant and aporetic to contemporary sensibilities. Did the redemptive love of the Drover's Boy romanticise frontier sexual violence and pastoral expansion? If Egan's exposé is true, then these white men perpetrated bride capture: an entrenched colonial trope of primitive masculinity in which Aboriginal women were abducted into marriage.

If white stockmen were abducting and forcing Aboriginal women into sexual concubinage, then they were replicating the behaviour associated with primitive black men. As such, their exculpation was critical to sustaining the picaresque masculinity of the pastoral industry. As Angela Woollacott argues, "the economic requirements of pastoralism made moral ambiguity a staple of settler life".[8] Indeed, the love of Aboriginal women functions to exonerate the white men whose suspected sexual appropriation associated them with the brutish primitive believed to violently abduct his wives. Humanitarians and missionaries often queried who was more civilised when decrying the abuse of "low-caste" white men against Aboriginal women and girls.

Implicit in that idea of redemptive love, this chapter argues, is a peculiarly colonial mystification around Aboriginal women's consent, already virtually unthinkable under anthropological theories. I first set out the history of the Drover's Boy type and the context for its emergence on the pastoral frontier. I then consider how typecasting Aboriginal women's sexuality attempted to fix the highly mutable meanings of interracial sexuality. Finally, I turn to Victorian anthropology to argue that the "primitive" woman's sexual consent was rendered unthinkable. Through the racialised type of the Drover's Boy, I ask, can the subaltern woman consent in colonial discourse?[9]

---

7 Howard Morphy, "Proximity and distance: Representations of Aboriginal society in the writings of Bill Harney and Bruce Chatwin," in *Popularising Anthropology*, ed. Jeremy McClancy and Christian McDonaugh (London: Routledge, 1996), 167; Liz Conor, *Skin Deep: Settler Impressions of Aboriginal Women* (Crawley: UWA Publishing, 2016), 222.

8 Angela Woollacott, "Ambiguity and necessity: Settlers and Aborigines in intimate tension in mid-nineteenth century Australia," in *Intimacies of Violence in the Settler Colony: Economies of Dispossession Around the Pacific Rim*, ed. Penelope Edmonds and Amanda Nettelbeck (Basingstoke: Palgrave Macmillan, 2018), 47.

9 See: Gayatri Chakravorty Spivak, "Can the subaltern speak?" in *Marxism and the Interpretation of Culture*, ed. Cary Nelson and Lawrence Grossberg (Houndmills: Macmillan, 1988).

Derivation of the "Drover's Boy" as a racialised typecast

The Drover's Boy first appeared in Australian print in an 1852 billing for an equestrian circus act, but had been discussed in Europe from the seventeenth century and probably earlier.[10] Not unlike "Black Velvet", the slang for white men's fantasy of unfettered sexual access to Aboriginal women, it was a favoured name for racing horses.[11] In a 1912 gallery of photographs a slight stockman is seated on a mule, though her features suggest she is a young woman. The caption "An Overland Drover's Boy" goes unremarked; so does the caption "Wild Spinifex Niggers" (Figure 3).[12] As "Sapphire Bill's" 1930s column in *The Chronicle* recalled, "I once ran a full team of lubras as drover boys par excellence", but divulges nothing further.[13] A correspondent to *The Queenslander* wrote, "It is an everyday occurrence in the north to meet travelers and teams accompanied by a black woman ... in a man's clothes and passing her off as a boy".[14] Authorities in different states were aware of this sartorial ruse to get around anti-cohabitation clauses. Both the Northern Territory and South Australia brought in ordinances outlawing crossdressing by Aboriginal women in 1911.[15]

Aside from these scattered references, however, the phenomenon of the Drover's Boy was virtually redacted from the Australian public sphere until Egan's song rather belatedly drew attention to it during the 1990s. Indeed, references to inter-racial sex tend to emerge in the fictional context of "ballads, poetry or novels" rather than through individual accounts.[16] The Drover's Boy, a vernacular racialised typecast derived from the classifications of scientific racism, inhered a curious yet foundational ambivalence about Indigenous women's consent.

10 *Sydney Morning Herald*, 6 February 1852, 1.

11 Ann McGrath, *Born in the Cattle: Aborigines in Cattle Country* (Sydney: Allen & Unwin, 1987), 68–95; Conor, *Skin Deep*, Chapter 5.

12 "Native life in the Northern Territory," *Leader*, 12 October 1912, 28.

13 "The tales of Sapphire Bill: Sun-burnt arms and gee gaws told by himself," *Chronicle*, 26 May 1938, 68.

14 Quoted in Rosalind Kidd, *The Way We Civilise* (St Lucia: University of Queensland Press, 1997), 30.

15 Mary Anne Jebb, *Blood, Sweat and Welfare: A History of White bosses and Aboriginal Pastoral Workers* (Crawley: UWA Publishing, 2002), 81. The subterfuge was relatively unknown in Queensland, see: Victoria Haskins, "'A troublesome gin like Annie': Masculinity, race and intimate violence in federation-era north Queensland," *law&history* 4, no. 2 (2017): 139, footnote 54.

16 Hannah Robert, "Disciplining the female Aboriginal body: Inter-racial sex and the pretence of separation," *Australian Feminist Studies* 16, no. 34 (2001): 70.

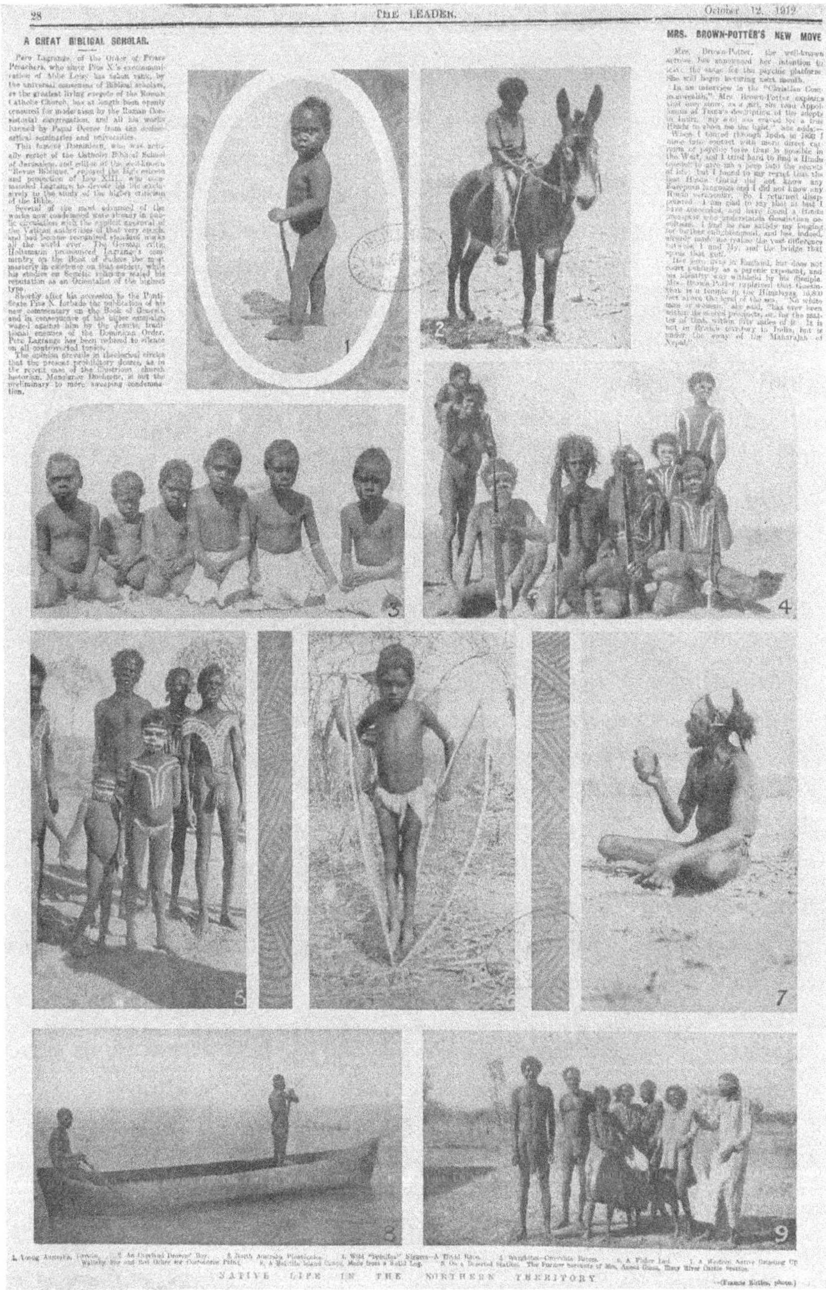

28 THE LEADER. October 12, 1912

A GREAT BIBLICAL SCHOLAR.

Pere Lagrange, of the Order of Friars Preachers, who since Pius X.'s excommunication of Abbé Loisy has taken rank, by the universal consensus of Biblical scholars, as the greatest living exegete of the Roman Catholic Church, has at length been openly censured for modernism by the Roman Consistorial congregation, and all his works banned by Papal Decree from the ecclesiastical seminaries and universities.

MRS. BROWN-POTTER'S NEW MOVE

NATIVE LIFE IN THE NORTHERN TERRITORY

(Francis Birtles, photo.)

Figure 3. *The Leader* (Melbourne) 12 October 1912, 28.
Photographer Francis Birtles. Courtesy of the National Library of Australia, MS079.9451.

How might we account for this quite recent, retrospective commemoration of the Aboriginal women who worked as drovers and sometimes as violently appropriated concubines? Egan's song emerged in the context of a series of tectonic shifts in Australian race relations, including: the 1992 Mabo High Court decision, which overturned the doctrine of Terra Nullius; the much contested 1988 bicentenary, which witnessed the largest Aboriginal rights protest march; the 1991 Royal Commission report into Aboriginal Deaths in Custody, a response to disproportionate Aboriginal deaths post-arrest; the homelands movement of close-kin from missions to small decentralised land to escape dysfunction and government policy; the presentation of the Barunga Statement, or bark petition, to Prime Minister Bob Hawke calling for land rights and a range of measures towards self-determination; and the first elections for the Aboriginal and Torres Strait Islander Commission, which operated from 1990 to 2005. Precisely in the years spanning Egan's initial protest song up to the 2014 documentary of tender outback forbidden love, Egan's indictment against frontier sexual violence and its exoneration in subsequent cultural production parallels these dramatic shifts in Aboriginal affairs and the onset of the Culture Wars.[17]

Egan says the song was prompted by an Aboriginal woman elder. Knowing he wrote songs, she exhorted: "when you gonna write one about us? All we hear are songs about white men".[18] Across the Kimberley women stockworkers were critical to the expansion of settler pastoralism. However, after the pastoral award of 1965, women were "written out of work in the pastoral industry".[19] No women stockworkers were recorded by 1971, a drop from 373 in 1966.[20] Women stockworkers remembered themselves as 'born in the cattle', having delivered cattle to far-flung markets such as Gepps Cross in Adelaide, Dajarra in Queensland and Wiluna in Western Australia.[21] Observing how women passed on valuable advice to both black and white drovers, Egan already knew they had a great deal of experience and authority about mustering.

---

17 See: Jim George and Kim Huynh, *The Culture Wars: Australian and American Politics in the 21st Century* (South Yarra: Palgrave Macmillan, 2009).

18 Personal correspondence with Ted Egan, 15 November 2017.

19 Paul Roth, "Indigenous voices at work," in *Voices at Work: Continuity and Change in the Common Law World*, ed. Alan Bogg and Tonia Novitz (Oxford: Oxford University Press, 2014), 106.

20 Mary Anne Jebb, *Blood, Sweat and Welfare*, 291.

21 This phrase became the title of Ann McGrath's ground-breaking history of Aboriginal workers on the pastoral stations.

Despite the Elder's prompting, Egan says he "had the song in my head" for many years. Only after a friend remembered how these women had been referred to as Drover's Boys was Egan able to write it – in half an hour. The women, who considered themselves better at handling cattle, unflinchingly described themselves as "owned" by the white men. Egan told me:

> I present the song always on the basis that the part played by so many Aboriginal girls and women in the biggest movements of cattle ever known in the world, deserves acclamation, indeed honour. Yes, many, probably most of them were brutally treated. But the women mainly wanted to remember, with pride, what good "stockmen" they were.[22]

For all their trials, Egan reports that the principle memory communicated to him was their pride in outdoing white and black men in tracking, as well as looking after cattle and horses.

Like historian Ann McGrath, Egan reports on the women speaking openly about past sexual activity or relationships with their white bosses. This was "one of the bloodiest of Australia's nineteenth century frontiers": it featured "sexual violence, abduction and brutal coercion against Aboriginal women by colonisers and their well-armed native police force".[23] For Aboriginal men who knew raids against cattle-spearers were also "recruitment drives" for their wives and daughters, McGrath notes, the loss of their women was profoundly emasculating and distressing.[24] On the northern Queensland frontier, Victoria Haskins writes, the "rampant rape and sexual abuse of Aboriginal women and girls" was "closely associated with the kidnapping of women and children for labour".[25] In the Kimberley, Mary Ann Jebb describes the circumstances of relationships between Aboriginal stockwomen and white bosses as involving "violence, coercion, social dislocation and fear". Jebb describes a "pattern of moving with white men" for protection against the armed police patrols which were arresting men for cattle-killing. But this was in fact about accessing their wives. Women, detained as witnesses, were raped en route, sometimes while chained. Upon being released to stations as stockworkers, these women were thereby "drawn into a sphere of limited protection".[26]

---

22 Personal correspondence with Egan.

23 Ann McGrath, "Consent, marriage and colonialism: Indigenous Australian women and coloniser marriages," *Journal of Colonialism and Colonial History* 6, no. 3 (2005).

24 McGrath, *Born in the Cattle,* 11.

25 Haskins, "'A troublesome gin'," 128.

26 Jebb, *Blood, Sweat and Welfare*, 26, 31, 131, 48, and 46.

The women generally had dual roles. As drover Matt Savage famously put it, "They would work all day in the cattle, then all night in the swag".[27] To Egan, they seemed to be accepting of the outcome of their recruitment: "There were obvious brutish white men in many of their lives, but these were usually written off: 'Oh, he hard man.'" As McGrath suggests:

> Entering any kind of union with a coloniser man thus became part of her wider community's ongoing negotiations with the coloniser state. In the absence of enforceable treaties, such negotiations could involve obtaining "protection" from the state by a member of the coloniser class or obtaining defined goods.[28]

Indigenous women could also be a form of currency by which to "broker" the loyalty of black station hands.[29] Tauri Simone's research into Aboriginal stockwomen found the Drover's Boy typecast to be common across pastoral stations in Queensland, the Northern Territory and Western Australia.[30] Egan's use of the Drover's Boy was therefore more likely to offend Aboriginal men, no doubt due to the "harrowing narratives" about their emasculation and displacement that Megan Davis believes influenced women to "sacrifice their own wellbeing and safety for the greater good."[31]

Women also liked this typecast for its celebration of their skills and labour. When Jebb interviewed women stockworkers in the Kimberley, they described their men's clothing. Yet "there was no indication that they were hidden from police or government protectors", despite some working well into the 1950s.[32] During the 1940s, moreover, "only a handful" of women stockworkers lived with white men as their spouses.[33] This was often due to the decimation of Aboriginal men by violence, as well as their removal to lock hospitals and compounds. As the campaign to remove Aboriginal men from the Kimberley through arrest receded from 1914 on account of spiraling costs, the "idea of detaining women to control the whole group became an important part of local relationships between European bosses

---

27 Quoted in McGrath, *Born in the Cattle*, 51.

28 McGrath, "Consent, marriage and colonialism."

29 Amanda Nettelbeck, "Intimate violence in the pastoral economy: Aboriginal women's labour and protective governance," in *Intimacies of Violence*, 78.

30 Simone, "Aboriginal stockwomen."

31 Megan Davis, "Aboriginal women: The right to self-determination," *Australian Indigenous Law Review* 16, no. 1 (2012): 81.

32 Jebb, *Blood, Sweat and Welfare*, 204.

33 Ibid.

and Aboriginal People".[34] Droving gave women protection from frontier violence; it offered a coping mechanism for their loss of food sources and connection to country.

Women were also avoiding the missions and the intertribal conflict which arose through administrative insensitivities. Some had their children removed, but pastoralists sometimes hid the children upon whose labour they relied – including as the next generation of stockworkers. When granted permission to marry their bosses, the "governance of the husband" effectively freed women stockworkers from the governance of the state. Indigenous women married under the tribal system did not share such entitlements.[35] The stockwomen also educated the station whites, including children, in their traditional knowledge of country. Intimate interracial relations were thus "highly complex, unfolding on a sliding scale between agency and disempowerment, consent and coercion."[36] The women rarely spoke of the violence they may have experienced. But in their retellings, women stockworkers focused less on Egan's romanticised notions of love, and more on their pride in their skills and contribution to the northern pastoral industry.

Aboriginal women acted as "intermediaries" between cultures, gaining status through knowledge and goods traded for sexual favours. They also created kinship obligations for white men, offering them and their families leverage which, if unmet, might lead to retaliation. According to Hannah Robert, "inter-racial sex was placed firmly in a context of sex and vice rather than of reproduction and family, thus making Aboriginal women and their children targets of disciplinary intervention by the state."[37]

White administrators were preoccupied with the sexual appropriation of Aboriginal women. The historical argument that the vulnerability of Aboriginal girls and women on the frontier furnished protection administrations with cause to drastically curtail their freedom of movement, mothering and employment is widely accepted. The Northern Territory ordinance of 1918, which replaced all previous legislation, was aimed at preventing the conception of "half-castes" through controlling Aboriginal women's marriage. It became an offence to "habitually consort" and unlawful to have carnal knowledge with an Aboriginal or "half-caste" woman. In an early but enduring analysis, historian C.D. Crowley wryly noted that

34 Ibid., 65 and 70.

35 McGrath, "Consent, marriage and colonialism."

36 Nettelbeck, "Intimate violence in the pastoral economy," 68.

37 Robert, "Disciplining the female Aboriginal body," 69.

such measures were "probably nothing more than a way of lessening the charge of rape by providing an alternative charge". The South Australian frontier was so dangerous for Aboriginal women and girls that "gin-busting" was the foremost reason for introducing an (ultimately rejected) protection bill of 1899.[38]

The refusal to recognise and even penalise permanent relationships tended to encourage casual exchanges. "The sexual and racial paranoia of white society," McGrath argues, "destroyed the possibility that relationships with white men could work out equitably for Aboriginal women".[39] A 1929 report by Queensland Chief Protector Bleakley recommended removing women not in employment to institutions such as the Kahlin Compound in Darwin where they lived under curfew. He reported that starvation on the pastoral stations and the camps forced women into prostitution, but that white men on "ginsprees" were sometimes "low enough" to "pay the women with bogus money".[40] Earlier in the Kimberley, massacres followed pastoral workers disputes over access to women.[41] The interventions of white feminists such as Mary Montgomery Bennett and Caroline Kelly at Aboriginal reserves further illustrate the depth of feeling around the vulnerability of Aboriginal women and girls.

Sexual violence was the principal cause of internecine violence on the Kimberley's "quasi-feudal" pastoral frontier from the earliest European incursion into the region.[42] Venereal disease was rife, with syphilis impacting the entire population as reported in the 1895 Aborigines Protection Board report.[43] Police who tried to intervene in the rape of women and girls were ignored and obstructed; those who were perpetrators were rarely admonished let alone penalised.[44] In this exceptionally perilous rapescape, the sexual consent of Aboriginal women and girls became virtually unthinkable.

Whether we view Drover's Boys as forced, coerced or cherished, it seems the role was inseparable from sexual service – and latterly in Egan's perception, from romantic love. Why was it even more absented from

38 Crowley, *Destruction of Aboriginal Society*, 236 and 211.

39 McGrath, *Born in the Cattle*, 70.

40 Crowley, *Destruction of Aboriginal Society*, 262 and 264.

41 Jebb, *Blood, Sweat and Welfare*, 115.

42 Chris Owen, *Every Mother's Son is Guilty: Policing the Kimberley Frontier of Western Australian*, 1882–1905 (Crawley: UWA Publishing, 2017), 278.

43 Ibid., 383; Alison Holland, "The campaign for women Protectors: Gender, race and frontier between the wars," *Australian Feminist Studies* 16, no. 34 (2001): 27–42.

44 Owen, *Every Mother's Son*, 410.

print media than Black Velvet? Why did Egan's initial quite outspoken exposé of the mistreatment of Aboriginal women and girls on the pastoral frontier transfigure into an outback love story? Is the sexual agency of Aboriginal women being credited, or is an unseemly amnesia over frontier sexual violence reasserting itself? A longstanding impasse, or ambivalence, about Aboriginal women's consent plays a significant role in the sorts of mythologising that shaped the typecasting of the Drover's Boy.

Racialised colloquial types

The Drover's Boy needs to be understood as a type, specifically a colloquial racialised typecast. In Elizabeth Povinelli's analysis, types create links between forms of intimacies and social governance developing a "social matrix out of which identities and their divisions emerge".[45] Studies of colloquialism and national idiom often sideline the role of types in assigning and articulating racial difference and identity.[46] On the pastoral frontier, the Drover's Boy is but one among a pantheon of colonial types. It needs to be considered *as a type* and thereby situated within a tradition of colloquial typecasting that has produced dozens of racialised and hierarchised types deriving from colonial incursion and expansion. Pastoral station types were occupational and included the *Jackaroo*, *Gun*, *Bagman*, *Lizard*, *Rouseabout*, *Maluka*, *Offsider*, *Sundowner*, *Overlander*, *Drover*, *Ringer*, *Missus*, *Pannikin Boss*, *Picker-up*, *Poddy-dodger*, *Deucer*, *Slushy*, *Snagger* and *Bushwhacker*. Significantly, the *Jackaroo* and *Burnt Cork* (white men sexually involved with Aboriginal women) also figured in scenarios of sexual relations with Aboriginal women on cattle stations. The sexual repertoire and coordinates of Black Velvet were also designated through types such as the *Spinifex Fairy*, *Stud*, *Gin burglar*, *Gin jockey*, *Gin shepherd*, *Combo*, as well as *Yeller Feller* and *Creamy* to indicate the ensuing "half-caste" children.

Colonial typologies created systematic grammars for packaging populations into regulatable identities. What is striking about the Drover's Boy is that it may have been cast retrospectively – almost as a commemorative type – in which attempts to disguise and circumvent the regulation of the Northern Territory's 1911 and 1918 ordinances were ultimately revealed

45 Elizabeth A. Povinelli, *The Empire of Love: Toward a Theory of Intimacy, Genealogy, and Carnality* (Durham: Duke University Press, 2006), 3.

46 Liz Conor, "Classification and its discontents," *Interventions: International Journal of Postcolonial Studies* 17, no. 2 (2015): 155–173.

decades after the fact. Typecasting negotiated the dependencies and intimacies which broached the racial cleave of the frontier, in category-shattering trysts across definitional bounds that colonial governments tried desperately to dissuade or regulate by channelling into White Australia through "biological absorption". These types were instrumental to the formulation of Indigenous work as sitting "at the very centre of exchange in colonial knowledge and emotion economies", revealing how "intimacy and violence were wound together at their heart."[47] Identifications made through racialised typecasts literally cast people within a melding of these occupational and intimate roles.

The Drover's Boy ruptured the authorities' regulatory and protection attempts – it was a category that specifically defied the respectable ontologies of colonial sexual exchange. The cross-dressing Drover's Boy destabilised binaries of gender and sexuality to expose them as performative – a mere guise.[48] Even so, it remains unclear whether this type served the prevailing sense of the uncontainable sexual needs of rampant frontier white masculinity at the expense of the safety of Aboriginal women and girls. Alternatively, perhaps it eulogised a hybrid, ordinance-defying mutual exchange, one that, as McGrath has more recently argued, radically entwined sovereignties and conquered the bifurcations and exclusions of colonial regulatory taxonomies with love.[49]

Construing these intimacies and/or abuses as a colloquial type is material to its comprehension. For Foucault, types are "functional discriminations" by which individuals are specified. Certain categories positioned subjects within certain group membership and thereby into designated modalities of power – juridical, disciplinary, spatial, and medico-administrative.[50] In the colonial scenario, types attempted to contain the hybridised and proliferating identity effects emanating from colonial mobility and frontier entanglements, creating the impetus for classificatory schema and providing the content for "regimes of difference".[51] Types were often a fruitless

---

47 Edmonds and Nettelbeck, ed. *Intimacies of Violence*, 13.

48 Lucy Chesser, "'Woman in a suit of male': Sexuality, race and the women worker in male 'disguise', 1890–1920," *Australian Feminist Studies* 23, no. 56 (2008): 175–194.

49 Ann McGrath, *Illicit Love: Interracial Sex and Marriage in the United States and Australia* (Lincoln: University of Nebraska Press, 2015).

50 Michel Foucault, "The politics of health in the eighteenth century," in *The Foucault Reader*, ed. Paul Rabinow (London: Penguin, 1984), 322

51 Patrick Wolfe, "Land, labour, and difference: Elementary structures of race," *American Historical Review* 103, no. 3 (2001): 866–905.

attempt to pin down and fix the inherently unstable and porous identity categories of colonial incursion. Types were pinned on people, particularly brown people, with little regard for their nomenclature. And as McGrath's work makes startlingly clear, nothing capsized those boundaries more than the exchange of bodily fluids, or, where love and desire were returned, within the exquisite pleasure and unholy chaos of passionate ardour across the cleave of race.

Classification is a cultural technology of rule but types provide the mechanism for exclusion as well as spaces for belonging. Sociologist Georg Simmel described this paradox, as the "fact of finding oneself simultaneously within and without".[52] The Drover's Boy shape-shifted across both gender and sexual identities. It was a cross-dressing typecast that feigned a racially striated fraternity with her pastoral co-workers, who often included men from her own community or other Aboriginal groups.

The masquerade of the Drover's Boy's masculinity served to efface sexual relations since homosexuality was even more unthinkable, it seems, than interracial intimacies. Russel Ward's iconic 1958 *The Australian Legend* argued that sexual access to Aboriginal women may have kept homosexuality out of mateship.[53] Yet in Egan's song, and the ensuing books and documentaries, recognition of the women's true identity transfigured from abduction and rape. It comes from their redemptive love and highly skilled labour. As drovers, Egan argues, the women became:

> Real pioneers. Uniquely Australian. Old Aboriginal women with their timeless, stoical faces, sitting in the dust, smoking pipes, wearing broad-rimmed stockmen's hats. Scanning the horizon with the look that tells you they understand the big distances, the long dry stages … The story of these pioneering women of northern Australia has never been told before.[54]

Yet there have been few popular representations extolling the hard work and full life experiences of elder Aboriginal women, until the figure of the "Aunty" gained white recognition. Instead, the Drover's Boy's youth intimates a certain romanticism. This type becomes a faithful helpmate to the colonial project, contributing in their own way to the "establishment of

52 Georg Simmel, "The poor," in *On Individuality and Social Forms*, ed. Don Levine (Chicago: University of Chicago Press, 1971), 150–178 and 171.

53 Cited in McGrath, *Born in the Cattle*, 68.

54 "About the drover's boy."

colonial hegemony".[55] Their sexual service becomes subsumed under their laboring and morphs, as in the quote above, into romantic intimacy.

"At a time when colossal numbers of cattle needed to be moved around the country, the women's slave-like contribution was both substantial and completely unacknowledged," one American review of Egan's book *The Drover's Boy* remarked. "Sometimes there also developed between the women and their white overseers a genuine love, a love often resulting in children – despite, ironically, the horribly violent way these women were often forced into their roles."[56] Although this reviewer confuses Egan's commemoration as historical source, she too emphasises the mutual dependencies of white men and Aboriginal women as forging love across racial difference and in spite of violent beginnings. Yet surely these working dependencies were also fostered between white and black stockmen? Yet such dependencies between stockmen did not forge love on the pastoral frontier, at least that we have any record of whatsoever.

Racialising consent in colonial thought

Aboriginal women's consent has been almost unthinkable in colonial knowledge production. Firstly, interracial sex comprised such a violation of social norms that it was confused with violation itself.[57] Secondly, Aboriginal women were characterised as so devoid of chastity or modesty as to be unable to be "outraged". Thirdly, they were routinely typed as "chattels", as brutally subjected to their men's tyranny and trafficking. While broaching European women's consent was generally couched in terms of the violation of men's property, Aboriginal men's capacity for property ownership was necessarily elided and as muddled as notions of Aboriginal women's sexual consent. These obfuscations are both critical as expedient descriptors of the 'primitive' within the discourse that served colonial dispossession.

Like all popular typecasts, the colloquial typecast of the Drover's Boy had its impetus in the classificatory taxonomies of scientific racism. This derivation provided the epistemological basis for the typecast and rendered Aboriginal women's consent a non sequitur to colonial discourse.

55 See: Elizabeth Furniss, "Timeline history and the Anzac myth: Settler narratives of local history in a North Australian town," *Oceania* 71, no. 4 (2001): 279–297.

56 Karen Jameyson, "News from down under: Brush strokes with history," *Horn Book Magazine* 75, no. 3 (1999): 364–368.

57 Conor, *Skin Deep*, 277.

A peculiarly colonial form of knowledge production, Aboriginal women's incapacity for consent – ultimately embodied in the Drover's Boy – transferred from the scientific to the vernacular.

Bride capture, a classic Victorian anthropological narrative, came to underwrite the purported sexual chaos of the "savage" horde. As Patrick Wolfe painstakingly explains, the tropes of bride capture and infanticide were premised on nescience – ignorance of paternity – and rapine, phenomena which could only be overcome by sons identifying their common mothers and thereby becoming each other's brothers, or kin. In the initial presocial stage imagined by Victorian anthropologists, the mother's capacity to identify her children, let along their fathers, was said to be thrown to the wind by their constant abduction through bride capture. But when the mothers were kept as common property by the horde, their sons were able to recognise themselves as brothers through their common mother. As kin they were able to claim the land of their birth as property in common. In Victorian anthropology, the evolutionary progression from "horde to house" referred to the territory of the father, which initially could not be held as property in common by the sons until they recognised their consanguinity.[58] This meant that property was bestowed by shared blood, kinship or mother-rite, effectively within matriarchal social organisation. The final stage in the progression from the presocial to the patriarchal social contract – ostensibly the pinnacle of social development – was through the stability of paternity, where fathers passed property held in common to their sons. For Victorian anthropologists this rather vaingloriously marked the shift from mother-rite to father-rite, from nature to culture, from god to science, from religion to rationality, from the material to the transcendent.

In the era of the Married Women's Property Act of 1882, this manifestly bonkers theory of father-rite was a "defense of patriarchal property" constituting "a kind of gendered variant of terra nullius" in its complete abnegation of women's property rights.[59] Women, mothers, daughters themselves became property, and their sexual consent was repressed, in the social contract of patrilineal agnatic inheritance. The dispossession of married women's property was then displaced onto the colonies where the "savage" was jettisoned in Victorian anthropology's narrative of social organisation – somewhere between the presocial horde and mother-rite. That is to say,

---

58 Patrick Wolfe, "Settler colonialism and the elimination of the native," *Journal of Genocide Research* 8, no. 4 (2006): 387–409.

59 Patrick Wolfe, *Settler Colonialism and the Transformation of Anthropology: The Politics and Poetics of an Ethnographic Event* (London: Cassell, 1999), 84.

"savages" never advanced to father-rite and property ownership. So the prevailing trope about bride capture served a very particular and expedient function in the colonial logic of elimination. It meant, rather conveniently to the colonial project of dispossession, that Aboriginal sons neither held property nor land in common.

Women's sexual consent is nowhere to be seen in this Victorian anthropological narrative of evolutionary succession. This is unsurprising, given mothers were said to be unable to recognise their own children – rather incredulously, mothers could only be recognised *by* sons. If women consented to their captors, or suitors for that matter, they stabilised both maternity and paternity: by rendering themselves mothers and their captive husbands fathers, both became recognisable to the sons who stood to inherit their father's territory. If the white social contract was effected by a maternal repudiation of such epic proportions, the effacement of Aboriginal women's sexual consent became constitutive – indeed, the very premise of civilisation itself. Its complete absenting provided the grounds for the Victorian fantasy of origin, not to mention the literal grounds of colonial conquest.

Property inheritance, and the indisputable agnatic bloodlines it depended on, could only be guaranteed by either the enforcement of women's sexual exclusivity (never entirely reliable) or their consent to monogamy (perhaps marginally more so). In 'native' women's sexual consent was the evolutionary pathway from primitivism to civilisation. Aboriginal women were stuck in the primordial because of their inability to consent. That was one of the things that identified them as primitive – the corollary in primitive men, of course, being that they never sought consent and were merely rapists and pimps. In origin theories of marriage, it is exogamy that progresses the rapacious horde through to Emile Durkheim's "simply polysegmental" "union of clans organised in the form of villages" on to the sexual contract of companionate marriage.[60] Arguably this instated the sexual consent of Indigenous women as the path to evolutionary progression. Women's consent was thus a central marker of civilisation.

The sexual consent of the ostensibly primordially promiscuous and brutalised native woman was thus foundational to the succession of evolutionary biology and the sequence from "horde" to "social contract". As Carole Pateman theorises, the much lauded "free agreement of the social contract" was advanced only after the consent of women to the repressed

60 Emile Durkheim, *The Rules of Sociological Method*, ed. Vani Prakashan (New Delhi: Nine Books, 1895, 2015), 123–124.

sexual contract. That is, a presumed and unacknowledged civic capacity in women is depended upon for the primitive form of mother-rite to become superseded by father-rite, itself founded in the sexual property of women's bodies. The sexual contract is "a repressed dimension of contract theory" – integral but unarticulated.[61] So too is the repressed but elemental function of Indigenous women's sexual consent, much like the Drover's Boy.

The interracial intimacies McGrath describes in *Illicit Love* were an affront to bourgeois landed patriarchy. This was not only because "entwined sovereignties" winkled Indigenous birthright into what was imagined to be an exclusively settler inheritance, but also because interracial marriage disrupted the entrenched notion that Indigenous women were incapable of sexual consent. Without women's consent, the horde could not progress beyond rapine and nescience; it remained incapable of apportioning property in the form of patrilineal inheritance. Indigenous women's consent was historically moribund, unthinkable and jettisoned in the primordial. Within settler knowledge production, the incapacity for Indigenous women to consent was more than one of the indices of civilisation: it was its very keystone.

Conclusion

Larissa Behrendt's work on sexual consent found that Aboriginal women were "able to exert their own power and control through their relations with white men and, once there was reliance on black labour, were able to exert more control over the situation".[62] Her findings are supported by reports of sexual autonomy made by Aboriginal women to scholars from Phyllis Kabbery to Diane Bell and Ann McGrath among others.[63] For McGrath, such marriage narratives "involved political and social ideas of 'civilisation', 'freedom' and 'consent', all of which – in English translation or not – had multiple, conflicting and shared meanings across cultural and colonising boundaries." In the colonising context marital consent is "a gendered form of nation-building and of state formation".[64]

---

61 Carole Pateman, *The Sexual Contract* (Polity: Cambridge, 1988), ix.

62 Larissa Behrendt, "Consent in a (neo) colonial society: Aboriginal Woman as sexual and legal 'other'," *Australian Feminist Studies* 15, no. 33 (2000): 355.

63 Phyllis M. Kaberry, *Aboriginal Woman: Sacred and Profane* (London: Routledge, 1939); Diane Bell, *Daughters of the Dreaming* (North Sydney: McPhee Gribble, 1983); McGrath, *Illicit Love.*

64 McGrath, "Consent, marriage and colonialism."

The confusion surrounding the Drover's Boy type – the victim of violent abduction and rape, or the cherished and unrecognised defacto wife or helpmate in pastoral national building – stems from the failure to credit the "primitive" woman with any capacity for sexual consent. This, conversely, made it almost impossible to credit her vulnerability to violence. In neither scenario does this typecast cathect a sexual agent: she is as passive to the love that overwhelms her trauma, resentment and wrath as she was to the violence that occasioned them.

I believe this structural ambiguity then seeks resolution through colloquial typecasting in which the indeterminate sexual and gendered identity of women stockworkers is fixed as a masquerade, but one the typecast itself exposes once a wider audience for national reckoning was established by Aboriginal activism and new frontier histories. The Drover's Boy is replaced by the Aboriginal Stockwoman, who is credited for her tenacity, skill and devotion. Concerns and confusion about Aboriginal women's sexual consent, deeply entrenched in Victorian anthropology, eventually find narrative resolution through this story of "outback forbidden love". The Drover's Boy is typecast in its unmasking and any national reckoning of the frontier as a rapescape is forestalled by romanticising the love of the Aboriginal Stockwoman, by which her consent becomes a foregone conclusion.

Chapter 8

SEX TRAFFICKING, LABOUR MIGRATION, AND THE STATE

Rae Frances

In May 2017, headlines in the Australian media proclaimed: "Victim of Alleged Human Trafficking Held Captive in Sydney Man's Home". The report concerned a 17-year-old girl from West Africa who allegedly travelled to Sydney with a man who offered her work as a cleaner. After arriving in early April, she was kept in a room where she was allegedly repeatedly sexually assaulted by a number of men. The girl only managed to escape from the house in the early hours of 27 April, running until she was picked up by an unknown woman who drove her to the Asylum Seeker Centre in Sydney's inner west. The teenager was taken to hospital for treatment following consultation with the Anti-Slavery Australia unit at the University of Technology Sydney, and was subsequently placed in the care of Family and Community Services. The Australian Federal Police and New South Wales Police Force pleaded for help from the public to find a man who is "either a Guinean national or an African male."[1]

This is but one of many cases of alleged sexual servitude reported in Australia since the late 1990s. Public interest has occurred in the context of increased international interest in issues of people trafficking and slavery, especially sex trafficking. Two months after this press report, the Commonwealth of Australia released *An Inquiry into Trafficking, Slavery and Slavery-like Practices* by its Parliamentary Joint Committee on Law

1 David Barden, "Victim of alleged human trafficking held captive in Sydney man's home," *Huffington Post*, 19 May 2017, accessed 31 May 2018, https://www.huffingtonpost.com.au/2017/05/18/victim-of-alleged-human-trafficking-held-captive-in-sydney-mans_a_22098075/.

Enforcement. The report made a number of recommendations, including funding the *National Action Plan to Combat Human Trafficking and Slavery 2015–19* "with a human rights-based approach to its implementation." This report confirms the direction in which Australian governments have been heading since the late 1990s, when the Commonwealth introduced offences relating to slavery, sexual servitude and deceptive recruiting for sexual services into the Criminal Code. A series of amendments to the Criminal Code in the twenty-first century have provided specific offences relating to trafficking in persons, forced labour, forced marriage and harbouring victims as well as protections for vulnerable witnesses. State and Territory Governments, responsible for regulating the sex work industry, have also enacted legislation relating to sexual servitude and deceptive recruiting.[2]

The *National Action Plan* (*NAP*), finalised in 2014, represents an attempt to provide a coordinated approach to the issue, bringing together a whole-of-government Commonwealth response working closely with State Governments, NGOs and sex worker organisations. The aim is to prevent and police trafficking, slavery and slavery-like practices as well as to provide appropriate support for the victims of these activities. The coordinated response described in the case of the African girl above reflects such an approach. It occurs within the broader context of an international anti-trafficking campaign coordinated by the United Nations (UN).[3]

While the scope of the *NAP* includes all forms of trafficking and slavery, until very recently the overwhelming focus has been on sex trafficking. Ongoing interest in the twenty-first century represents only the most recent chapter in a long history of Australian engagement with sex trafficking, dating to at least the last decades of the nineteenth century. This chapter provides a broader historical context for this very live contemporary issue. The history of migrant sex work, sex trafficking and official responses to these questions sheds light on theoretical and policy issues which arise in relation to the conceptualisation of commercial sex and its relationship to migration, trafficking and slavery today.

---

2 Commonwealth of Australia Parliamentary Joint Committee on Law Enforcement, *An Inquiry into Human Trafficking, Slavery and Slavery-like Practices* (Canberra: Senate Printing Unit, Parliament House, July 2017), 3; Commonwealth of Australia, *National Action Plan to Combat Human Trafficking and Slavery 2015–19* (Barton: Attorney-General's Department, 2014), 10.

3 Australia ratified the Supplementary Slavery Convention in 1958 and the UNTOC in 2004 and the Trafficking Protocol in 2005, Commonwealth of Australia, *National Action Plan*, 7.

Defining the problem: Sex trafficking and migrant labour

It is important to be clear about definitions, as much confusion arises from lack of clarity in relation to terminology and concepts. In particular, the difference between sex trafficking and migrant sex work must be clear.[4] The *NAP* defines human trafficking as "the physical movement of people across or within borders through coercion, threat or deception for the purpose of exploiting them when they reach their destination. Where the person is a child, ... the element of coercion, threat or deception is not required."[5] This is a succinct version of the definition given under the UN Protocol to Prevent, Suppress, and Punish Trafficking in Persons, Especially Women and Children (2000).[6]

The *NAP* defines slavery as occurring "when a person exercises the rights of ownership over another person." As well as activities that fit this definition, there are a range of "slavery-like practices" that include servitude, forced labour, deceptive recruiting, debt bondage and forced marriage.[7] Trafficking is not the same as people smuggling: the key difference is the former's element of exploitation.[8] While neither the *NAP* nor the UN

4 Biljana Meshkovska, Milissa Siegel, Sarah E. Stitterheim and Arjan E.R. Bos, "Female sex trafficking: Conceptual issues, current debates, and future directions," *The Journal of Sex Research* 52, no. 4 (2015): 382–383.

5 Commonwealth of Australia, *National Action Plan*, 4.

6 See: United Nations Human Rights Office of the High Commissioner, "Protocol to prevent, suppress and punish trafficking in persons especially women and children, supplementing the United Nations convention against transnational organized crime," *Office of the United Nations High Commissioner*, accessed 15 September 2017 http://www.ohchr.org/EN/ProfessionalInterest/Pages/ProtocolTraffickingInPersons.aspx. See also: *Report of the Special Rapporteur on Trafficking in Persons, especially Women and Children*, 28 July 2014, UN GAOR 69th sess, Item 69(b) of the provisional agenda, UN Doc A/69/33797, 6. The US State Department has a slightly different definition, which emphasises the critical role of exploitation via coercive and/or deceptive practices but places less importance on movement. "Human trafficking can include, but does not require, movement." Department of State (USA), *Trafficking in Persons Report June 2016*, 30, accessed 13 June 2018, https://2009-2017.state.gov/documents/organization/258876.pdf.

7 The Criminal Code defines debt bondage as the status or condition of a person that arises from a pledge of personal services as security for a debt owed, or claimed to be owed if the debt is manifestly excessive, the reasonable value of those services is not applied toward the liquidation of the debt or purported debt, or the length and nature of those services are not respectively limited and defined. Debt bondage is an offence under section 217.8 of the Criminal Code. Commonwealth of Australia, *National Action Plan*, 77.

8 Although as the NAP notes, there are other differences and some intersections/overlap where smuggled persons may experience human trafficking or slavery once they arrive in their destination country. Commonwealth of Australia, *National Action Plan*, 10.

Protocol specifically define sex trafficking, this can be understood as trafficking for the purposes of sexual exploitation.[9]

It is important to note, however, that this simple definition conceals a highly contested issue in relation to sex trafficking and migrant sex work. There are two major camps, derived from fundamentally different approaches to the meaning of commercial sex: the exchange of sexual services for payment as a form of service work versus commercial sex as essentially a form of violence against women. In the former, those who travel from their home country to engage in the sex industry are regarded as migrant sex workers. In contrast, when "all women who are in the sex industry" are viewed as "violated and sexually exploited,"[10] any women who travel to another country to engage in the sex industry are regarded as trafficked persons rather than workers.

The distinction is not just theoretical. The "sex work camp" is primarily concerned with protecting sex worker rights without attempting to eliminate prostitution and generally favour the decriminalisation of most aspects of the sex industry. In contrast, those who see prostitution as always violence against women are opposed not just to coercive or deceptive trafficking but prostitution *per se*. They tend to advocate for various criminal sanctions against persons engaged in the sale or purchase of sexual services. The *NAP* adopts the former approach, as does this chapter. However, both approaches have been important historically and continue to shape contemporary debates, policies and laws.

The nature and scale of the problem

Just as the definition of sex trafficking is contested and politicised, so too is any attempt to be precise about its scale. As Lisa Fedina has pointed out, "many sources of literature continue to cite flawed data and some misuse research in ways that seemingly inflate the problem, which can have serious implications for anti-trafficking efforts, including victim services and anti-trafficking legislation and policy."[11] Arguably, those interested in abolishing prostitution exaggerate the scale of the issue in order to create a "moral panic" and so pressure governments into action. Their critics, in contrast,

9 Meshkovska et al, "Female sex trafficking," 382.

10 Monica O'Connor and Grainne Healy, *The Links between Prostitution and Sex Trafficking: A Briefing Handbook* (Dublin: Coalitition Against Trafficking in Women, 2006), 5.

11 Lisa Fedina, "Use and misuse of research in books on trafficking: Implications for interdisciplinary researchers, practitioners, and advocates," *Trauma, Violence and Abuse* 16, no. 2 (2015): 188.

have identified sex trafficking as a "myth", or at least a largely inflated problem.[12] While some commentators suggest that 27 million people are subject to forced labour, or slavery, worldwide, in 2012 the International Labour Office (ILO) estimated this figure to be 20.9 million, although recognising this is likely an underestimate. Of these almost 21 million people, the ILO estimates that 58 per cent are trafficked for the purposes of sexual exploitation, the overwhelming majority being women and girls.[13]

However, all such data must be treated with caution. The clandestine nature of trafficking means much of this activity is concealed. It is therefore impossible to obtain precise statistics.[14] Scarlet Alliance, the peak body representing sex worker organisations in Australia, argues that trafficking is "a relatively isolated phenomenon in the Australian sex industry." This is based on evidence from their membership, who are in regular contact with migrant sex workers in their workplaces.[15] Despite intensive surveillance and legislation that expanded the offenses now covered by anti-trafficking laws, only 17 cases have been successfully convicted under Australia's anti-trafficking legislation. The *NAP* agrees, arguing that opportunities to traffic people into, or exploit people within, Australia are limited because of strong migration controls, geographic isolation, and a high degree of regulation, compliance and enforcement.[16]

The question of migrant sex workers is separate, although related, to the question of persons trafficked to work in the sex industry. Arguably, migrant sex workers who may have migrated voluntarily are more vulnerable to exploitation than local workers, especially if they are in Australia illegally. The stigma and sometimes illegal nature of sex work in Australia makes it difficult to be precise about the numbers working in the industry, but recent estimates put the figure at around 20,000 nationwide. Of these, a substantial proportion are believed to be migrants predominantly from Asia.[17]

---

12 Ibid; Ronald Weitzer, "The movement to criminalize sex work in the United States," *Journal of Law and Society* 37, no. 1 (2010): 61–84; Johnny E. McGaha and Amanda Evans, "Where are the victims? The credibility gap in human trafficking research," *Intercultural Human Rights Law Review* 4 (2009): 243–244.

13 International Labour Organisation, *Global estimate of forced labour* (2012), in Commonwealth of Australia, *National Action Plan*, 6.

14 For just one example of this vagueness, see: Department of State (USA), *Trafficking in Persons Report June 2016*, 80.

15 Scarlet Alliance submission to Commonwealth of Australia, *Inquiry into Human Trafficking*, 4.

16 Commonwealth of Australia, *National Action Plan*, 6.

17 Lauren Renshaw, Jules Kim, Janelle Fawkes and Elena Jeffreys, *Migrant Sex Workers in Australia* (Canberra: Australian Institute of Criminology, 2015), viii.

The longer history

Australia's first encounter with sex trafficking occurred in the late nineteenth century, when thousands of women joined the throngs of people moving around the globe to work in a range of industries. This labour migration coincided with a widespread moral panic about the so-called "white slave traffic" – the nineteenth-century term for sex trafficking.

One of the clearer cases of sex trafficking was not "white slavery" but involved Japanese women and girls who were recruited from Japan and sent throughout Southeast Asia, the Pacific, Australia and as far afield as South Africa.[18] In the 1890s, there were approximately 300 such women, known now as *Karuyki-san*, at any given time working in mining, pearling and sugar cane centres throughout Australia. Girls as young as seven were sold by their impoverished parents to entrepreneurs who smuggled them out of the country in the coal-holds of steamers. Others were tricked, lured or kidnapped by procurers. The conditions of these journeys were horrific, often resulting in tragedy when the coal shifted in heavy seas or caught alight. Those who did survive these voyages were taken to Singapore, Kuala Lumpur and Hong Kong and trained in brothel-work before being re-shipped to Australia and other parts of South-East Asia and the Pacific.[19]

The precise terms of their engagement varied, but the girls seemed to operate under a form of debt bondage whereby they worked for many years to pay back "debts" – the amount of which was calculated by their captors.

---

18 Nicole Keusch, "The phenomenon of the *'Karayuki-san'*: A transnational network of prostitution, 1870–1940," in *Selling Sex in the City: Global history of prostitution*, ed. Magaly Rodríguez García, Lex Heerma van Voss and Elise van Nederveen Meerkerk (Leiden: Brill, 2017); Bill Mihalopoulos, *Sex in Japan's Globalization, 1870–1930: Prostitutes, Emigration and Nation-building* (London: Pickering & Chatto, 2011); Peter J. Rimmer and Lisa M. Allen, ed. *The Underside of Malaysian History: Pullers, Prostitutes, Plantation Workers* (Singapore: Singapore University Press, 1990); Tomoko Yamazaki, "Sandakan No. 8 Brothel," *Bulletin of Concerned Asian Scholars* 7, no. 4 (1975): 52–60; Bill Mihalopoulos, "世界か Women, overseas sex work and globalization in Meiji Japan 明治日本における女性, 国外性労働、海外進出," *The Asia-Pacific Journal* 10, no. 35/1 (2012): 1–24; Nagata Yuriko, "The Japanese in the Torres Strait," in *Navigating Boundaries: The Asian Diaspora in Torres Strait*, ed. Anna Shnukal, Guy Ramsay and Yuriko Nagata (Canberra: Pandanus Books, 2004), 138–159. For other historical accounts of the *karayuki-san*, see: Raelene Frances, *Selling Sex: A Hidden History of Prostitution* (Sydney: University of New South Wales Press, 2007), 46–60; Hiroshi Shimizu, "Karayuki-san and the Japanese economic advance into British Malaya, 1870–1920," *Asian Studies Review* 20, no. 3 (1997): 107–132; Motoe Terami-Wada, "Karayuki-san of Manila: 1880–1920," *Philippine Studies*, no. 34 (1986): 287–316.

19 James F. Warren, *Ah Ku and Karayuki-San: Prostitution and Singapore Society, 1870–1940* (Oxford: Oxford University Press, 1993), 75.

Although they might be bought from their parents for as little as 300 yen, subsequent charges levied for transport, food, clothing and medical expenses meant that it could cost a woman up to 2,000 yen to "buy back her freedom".[20]

Once in Australia, the conditions under which these women worked depended very much on geographical location. Often among the first settlers in new mining and pearling areas, many led transient and uncomfortable lives, operating in tents or makeshift dwellings. The more fortunate led more stable lives in the bigger towns. Those who had paid their debts had more control over their lives. Some seem to have accumulated considerable wealth. A study of almost 200 Japanese women in Western Australia revealed that most were in their twenties when they arrived in the 1890s, had several trips overseas and returned to Japan in old age. During the course of their careers, they were often more than prostitutes: some owned and managed brothels, pearling interests and other small businesses, financed originally through prostitution. Many married Japanese, Chinese and sometimes European, Filipino or Malay men. Others remained single but moved from prostitution to other enterprises, such as running boarding-houses or dressmaking. However, judging from surviving police records, like contemporary Thai sex workers, the Japanese women who were engaged in the sex industry seem to have been particularly prone to violence from customers.[21]

Of course, these Asian women were not referred to as "white slaves". Indeed, part of their attraction was the fact that they were not white. Late colonial Australia was a much more ethnically-diverse society than it was to become in the twentieth century, especially in the north. Large numbers of Chinese were engaged in mining, while Japanese and Malays worked in the maritime industries around the northern coast. The sugar cane plantations also depended on the labour of Melanesian men, known generally as Kanakas. This presented a problem for colonial authorities, who believed that dire social consequences would follow unless a "suitable outlet for their sexual passion" could be found.[22] They were especially worried about "coloured" men raping white women. The importation of Japanese

20 Tomoko, "Sandakan No. 8 Brothel," 52.

21 Susan Jane Hunt, *Spinifex and hessian: Women's lives in North-Western Australia, 1860–1900* (Perth: University of Western Australia Press, 1979), Chapter 5.

22 Report by Police commissioner W.E. Parry-Okeden, February 1899, in Raymond Evans, "'Soiled doves': Prostitution in colonial Queensland," in *So Much Hard Work: Women and Prostitution in Australian History*, ed. Kay Daniels (Melbourne: Fontana/Collins, 1984), 139.

prostitutes was seen as a good solution to the need to provide some sexual outlet for "coloured" men, whilst maintaining the status of the white race. As the Queensland Commissioner of Police argued:

> Social evil [prostitution] exists and flourishes nearly everywhere in districts where large numbers of coloured aliens are located ... The supply of Japanese women for the Kanaka demand is less revolting and degrading than would be the case were it met by white women.[23]

Japanese were also preferred for this function over Aboriginal women, who were popularly regarded as dirty, diseased and more likely to produce children of mixed descent (Figure 1).

After the introduction of the White Australia Policy and the deportation of most non-white immigrants in the early twentieth century, the perceived problem of satisfying the lusts of a large population of so-called "coloured" men disappeared. Japanese women found themselves no longer welcome in White Australia, and most left. But this did not mean Australia ceased to be a destination for itinerant sex workers, for there was another traffic in women which had also begun in the late nineteenth century that continued well into the twentieth: the movement of women between continental Europe and Australia via South America or Egypt. This traffic came to be referred to as "white slavery".

Although its clandestine nature means we will never know the precise dimensions of this traffic, some insight into its operations can be gleaned from those cases that came under police investigations. In 1902, sixteen-year-old Assunta Spazziani was recruited in Rome through an employment agency to work as a general servant for an Italian couple about to embark for the West Australian goldfields. According to her account, her employers, Charles Cozzi and Marie Guidotti, told Assunta that Charles was engaged in the mining industry and that she would be paid her fare and good wages. The three sailed from Naples in 1902 and on disembarking at Fremantle took the train to Kalgoorlie. The couple rented a house in Brookman Street – a notorious red-light area. Gradually the real nature of her employment dawned on the young woman. Looking out her window, Assunta saw "a lot of women on the other side of the street, sitting or standing at the doors of their houses, dressed in coloured, gay, loose wrappers". Marie explained what they were doing and told her that she too would soon "be in the fashion". The next day Assunta was forced

23 Report by Police commissioner W.E. Parry-Okeden, February 1899, quoted in Evans, "Soiled doves", 139.

to solicit customers, her employers assuring her that she would soon get used to the work. Unfortunately for them, Assunta was not so co-operative. Whenever she was sent to a room with a man, she screamed so much that the customer was happy to retreat. Despite beatings administered by Cozzi, she continued to resist and seek a way to escape.

Three months after arriving in Kalgoorlie, an opportunity presented itself in the person of a young Italian tradesman employed to do renovations on the house. Ricchiardo agreed to help Assunta, fleeing with her to Perth where she was deposited with friends of his. Assunta was later moved to the Salvation Army Refuge, where the officials reported the matter to the police. Cozzi and Guidotti were arrested, found guilty of procuring and sentenced to two years imprisonment with hard labour.[24]

Assunta's case was not unique. Seventeen-year-old Natalina Appendino, also Italian, was working in a Marseille factory in France when she was offered a job at much higher wages in Western Australia. For two pounds per month, plus board, washing and her return fare, Natalina agreed to accompany a man and his female companion to work as an assistant in a confectionery shop in Kalgoorlie. Like Assunta, it was only on arriving in Australia that she discovered she would be selling sex rather than candy, but her inability to speak English made escape difficult. However, also like Assunta, Natalina proved resourceful. First, she feigned illness and was admitted to the hospital. Unfortunately, less than a week later she was visited by a Frenchwoman, Madam Galliard, who persuaded Natalina to go home with her on the promise that she would care for her. She told the girl she had bought her freedom for the sum of 65 pounds. This woman also turned out to be in the sex industry, and Natalina found herself once more in a brothel. Madam Galliard's investment did not pay off: Natalina showed no enthusiasm for sex work and was soon sold to another Frenchman, Paul Loubens, for 35 pounds. He placed her in Annie Smith's brothel, but she escaped and sought refuge at an Italian wine saloon. Natalina formed a relationship with an Italian contractor who encouraged her to go to the police and lay a complaint. Although there was no case of procuring against Loubens, he was convicted of living off the earnings of prostitution and sentenced to six months gaol.[25]

---

24 "Capture of Cozzi," *Sunday Times*, 24 August 1902, 3; "Brothels, Bawds, and Bludgers," *Sunday Times*, 14 September 1902, 7.

25 Raelene Davidson (now Frances), "Prostitution in Perth and Fremantle and on the eastern goldfields, 1895–1939" (MA thesis, University of Western Australia, 1980), 172; Police vs Loubens, Kalgoorlie Police Court Minutes, 18 May 1900, Battye Library, acc. no. 1340/12.

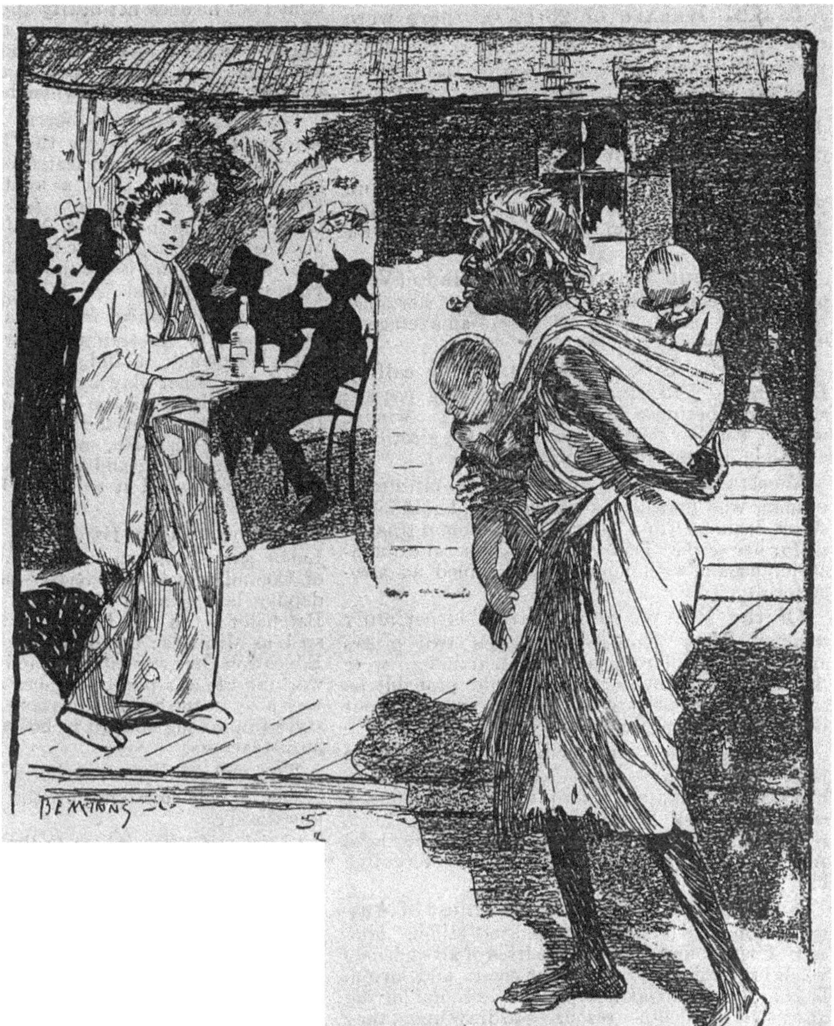

Figure 1. "Asiatic Australia – A Phase that is Passing Away,"
Bulletin, 7 January 1904, 16.
Courtesy of the National Library of Australia.

These cases were unusual in that they resulted in prosecution and conviction. Other instances of European women's procurement by deception and violence were reported in the press, forming part of a growing international concern about the so-called "white slave traffic". This concern, and the terminology of sexual slavery, was originally used to apply to the procuration of young English girls for sale to brothels in Belgium and France. A famous case in 1885 in which the London publicist, W.T. Stead, purchased such a girl provided the opportunity for widespread discussion in the press. A growing movement aimed at ending this traffic culminated in the first of a series of international conferences in 1899. This concern was evident in Australia, where people were on the lookout for anything resembling white slavery in their midst. The cases of Assunta Spazziani and Natalina Appendino seemed to confirm the existence of this traffic and fuelled public imagination.

However, the issue was rather more complicated than the discourse of white slavery implied. Leaving aside the difficult question of choice in the context of limited economic options, these two women fit the classic stereotype of the "white slave": young, sexually innocent white women lured to a life of enforced whoredom in a foreign country. As well as serving the men of European descent who dominated the goldfields population, these women would also have been expected to service the large numbers of "coloured" men who visited the brothels: principally "Afghan" camel drivers and traders but also a smaller number of Japanese.[26] The evidence presented to the court in these cases indicates that the "white slave traffic" was not simply a creation of the sensationalist press. The question is, how representative were they?

We will never be able to say for sure. It seems likely, though, that such extreme cases of deception and coercion were the exception rather than the norm. By their own reports, most of the French and Italian women who encountered the law in Western Australia had worked in the sex industry previously. They were less innocent victims decoyed to "a fate worse than death" than professionals seeking the best market opportunities.[27] Even if not professionals in their own country, they were prepared to engage in commercial sex once abroad. Women were often assisted by a number of men with whom they had a variety of relationships: as lovers, business partners, exploiters, and protectors. Other women came independently of

26 For police reports of men observed visiting the premises of Molly Young, see: Kalgoorlie Police Court Minutes, 17 October 1910, Battye Library, acc. no. 1340/22.

27 Kalgoorlie Detectives Occurrence Book, 20 October 1898; 1 April 1903.

men and the so-called "syndicates", operating either alone or with other women. These were in fact migrant sex workers rather than trafficked women.[28]

Once in Australia, they found their presence tolerated, if not welcomed. The large numbers of "foreign" women engaged in sex work allowed local commentators to congratulate themselves on the advanced status of Australia. In 1915, a West Australian politician, the Honourable R.H. Underwood, told the Legislative Assembly:

> We can take credit, and I think should take credit to ourselves in WA for our social conditions when we reflect that the supply of prostitutes in this country has given out. Most honourable members know that prostitutes in WA are supplied chiefly from France, Japan, and Italy. As a matter of fact the Australian social system has kept the Australian women out of it.[29]

This was a comfortable illusion rather than a reality: Australian-born women actually constituted the majority in the local sex industry. But it was true that non-Australian and non-British women were disproportionately represented amongst the ranks of sex workers.[30] All this was about to change, however, as Australia determined to create a specifically British version of White Australia after the First World War, and also became more conscious of its status as an emerging nation on the world stage.

Although popularly understood as a policy of racial exclusion – hence its popular designation as a White Australia Policy – the Immigration Restriction Act of 1901 was not framed in explicitly racial terms. On the contrary, there was no specific mention of racial attributes in the selection of immigrants. The primary mechanism for exclusion was a dictation test in a European language, used in the twentieth century to exclude not just "coloureds" but also others considered subversive to Australia's political and social institutions. The case of the Communist Egon Kisch, excluded in 1934 after failing a test in Gaelic, is well-known.[31] Less well known is the use of this dictation test to exclude persons of suspect sexuality.

28 Nor was the traffic in one direction only; some entrepreneurs brought young women from Europe to Australia and New Zealand while others recruited women to take back to brothels in Buenos Aires and London.

29 Hon. R.H. Underwood, *Western Australian Parliamentary Debates: Legislative Assembly*, 51 (7 September 1915), 637.

30 Davidson (now Frances), "Prostitution in Perth and Fremantle," Chapter 5.

31 Stuart Macintyre, *The Reds: The Communist Party of Australia from Origins to Illegality* (Sydney: Allen & Unwin, 1998), 270–273.

The prosecution of Cozzi and Guidotti in 1902 coincided with an increase in international concern about the traffic in women. The international movement arising from this concern had close connections with "abolitionist" groups who sought an end to all systems of state-regulated prostitution. Before 1914, there were three international conventions aimed at suppressing the so-called "White Slave Traffic"; Australia was a signatory to each.[32] Australian feminists were active in this campaign, both locally and internationally, but the authorities were not convinced that traffic in women was a serious problem in Australia. The 1914 Premiers' Conference refused to hear from a delegation, led by the Women's Political Association of Victoria, on the issue.[33]

The outbreak of war in 1914 changed government and feminist reactions to the international sex industry. Australian troops fighting in the Middle East frequented Cairo brothels, a fact generally known in Australia.[34] This drew attention both to the extent of the traffic in women in Egypt and also heightened concerns about the relationship between prostitution and venereal disease (especially the importation of new, "foreign" strands to Australia).[35] After the war, feminist concerns about the traffic in women overlapped with eugenicist fears about the impact of sexually transmitted diseases on racial vigour. The post-war government, sharing fears about racial decline, was concerned that Australia be seen to acquit itself on the international stage as a "civilised" and "advanced" society. When the League of Nations took over the administration of the international conventions on the traffic in women and children, Australia was keen to become a signatory and to carry out its obligations under the convention.[36]

By the mid-1920s, most Australian governments no longer regarded the presence of foreign prostitutes as beneficial or even benign. Since the White Australia Policy had ceased the importation of Pacific Island and Chinese labourers and enforced the repatriation of most of Australia's existing "coloured" populations, the racial rationale for tolerating foreign prostitutes

32 AA Series A1108, item vol. 31, National Archives of Australia (NAA). See: Sheila Jeffreys, *The Idea of Prostitution* (Melbourne: Spinifex Press, 1997), Chapter 1.

33 AA Series A1, item 1915/5651, NAA; also AA Series A1108, item vol. 31, NAA.

34 AA series CP78/23/1. item 14/89/252 Pt 1, NAA; Bruce Scates and Raelene Frances, *Women and the Great War* (Cambridge: Cambridge University Press, 1997), chapter 6.

35 Judith Smart, "The Great War and the 'scarlet scourge': Debates about venereal diseases in Melbourne during World War I," in *An Anzac Muster: War and Society in Australia and New Zealand 1914–18 and 1939–45*, ed. Judith Smart and Tony Wood (Clayton: Monash University Press, 1992), 58–85.

36 The first two conventions (1904 and 1910) were administered by the French Government.

to service a large non-white male population no longer existed. Japanese prostitutes were themselves victims of the new immigration laws: the door was firmly closed against new arrivals, while most already in Australia were required to leave. French prostitutes were now targeted as the main contaminating influence, both morally and physically. After Australia's wartime experiences, it was not hard for the government to be convinced that a traffic in women did exist and that the Middle East played a particular role as a staging post en route to Australia.[37]

The question was, what action should be taken? In retrospect, it is not hard to see why the policy of exclusion commended itself to the authorities. The Director of the Attorney General's Department explained:

> As principal executive officer in Australia under the White Slave Convention of the League of Nations, I am of opinion that one of the best practical methods of dealing with the question of White Slavery is to make it impossible for the unscrupulous foreigners to import women of the unfortunate class to Australia, and that the best way to do this is to deport any such women who manage to enter and who immediately practise their profession here.[38]

Although convenient for the government, the effects of Australia's approach to the "white slave traffic" were much more ambiguous from the point of view of the abolitionists. The activities of the International Abolitionist Federation had considerable impact on immigration policy and policing within Australia. Activists would no doubt have been most gratified at the exclusion or deportation of men allegedly involved in trafficking women. However, the wholesale deportation of foreign prostitutes, which was carried out as a Government strategy to discourage the international movement of sex workers, was more problematic from a feminist perspective. Indeed, the question of the compulsory repatriation and exclusion of prostituted women was a contentious issue for the League of Nations, with feminists and civil libertarians arguing against discriminatory measures which would result in "the prostitute … being considered as a special class which could be driven from place to place".[39]

---

37 H.E. Jones to Director, Attorney-General's Department, to The Secretary, Home and Territories Department, 29 July 1927, AA Series 2998/1, item 51/576, NAA.

38 Ibid.

39 International Bureau for the Suppression of the Traffic in Women and Children, *Congress Reports*, London, 1930, cited in Jeffreys, *The Idea of Prostitution*, 24.

Several sensational cases involving French and Italian nationals in the late 1920s and early 1930s proved these concerns justified. The first case involved a French woman of ill-repute who had married an Australian war veteran to escape deportation. She soon became bored with her marriage and returned to her former acquaintances. In April 1929, she was charged with being a prohibited immigrant; failing to pass a dictation test in German, she was sentenced to six months' imprisonment and deportation.[40] Four days later the Sydney *Sun* reported the deportation of one of her associates after failing to pass a dictation test in English, reporting the item with a bold caption: "WHITE SLAVERY INQUIRY". The government claimed it had only acted after receiving "a communication from the White Slavery Committee of the League of Nations".[41]

Earlier cases made the same connections. In July 1928, the Melbourne *Argus* reported that two French women, residents of Perth who allegedly kept a house of ill fame, were to be deported after failing to pass the language test in English.[42] The Melbourne *Age* went into more detail, reporting how the women had lived in Egypt before coming to Australia with 2000 pounds, which they invested in a house in Roe Street, Perth. As most Australians were aware, Roe Street was a notorious red-light district, while European women who had lived in Egypt were immediately suspect.[43] In their defence, the women argued that the Immigration Act should not have been applied as their investments made it clear that they intended to settle in Australia permanently. As such, they were "citizens", not "immigrants". Unconvinced, the Chief Justice emphasised that the dictation test could be administered anytime within the first three years after arrival, during which time persons who entered Australia were here "on approval."[44] Clearly, Australia did not approve of prostitutes. The authorities, it was implied, were behaving in the nation's best interests. The references to the League of Nations also suggested that Australia was carrying out broader agendas as part of its responsibilities as a member of the community of (civilised) nations. What is clear from all of these cases is the importance of an association with prostitution as a criterion for exclusion, regardless of the wealth or property of the individuals concerned.

---

40 "£1000 round a slim waist," *Smiths' Weekly*, 20 April 1929, 4.

41 "Three months: Teboul Sentenced: White slave inquiry," *Sun*, 24 April 1929, 13.

42 "Women to be deported," *Argus*, 13 July 1928, 7.

43 "French immigrants," *Age*, 13 July 1928, 11.

44 "Prohibited immigrants," *Advertiser*, 13 July 1928, 14.

Nor were women the only targets of these deportations: men believed to be involved as procurers or associates of prostitutes were also excluded.

The description of these cases as examples of white slavery, terminology which the government and press were keen to embrace, is also interesting. In fact, the situation of the women and their male companions, as reported both by the police and themselves in evidence, suggests that the relationship was a far cry from the popular idea of white slavery. The women were neither young nor inexperienced; they did not appear to be vulnerable to the men with whom they associated. However, by using the language of white slavery, the government was better able to justify its actions – and no doubt the newspapers sold more copies.

The women who were subsequently deported from Australia had previously left Egypt in the wake of changes brought about by the activities of the International Bureau for the Suppression of the Traffic in Women, working in conjunction with the local police.[45] As the official files relating to the 1920s deportations show, many – perhaps even most – of the women who came to Australia from France via Egypt intended to become long-term residents, bringing property and establishing businesses in the relatively lucrative and safe environment of Perth's Roe Street. These women became the unintended victims of the anti-trafficking campaign, forced to sell their property at a loss and leave a country where they had hoped to achieve modest comfort and security. What became of the women forced to move on from Australia remains unknown. Contrary to the intention of those attempting to stop the exploitation of women's sexuality, such deportations probably prolonged the working life of prostitutes by forcing them to recoup their Australian losses elsewhere.

Conclusion

There are many parallels between the history of sex trafficking and migrant sex work in the late nineteenth and early twentieth centuries and the contemporary situation. In both cases, there is clear evidence that some women and girls from other countries were coerced or tricked into exploitative conditions in the sex industry. However, these seem to represent a small minority of the total number of migrant sex workers in Australia. The failure to distinguish between trafficked women and migrant

45 Extract from *Vigilance Record*, March-April 1929, in International Bureau for the Suppression of the Traffic in Women Papers, Josephine Butler Archives, Fawcett Library, London, ms. 4/1BS, box 112.

workers in the past led to migrant sex workers being discriminated against by the Australian authorities. By the interwar period, they were excluded, deported and in some cases imprisoned because of their involvement in the sex industry. Arguably, this was the result of a failure to take a human rights approach to sex trafficking, which would instead have meant a clearer focus on how interventions would impact sex workers. The emphasis on stopping all transnational movements had clearly negative consequences for migrant sex workers.

The lessons from this history have continuing relevance today, both in Australia and more broadly. While the Australian government currently adopts a human rights approach, there is a growing movement internationally to pursue a vigorous abolitionist approach. This is most evident in the United States where twenty-first-century "neo-abolitionist" pressure groups have aligned with right-wing politicians on this issue. Thus, George W. Bush linked the moral grounds for his war on terror with a war against trafficking.[46] Government finances, through USAID, are only directed to organisations which are clearly against prostitution. Other organisations – many of which supply health services to sex workers – are deprived of such funding, with obvious negative effects on women in the sex industry.[47]

This is in marked contrast to the situation in Australia, where the explicitly human rights approach means that government policies support sex worker groups and other organisations to deliver services to sex workers. Thus, both the longer and more recent history of migration and the sex industry support a human rights approach to this issue, delivering the best outcomes for both trafficked women and migrant sex workers.

---

46 Meshkovska et al, "Female Sex Trafficking," 383; Ronald Weitzer, "The social construction of sex trafficking: Ideology and institutionalization of a moral crusade," *Politics and Society* 35 (2007): 447–475.

47 Cheryl Overs and Kate Hawkins, "Can rights stop the wrongs? Exploring the connections between framings of sex workers' rights and sexual and reproductive health," *BMC International Health and Human Rights* 11, no. 3 (2011): S6.

Chapter 9

GENDER-BASED VIOLENCE IN OUT-OF-HOME CARE

Shurlee Swain

Since the 1990s, a series of inquiries into historical institutional abuse across the Western world have consistently disclosed high levels of physical and sexual violence experienced by children living apart from their families. Many conclude that such abuse has been endemic across the sector for many years. Drawing primarily on survivor testimony, these inquiries focus on establishing why abuse occurred and on making recommendations to prevent such abuse in the future. While they attempt to document the prevalence of abuse, few apply a gender lens to their analysis. This chapter aims to fill that gap, using the key Australian inquiries into historical institutional abuse over the past half century to examine the degree to which the experience of physical and sexual violence in out-of-home care has been gendered.

Family violence and sexual abuse were both forced onto the public agenda through the activities of the women's movement from the 1970s. By sharing individual stories participants came to recognise such experiences not as personal but political, indicative of gendered inequalities inherent in the world in which they lived.[1] Subsequent research, analyses and policy formulation have been developed through this feminist lens. While such an approach has proved fruitful in opening up silences around gendered violence, it has also risked, at times, reinscribing stereotypical notions of

1 Paula Reavey and Sam Warner, eds. *New Feminist Stories of Child Sexual Abuse: Sexual Scripts and Dangerous Dialogues* (London & New York: Routledge, 2003), 2–3.

men as aggressors and women as victims.[2] This has been a particular risk in relation to studies of intra-familial child abuse where the centrality of the mother as care giver has demanded a more textured feminist response. Positioning child sexual abuse as a product of gendered power inequalities within the family home proved to be more convincing than applying a similar explanation to the prevalence of physical abuse where analyses grounded in personal and social dynamics have prevailed.[3] Despite such feminist interventions, elements of mother-blaming – derived from older Freudian analyses – remain, grounded in essentialist understandings of the protective role of the mother.[4] But feminist campaigning around child abuse ignored the abuse of children in out-of-home care, already removed from their families. Preoccupied with an analysis of power relations within the family, the theories they developed have yet to be applied to the extra-familial settings that have been the focus of the public inquiries examined in this chapter. That is not to argue, however, that they could not benefit from a similarly gendered analysis.

The sequence of testimony-driven inquiries in Australia began with the Human Rights and Equal Opportunity Commission's investigation of the separation of Aboriginal and Torres Strait Islander children from their families which reported in 1997.[5] These separations arose as part of both protection and assimilation policies which, from the late nineteenth century, predominantly saw children of mixed descent forcibly removed from Indigenous communities and placed in church or government run institutions in order to be trained to work in the non-Indigenous economy. After World War II growing numbers of removed children bypassed institutional care and were placed directly in foster or adoptive homes, and denied contact with – and sometimes also knowledge of – their Indigenous origins.[6] Although the focus of the inquiry was on the justification and

2 The most influential article in this respect was Linda Gordon, "The politics of child sexual abuse: Notes from American history," *Feminist Review* 28, no. 1 (1988): 56–64.

3 For an early analysis of these dilemmas, see: Brid Featherstone and Barbara Fawcett, "Feminism and child abuse: Opening up some possibilities," *Critical Social Policy* 14, no. 42 (1994): 61–80.

4 Corry Azzopardi, Ramona Alaggia and Barbara Fallon, "From Freud to feminism: Gendered constructions of blame across theories of child sexual abuse," *Journal of Child Sexual Abuse* 27, no. 3 (2018): 254–275.

5 Human Rights and Equal Opportunity Commission (HREOC), *Bringing Them Home: Report of the National Inquiry into the Separation of Aboriginal and Torres Strait Islander Children from Their Families* (Sydney: HREOC, 1997).

6 For the history of this policy, see: Anna Haebich, *Broken Circles* (Fremantle: Fremantle Arts Centre Press, 2000).

after effects of removal, the disclosure of high levels of physical and sexual violence (alongside neglect, excessive levels of child labour and emotional abuse) created a space in which other care-leavers could speak of their experiences. Subsequent inquiries at both state and national levels validated the claims that child migrants brought to Australia from the 1920s to the 1960s,[7] children removed from their families within Australia across the twentieth century,[8] and single women forcibly separated from their children by adoption from the 1950s to the 1970s were similarly subject to abuse in the institutions entrusted with their care.[9] There has been no inquiry to date into the abuse of children in the disability sector (one was announced in February 2019), though there is evidence in the existing inquiries that violence there was also endemic.[10] When attention shifted in the twenty-first century to concentrate upon sexual abuse, widening the focus to include abuse in churches, schools and sporting organisations, survivors of institutional care continued to be over-represented amongst those who came forward to testify.[11] While most of the allegations made before such inquiries have not been tested in a court of law, the weight and consistency of the claims gives them a veracity beyond individual accounts. The reports and evidence presented to such inquiries therefore provides a rich evidence base from which to investigate the degree to which the experience of institutional abuse has been gendered.

---

7 Australian Senate Community Affairs References Committee (ASCARC), *Lost Innocents: Righting the Record Report on Child Migration* (Canberra: Senate Printing Unit, 2001).

8 Australian Senate Community Affairs References Committee (ASCARC), *Forgotten Australians: A Report on Australians Who Experienced Institutional or Out-of-Home Care as Children* (Canberra: Senate Printing Unit, 2004); Leneen Forde, *Report of the Commission of Inquiry into Abuse of Children in Queensland Institutions* (Brisbane: The Inquiry, 1999).

9 Australian Senate Community Affairs References Committee, *Commonwealth Contribution to Former Forced Adoption Policies and Practices* (Canberra: Senate Printing Unit, Parliament House, 2012).

10 ASCARC, *Forgotten Australians*, 61–62; Hon E.P. Mullighan, *Children in State Care Commission of Inquiry: Allegations of Sexual Abuse and Death from Criminal Conduct* (Adelaide: Children in State Care Commission of Enquiry, 2008), 8; Royal Commission into Institutional Responses to Child Sexual Abuse (RCIRCSA), *Interim Report* (Sydney: Commonwealth of Australia, 2014), 112.

11 Mullighan, *Children in State Care Commission of Inquiry*; Family and Community Development Committee Parliament of Victoria (SCDCPV), *Betrayal of Trust: Inquiry into the Handling of Child Abuse by Religious and Other Non-Government Organisations*, vol. 1 (Melbourne: Parliament of Victoria, 2013). RCIRCSA website, accessed 29 October 2017, http://www.childabuseroyalcommission.gov.au/.

Structures of welfare and care

To comprehend this body of evidence it is important to understand the structure of out-of-home care for children in Australia. The earliest institutions were large orphanages established in most major centres in the early years of colonisation. Orphanages under Protestant auspices usually accommodated both boys and girls. Although overwhelmingly staffed by women, such institutions often had a male superintendent and a small number of men responsible for the older boys. Catholic orphanages, staffed by members of religious orders, were usually segregated by gender in terms of both staff and residents. In the second half of the nineteenth century, most colonies established their own state children's departments, initially conducting industrial and reformatory schools but increasingly relying on placing children out with individual families. However, the inability of such foster care to provide for all children meant most departments continued to rely on non-government organisations. Occasionally, instances of abuse in both forms of care surfaced in nineteenth-century newspaper reports. However, they were generally dismissed as individual aberrations rather than seen as evidence that the systems themselves were abusive.[12]

From the early twentieth century, institutions for children softened their image. Labelled as homes, many attempted to develop a more family-like atmosphere. But the denominationally-based gendered patterns nonetheless survived, with the bulk of care in all but boys' only institutions being provided by women – now addressed as aunties or sisters, or even on occasions mother. While, over time, most children came to be accommodated in mixed aged and gender settings, segregated institutions continued to accommodate older boys, and girls classified as "difficult".[13] In institutions, as in the community as a whole, perpetrators of both physical and sexual violence were overwhelmingly male.[14] However, given the predominance of female staff, this statistic takes on added significance

12 See: "Flogging at an orphan school," *Sydney Mail*, 5 March 1870, 9; "Geelong Protestant Orphan Asylum," *Geelong Advertiser*, 29 January 1875, 3; "Boarding-out abuses," *South Australian Weekly Chronicle*, 28 June 1884, 5; "Cruelty to a child," *Daily Telegraph*, 13 September 1890, 10; "Cruelty to a state orphan," *Gympie Times and Mary River Mining Gazette*, 27 June 1891, 4.

13 For a fuller study of the range of institutions in Australia, see: Shurlee Swain, *History of Institutions Providing out-of-Home Care for Children* (Sydney: Royal Commission into Institutional Responses to Child Sexual Abuse, 2014).

14 Bridget Penhale, "Introduction," in *Institutional Abuse: Perspectives across the Life Course*, ed. Nicky Stanley, Jill Manthorpe, and Bridget Penhale (London: Routledge, 1999), 1.

in institutional settings.[15] Amongst victims the gender profile is more complex, with differences emerging both between physical and sexual violence, and in different institutional contexts.

Physical abuse

Despite the recent focus on sexual abuse, physical abuse was more frequently reported by witnesses before earlier inquiries.[16] "Sexual abuse is always highlighted as if it was the 'worst' abuse", writes Care Leavers of Australasia Network co-founder, Joanna Penglase. "What gets lost here is that children were violated in every sense in an institution, and being used sexually was just one of those violations."[17] Hence, in examining the gendered dimensions of institutional violence, it is important both to acknowledge the widespread (but less visible) emotional and psychological abuse, and to first consider the physical abuse which was not only more prevalent but also created the environment in which sexual abuse was able to flourish.[18]

Although none of the inquiry reports breaks down frequency statistics by gender, the explanations they offer as to the contexts in which physical violence took place have a gendered dimension. Central to such explanations was the quantity and quality of staff in such institutions. In both single sex and non-gendered institutions, a small number of poorly trained staff were too often left in charge of large numbers of children and then resorted to violence in order to maintain control. In oral histories of such institutions and evidence before various inquiries, former staff members recall how they were inducted by older colleagues into a culture in which the use of physical violence against children was a way of exercising authority in a threatening environment.[19] The low status of childcare work (even within religious congregations) meant that institutions, desperate for

---

15 Christine Barter, "Independent investigations into institutional child abuse: Developing theory and practice," in *Institutional Abuse*, 74; Dick Sobsey, Wade Randall, and Rauno K.Parrila, "Gender differences in abused children with and without disabilities," *Child Abuse and Neglect* 21, no. 8 (1997): 717–718.

16 ASCARC, *Lost Innocents*, 80; HREOC, *Bringing Them Home*, 162.

17 Joanna Penglase, *Orphans of the Living: Growing up in "Care" in Twentieth-Century Australia* (Fremantle: Curtin University Books, 2005), 145.

18 RCIRCSA, *Final Report: Historical Residential Institutions*, vol. 11 (Barton: Commonwealth of Australia, 2017), 64–65.

19 See: Jill Barnard and Karen Twigg, *Holding onto Hope: A History of the Founding Agencies of Mackillop Family Services 1854–1997* (Melbourne: Australian Scholarly Publishing, 2004), 193–194. RCIRCSA, *Report of Case Study No. 5: Response of*

staff, could provide a safe place for damaged individuals with a particular penchant for violence. Given the gendered nature of care work, it is possible that this may have been more the case with male than female staff, but in the evidence presented before the various Australian inquiries, there are instances of both men and women who fell into this category. Leneene Forde's report, for example, employed this explanation to describe the conditions in one Queensland institution. The married couple in charge during the 1940s and 1950s carried straps, which were freely used to beat the boys into submission.[20]

However, much of the reported violence was part – or an extension – of existing disciplinary practices considered appropriate for the 'type' of children in institutional care. Seen simultaneously as victims and threats, they were believed to require a stricter level of discipline if they were to be transformed into responsible adults.[21] Such attitudes show a remarkable persistence over time, with the need for discipline and restraint a central theme from the earliest nineteenth-century inquiries into institutional care through to the most recent inquiry into the detention of children in the Northern Territory.[22] While there were regulations governing corporal punishment, evidence from both survivors and regulatory authorities would suggest that they were little known and even less likely to be enforced, especially when beds were in short supply.[23] A magisterial inquiry into the death of a child at the Myora mission in Queensland in 1896 heard evidence of flogging, dunking and dragging by the matron, who was subsequently found guilty of manslaughter but released into the care of the Salvation Army in lieu of serving a prison sentence.[24] A 1908 Victorian Government inquiry into allegations that veteran Victorian child rescuer, Selina Sutherland, had used excessive forms of punishment dismissed the

---

the Salvation Army to Child Sexual Abuse at Its Boys Homes in New South Wales and Queensland (Sydney: Royal Commission into Institutional Responses to Child Sexual Abuse, 2015), 68.

20 Forde, *Report of the Commission of Inquiry*, 71.

21 For a fuller exploration of this phenomenon, see: Harry Ferguson, "Abused and looked after children as 'moral dirt': Child abuse and institutional care in historical perspective," *Journal of Social Policy* 36, no. 1 (2007): 123–139.

22 For an example of the longevity of such concerns, see: "The training ship Vernon," *Sydney Morning Herald*, 16 April 1869, 3; *Report of the Royal Commission and Board of Inquiry into the Protection and Detention of Children in the Northern Territory*, vol. 2A (Darwin: Northern Territory Government, 2017).

23 Barnard and Twigg, *Holding onto Hope*, 193–196.

24 "Death of a child at the Myora Mission," *Brisbane Courier*, 26 September 1896, 6; "Editorial," *Brisbane Courier*, November 18 1896, 4.

charges, accepting her defence counsel's argument that she had only hit the children "when they really deserved it".[25]

Witnesses before each of the inquiries, both male and female, reported punishments which far exceeded those sanctioned by the community standards of the time, and on occasions bordered on criminal assault.[26] Recalling his time at the female-staffed Colebrook Home in South Australia in the 1950s, an Indigenous man saw "beatings and hidings" as a routine response both to children "playing up" and for bedwetting.[27] The report of the inquiry into child migration went so far as to describe the "systemic beatings designed to break down the will and subjugate the child migrants" as similar to the "stratagems used in concentration camps".[28] In severely understaffed institutions, the authority to administer such harsh punishments was extended to older residents, both males and females, whose use of violence against younger children was ignored and at times officially sanctioned.[29]

Violent punishment increased in severity in institutions for older children. Given the over-representation of boys in such contexts, the most brutal accounts come from male-only institutions, predominantly but not exclusively those operated by the Catholic Church and the Salvation Army. Girls, however, were not exempt. Although by regulation they were not meant to be subject to corporal punishment, testimony suggests that the regulations were often ignored. Physical violence, administered by female staff, was an integral part of the disciplinary regime in girls' reformatories, with some having access to a small number of male staff called in to deal with residents considered to be beyond female control.[30] In maternity homes, harsh physical punishment was less often reported, although some mothers recall physical examinations being conducted in an unnecessarily violent way as part of the punishment for their moral fall.[31]

Organised peer violence to control behaviour was more prevalent in boys' institutions. The use of older residents to "discipline" younger children created a chain of command in which victims became perpetrators.

---

25 "Miss Sutherland," *Argus*, 13 October 1908, 7; "Miss Sutherland," *Argus*, 20 October 1908, 9.

26 ASCARC, *Forgotten Australians*, 101–102.

27 HREOC, *Bringing Them Home*, 160.

28 ASCARC, *Lost Innocents*, 80.

29 Forde, *Report of the Commission of Inquiry*, 72 and 147.

30 Ibid., 155.

31 ASCARC, *Commonwealth Contribution to Former Forced Adoption Policies and Practices*, 38–39.

"Welcoming" rituals administered by older residents, for example, were an essential part of establishing and sustaining the institutional hierarchies that staff often relied upon to maintain order. A regular feature of the Salvation Army home in Goulburn, New South Wales was "the tunnel of love" where younger residents "had to run between bully boys in a line on each side of you, much like a rugby scrum as they kicked and thumped you".[32] Setting boys to fight each other as a form of both punishment and entertainment was a widespread practice, one child migrant claimed, describing it as "a human cockfight" set up by the Christian Brothers "for their enjoyment".[33] In one variation, boys were organized into "dingo packs" to pursue absconders. "When caught, the pack would bash into their 'victim' and drag him back", receiving a reward for their efforts.[34]

Sexual abuse

While any gendered differences that are evident in the prevalence of physical violence in institutional care can largely be explained in terms of staff and resident profiles, the situation in relation to sexual violence is more stark. The early Australian inquiries found that, like physical abuse, sexual violence was endemic in out-of-home care.[35] More recent inquiries, focused specifically on child sexual abuse, have confirmed these findings. Mullighan's report on South Australia concluded that "sexual abuse occurred in every type of care from the 1940s onwards".[36] The Royal Commission into Institutional Responses to Child Sexual Abuse (RCIRCSA), which ran from 2013 to 2017, extended its scope beyond out-of-home care to expose widespread child sexual abuse across a range of extra-familial settings. As in the broader community, men are identified as the main perpetrators against both boys and girls, although some work in

32 Submissions 248 and 282 of Forgotten Australians Submissions, *Parliament of Australia*, 2005, accessed 29 October 2017, https://www.aph.gov.au/Parliamentary_Business/Committees/Senate/Community_Affairs/Completed_inquiries/2004-07/inst_care/submissions/sublist.

33 Witness statement HIA 312, in *Northern Ireland Inquiry into Historical Institutional Abuse 1922 to 1995*, Module 2, accessed 29 October 2017, https://www.hiainquiry.org/sites/hiainquiry/files/media-files/hia_312_redacted_opt.pdf.

34 Submission 15, Wayne Laird of Forgotten Australians Submissions.

35 Forde, *Report of the Commission of Inquiry*, 87.

36 Mullighan, *Children in State Care Commission of Inquiry*, xiii. Mullighan's investigation was limited to the 1940s and beyond.

collaboration with a female offender.[37] There are suggestions, however, that female perpetration could be under-reported given societal pressures that may prevent males from reporting such abuse – either for fear of not being taken seriously, or because victims are constrained by the cultural scripts of male sexuality.[38] Reports of female perpetrators acting alone have also come from female-only institutions, but these are comparatively rare in the case of children's homes.[39] Women perpetrators are more frequently reported by survivors of girls' reformatory institutions and maternity homes where medical investigations could be excessively violent and peer sexual abuse was also widespread.[40]

Amongst victims, females still predominate. Yet males appear to have been more vulnerable than they would have been had they not been living in an institution. Additionally, males have certainly been more visible amongst witnesses to recent inquiries. This has led to accusations that a narrative of boys abused by priests and other religious figures diverts attention from the very real risk faced by girls both within and outside the family home.[41] As statistics compiled for the Royal Commission found, while 67 per cent of the victims of institutional child sexual abuse in Queensland from 2008 to 2013 were female, they constituted less than 8 per cent of female child sexual abuse victims in that state. By contrast, male victims of institutional child sexual abuse constituted more than 14 per cent of Queensland's male

---

37 Leah Bromfield, Craig Hirte, Olivia Octoman and Ilan Katz, *Child Sexual Abuse in Australian Institutional Contexts 2008–13: Findings from Administrative Data* (Sydney: Royal Commission into Institutional Responses to Child Sexual Abuse, 2017), 208; Margaretha C. Timmerman and Pauline R. Schreuder, "Sexual abuse of children and youth in residential care: An international review," *Aggression and Violent Behavior* 19 (2014): 718.

38 RCIRSCA, *Interim Report*, 104–105. The disparity observed by the Victorian Betrayal of Trust Inquiry between survivor testimony and the documentation of abuse in case files would appear to support this assertion. SCDCPV, *Betrayal of Trust*, vol. 1, 55; Steven Angelides, "Sexual offences against 'children' and the question of judicial gender bias," *Australian Feminist Studies*, 23, no. 57 (2008): 364.

39 HREOC, *Bringing Them Home*, 163. Mullighan, *Children in State Care Commission of Inquiry*, 36.

40 RCIRCSA, *Report of Case Study No. 30: The Response of Turana, Winlaton and Baltara, and the Victoria Police and the Department of Health and Human Services Victoria to Allegations of Child Sexual Abuse.* (Sydney: Royal Commission into Institutional Responses to Child Sexual Abuse, 2016), 33–35. RCIRCSA, *Report of Case Study No. 7. Child Sexual Abuse at the Parramatta Training School for Girls and the Institution for Girls in Hay* (Sydney: Royal Commission into Institutional Responses to Child Sexual Abuse, 2014), 17.

41 SCDCPV, *Betrayal of Trust*, vol. 1, 128.

child sexual abuse victims.[42] There have been few attempts to explain the gender disparity. However, the Betrayal of Trust report suggested that higher levels of recidivism amongst perpetrators who target boys may lead to more male victims in institutional settings.[43] The difference between the gendered incidence of sexual abuse in institutional and community settings is at its greatest in relation to large congregate care institutions, diminishing as the care settings more closely equate to the patriarchal family. Amongst the 16 male survivors (7.7 per cent) who told their stories of sexual abuse to the Bringing them Home inquiry, for example, 10 had been abused in institutions, whereas for the 50 sexually-abused females (11.7 per cent), all but 19 had been abused in family-like situations.[44] Similarly, while the Mullighan inquiry heard from slightly more males than females overall, of the 103 survivors who reported being sexually abused in foster care, 72 were women.[45]

The Victorian Betrayal of Trust inquiry argued that while there was no typical perpetrator, most would fit into one of three groups: the situational offenders who reacted to the environment in which they found themselves; the opportunistic offenders who, although able to restrain themselves most of the time, succumbed occasionally, and later developed elaborate justifications for their behaviour; and the predatory offenders or paedophiles who actively sought out potential victims.[46] Large congregate care settings were highly sexualised environments in which children were vulnerable to all three types of offenders, yet the risks and challenges which such sexualisation posed were routinely ignored and at times actively denied, leaving young residents unsure as to the limits of acceptable or "normal" behaviour.[47] In his submission to the Forgotten Australians inquiry, Bryan Cronin described himself arriving at Nazareth Boys Home, Ballarat, as a "pore [*sic*] defenceless child, an infant, fresh meet in a meet market [*sic*]".[48]

In such environments children's bodies were frequently exposed, creating situations in which situational or opportunistic offences could occur. Communal bathing, naked swimming, and harsh physical punishments

42 Bromfield et al., *Child Sexual Abuse in Australian Institutional Contexts 2008–13*, 207. Although parallel data was not available from all states and territories there was no reason to believe that the Queensland data was not typical of Australia as a whole.

43 SCDCPV, *Betrayal of Trust*, vol. 1, 137.

44 HREOC, *Bringing Them Home*, 162.

45 Mullighan, *Children in State Care Commission of Inquiry*, 216.

46 SCDCPV, *Betrayal of Trust*, vol. 1, 135.

47 Timmerman and Schreuder, "Sexual abuse of children and youth," 717.

48 Submission 290 in ASCARC, *Forgotten Australians*, 2004–2007.

could veer into the sexual where the perpetrator was so inclined, but there were also institutions that became the target of more organised paedophilia. The perpetrators were not only staff members, but professionals such as priests, doctors and social workers who had access to the children, and visitors who were allowed to take them for outings or holidays.[49] Mark McCabe, who was living at Vincent's, South Melbourne in the 1950s, came to believe that an annual picnic organised for the boys served as a "market" with "some people ... selecting the boys they wished to billet out at Christmas ... [alleging] there was plenty of anecdotal evidence that boys were sexually assaulted during the Christmas holiday period".[50] As the beneficiaries of such "kindness" the children were poorly positioned to report the offences, nor were they likely to be believed if they did so.

Witnesses before the Royal Commission's case study of Salvation Army institutions in Queensland and New South Wales talked of individual officers inappropriately touching boys while showering, "frothing at the mouth" when flogging them while naked, assaulting residents in the dormitories or during supposed medical examinations, and turning a blind eye when older boys sexually abused their juniors.[51] The case study of the Christian Brothers institutions in Western Australia found that abuse took place in the showers, the dormitories and the brothers' rooms, as well as in more isolated situations such as the projector room, farm buildings and surrounding bushland.[52] To survivor James McGregor, these institutions were "the kingdom and reign of the paedophile".[53]

The victims of paedophile rings were primarily but not exclusively boys. Evidence from both Catholic and Salvation Army boys' homes shows how perpetrators preyed on the vulnerability of lonely and isolated children, tempting and rewarding them with affection and treats, thus compromising their ability to resist.[54] Having succumbed to such temptation, many young victims initially struggled to recognise the perpetrator's behaviour as abusive and felt somehow complicit in the offence. Seduced by one of the

---

49 Mullighan, *Children in State Care Commission of Inquiry*, 34 and 90.

50 Submission 38 of Forgotten Australians Submissions.

51 RCIRCSA, *Report of Case Study No. 5*, 18–37.

52 RCIRCSA, *Report of Case Study No. 11. Congregation of Christian Brothers in Western Australia Response to Child Sexual Abuse at Castledare Junior Orphanage, St Vincent's Orphanage Clontarf, St Mary's Agricultural School Tardun and Bindoon Farm School* (Sydney: Royal Commission into Institutional Responses to Child Sexual Abuse, 2014), 22–25.

53 Submission 34 of Forgotten Australians Submissions.

54 ASCARC, *Forgotten Australians*, 104.

Brothers at St Augustine's, Geelong, Bryan Glanville thought he "had a friend and as I had never been shown affection by another human being that I could remember, I welcomed it".[55] Once trapped in such a paedophile ring, boys were repeatedly raped, with knowledge of their vulnerability passed between the offenders, allowing the abuse to continue even when staff or residents changed location over time. The Lost Innocents report emphasised that unlike the endemic physical abuse, such paedophile rings were confined to a small number of institutions. In the case of child migrants such activity centred on the Christian Brothers orphanages in Western Australia, but occasional or situational instances of sexual abuse of both boys and girls occurred in other locations.[56] The Royal Commission has investigated one such instance in its case study of the Anglican North Coast Children's Home where both boys and girls reported being sexually abused by a group of clergy who had privileged access to the home.[57] Similarly, at the Neerkol Orphanage, Rockhampton, both boys and girls were prey to a series of visiting priests as well as male workers on the property.[58]

In secure units and reformatory institutions, sexual abuse perpetrated by both staff and fellow residents occurred in conjunction with the endemic physical violence. Officers who maintained order in boys' institutions through physical violence used the fear that this engendered in their charges to take advantage of them sexually, while boys known to have succumbed were subject to sexual violence from other residents as well.[59] Too many of the male superintendents appointed to take charge of girls' reformatory institutions seem to have regarded sexual access to the residents as a privilege of their office. The Royal Commission case study of the girls' homes at Parramatta and Hay heard allegations that 11 men who occupied senior positions from 1957 to 1963 had indecently assaulted or raped residents under their charge.[60] The widespread use of isolation as

---

55 Submission 129 of Forgotten Australians Submissions.

56 ASCARC, *Lost Innocents*, 76 and 79.

57 RCIRCSA, *Report of Case Study No. 3: Anglican Diocese of Grafton's Response to Child Sexual Abuse at the North Coast Children's Home* (Sydney: Royal Commission into Institutional Responses to Child Sexual Abuse, 2014), 13–14.

58 RCIRCSA, *Report of Case Study No. 26. The Response of the Sisters of Mercy, the Catholic Diocese of Rockhampton and the Queensland Government to Allegations of Child Sexual Abuse at St Joseph's Orphanage, Neerkol* (Sydney: Royal Commission into Institutional Responses to Child Sexual Abuse, 2016), 45.

59 RCIRCSA, *Case Study 30*, 30–3.

60 RCIRCSA, *Case Study 7*, 17.

a disciplinary mechanism provided such managers with access to girls who had little opportunity to either resist or report the offence. Former residents of Melbourne's Winlaton between the 1950s and 1970s reported that their male social workers assumed similar privileges.[61]

Family-like environments such as cottages or foster homes created a different dynamic, one that more closely equated to the patriarchal home. In such contexts, men were far more likely to have unsupervised access to young female bodies than in institutional settings where girls and older boys lived and bathed in separate facilities under the supervision of staff of their own gender. In an environment lacking the protection offered in institutions divided by gender, girls were preyed upon by cottage or foster fathers and male siblings, as well as male peers. Having moved from a female dormitory to cottage accommodation at the Retta Dixon Home in the Northern Territory, Indigenous woman Sandra Kitching was subject to escalating sexual violence from her cottage father, who moved from watching to touching as his sense of entitlement grew.[62] He was not the only offender at the home; another house father was named as an abuser by five other residents.[63] At Melbourne's Methodist Homes for Children, the first three men employed as cottage fathers were all dismissed after they became sexually involved with older girls who had been returned from employment placements.[64] Condemned as seductive or untruthful when they attempted to disclose their experiences, some survivors came to believe that sexual violence was a part of "normal" family life.[65] Repeatedly abused by her foster father, Helena Dam had no standard against which to name his behaviour as aberrant. "Young as I was," she explained, "I wasn't aware of many things, I had never been educated or anything like that".[66]

---

61 RCIRCSA, *Case Study 30*, 34.

62 RCIRCSA, *Report of Case Study No. 17, The Response of the Australian Indigenous Ministries, the Australian and Northern Territory Governments and the Northern Territory Police Force and Prosecuting Authorities to Allegations of Child Sexual Abuse Which Occurred at the Retta Dixon Home* (Sydney: Royal Commission into Institutional Responses to Child Sexual Abuse, 2015), 21–22.

63 RCIRCSA, *Case Study 17*, 23–27.

64 Renate Howe and Shurlee Swain, *All God's Children: A Centenary History of the Methodist Homes for Children and the Orana Peace Memorial Homes* (Canberra: Acorn Press, 1989), 52–53.

65 HREOC, *Bringing Them Home*, 164.

66 Submission 237 of Forgotten Australians Submissions.

Concluding reflections

The heightened danger which girls and young women face in family-like care would come as no surprise to the feminists who, since the 1980s, have insisted that the most dangerous place for the girl child was the family home.[67] To some critics the series of inquiries into institutional abuse threatened to divert attention from this reality.[68] However, by analysing the reports of these inquiries through the lens of gender, this chapter has shown that the focus on institutional abuse reaffirms the feminist claims.

Such a conclusion should offer little comfort to those who would like to argue that the closure of the large institutions of the past has made children who need to live apart from their parents somehow safer. Many of the attitudes that made children in care vulnerable to both physical and sexual abuse have carried over into the new, smaller units where most boys and girls are placed today. It is also clear that the more family-like the accommodation, the greater the risk that girls in particular will be vulnerable to sexual abuse.

The Royal Commission has made a series of recommendations designed to make institutions safer for children of both genders.[69] However, unless the attitudes that cast such children as somehow lesser than other children as well as the patriarchal structures which underpin male violence towards women are addressed, children in care will continue to be vulnerable to abuse. The challenge facing welfare authorities in the future is not simply to prevent children from being preyed upon by damaged or disturbed individuals, but to develop environments in which sexual and physical violence are no longer allowed to develop or persist.

---

67 Gordon, "The politics of child sexual abuse," 63.

68 For a recent reflection of this disquiet see the discussion following Robert Llewellyn-Jones, "Child Abuse Royal Commission's work must continue," *Australian*, 12 September 2017.

69 RCIRCSA, *Final Report: Making Institutions Child Safe*, 17 vols., vol. 6 (Sydney: Commonwealth of Australia, 2017).

Chapter 10

"IT WAS QUITE A SCARY TIME"

Lesbians and violence in post-war Australia

Rebecca Jennings

In 1993, the Australian Institute of Criminology described levels of anti-gay and lesbian violence as "worrying", reflecting a new concern with the prevalence of the phenomenon in Australian society.[1] A survey conducted by Victorian activist group Gay Men and Lesbians Against Discrimination between 1990 and 1993 found that 70 per cent of the 492 women surveyed had experienced some form of verbal or physical abuse and 11 per cent had been bashed or physically abused.[2] In 1997, Chris Puplick, President of the Anti-Discrimination Board of New South Wales, claimed that lesbians were six times more likely than other women to be the victims of assault.[3] Initiatives were launched by police forces and NGOs in an attempt to facilitate the reporting of such crimes and tackle the causes of anti-gay violence.

This concern with documenting rates of anti-gay and lesbian violence was matched by a growing academic interest in explaining the causes and history of hate crimes. Much of this literature drew on the psychological concept of "homophobia" and the sociological concept of "heterosexism" to give meaning to the violence experienced by lesbians and gay men. Michael

---

1 Duncan Chappell, in Gail Mason, "Violence against lesbians and gay men," *Violence Prevention Today* no. 2 (Canberra: Australian Institute of Criminology).

2 Gay Men and Lesbians Against Discrimination (GLAD), *Not a Day Goes By: Report on the GLAD Survey into Discrimination and Violence against Lesbians and Gay Men in Victoria* (Melbourne: GLAD, 1994).

3 Chris Puplick, 'Foreword,' in *Homophobic Violence*, ed. Gail Mason and Stephen Tomsen (Sydney: Hawkins Press, 1997), iii.

Flood and Clive Hamilton's 2008 study of homophobia in Australia noted: "The term 'homophobia' has become a popular descriptor for attitudes, beliefs, stereotypes, and other cognitive and affective responses based on hostility towards and fear of gay men and lesbians," while "heterosexism" is "useful in emphasising the *system* of injustice and oppression organised around sexuality".[4] However, Gail Mason has also drawn attention to the importance of gender discourses in making sense of violence against lesbians. Drawing on feminist approaches to gendered experiences of violence, Mason argued that anti-lesbian violence differed from anti-gay violence in some important respects in that it sometimes more closely reflected patterns of violence against all women. More recently, Mason and Stephen Tomsen have noted that policing gender conformity is a key factor in both anti-gay and lesbian violence.[5]

These contemporary patterns of anti-gay and lesbian violence have a much longer history. Shirleene Robinson asserts that, although the term "homophobia" originated in the context of 1970s lesbian and gay activism, the phenomenon of an "identifiable set of prejudices" could be traced back to the late nineteenth century.[6] Historians have noted the historical specificity of forms of homophobia. Ruth Ford has explored post-war "homophobia-related" violence and discrimination in relation to women's same-sex love. Specific forms of abuse, Ford observed, drew upon notions then circulating in Australian society and elsewhere about female homosexuality being a sickness.[7]

Considerable scholarship from a range of disciplines has noted the connections between homophobic violence and visibility, emphasising the role of anti-gay and lesbian violence in policing the expression of gay and lesbian identities and behaviours.[8] Understanding anti-lesbian violence as a form of policing highlights the extent to which it has been a mechanism of control in the broader social, cultural and personal context of lesbianism in the past. Focusing on the post-war period from the 1950s to the early

4 Michael Flood and Clive Hamilton, 'Mapping homophobia in Australia,' in *Homophobia: An Australian History*, ed. Shirleene Robinson (Sydney: The Federation Press, 2008), 16–17.

5 Gail Mason, "Heterosexed violence: Typicality and ambiguity," in *Homophobic Violence*, 23; Stephen Tomsen and Gail Mason, "Engendering homophobia: violence, sexuality and gender conformity," *Journal of Sociology* 37, no. 3 (2001): 270.

6 Robinson, ed. *Homophobia*, 3–4.

7 Ruth Ford, "'Filthy, obscene and mad': Engendering 'homophobia' in Australia, 1940s-1960s," in *Homophobia*, 86–112.

8 Gail Mason, "Body maps: Envisaging homophobia, violence and safety," *Social and Legal Studies* 10, no. 1 (2001): 23–44.

1990s, this chapter explores some of the most frequent forms of violence experienced by women attracted to other women. Younger lesbians in particular experienced violence from their families and peers as well as from a range of authority figures, including medical professionals and the police. Women's experience of random acts of physical and sexual assault also indicates the extent to which violence was used to contain lesbian visibility in public spaces.

This chapter utilises oral history interviews with lesbian-identified women to trace patterns of anti-lesbian violence. Oral history has been widely used in lesbian and gay history, both as a means of recording minority experiences absent from the historical record and to enable historians to explore the subjective meanings which individuals have ascribed to these experiences.[9] Drawing on personal narratives, this chapter will therefore consider the ways in which women sought to make sense of violent encounters in the context of wider social attitudes to same-sex desire. Life history interviews, in which women recount their experiences of violence in the context of a much broader narrative of personal identity and experience, also highlight the extent to which lesbians have been subjected to violence – not only at the hands of "homophobic" perpetrators external to the lesbian community, but also from other lesbians in bars and from lovers within the home. Violence as a mechanism of control was evident in many different aspects of women's lives, as both recipients and perpetrators.

In his work on intimate relations between workingmen in interwar London, Matt Houlbrook has argued that "[i]ntimacy, sex, blackmail, theft, and assault constituted a continuum within the same cultural terrain"; it was the deployment of pejorative terms by workingmen which enabled their intimate relations with the queer.[10] While violence against or control of women within post-war lesbian communities did not facilitate intimate relationships in the way described by Houlbrook, it is clear that a cyclical relationship existed between the violent and repressive historical context in

9 For example, see: Madeline Davis and Elizabeth Lapovsky Kennedy, "Oral history and the study of sexuality in the lesbian community: Buffalo, New York, 1940–1960," *Feminist Studies* 12, no. 1 (1986): 7–26; Nan Alamilla Boyd and Horacio N. Roque Ramírez, ed. *Bodies of evidence: the practice of queer oral history* (New York: Oxford University Press, 2012).

10 Matt Houlbrook, *Queer London: Perils and Pleasures in the Sexual Metropolis* (London: University of Chicago Press, 2005), 178. See also: Amanda Kaladelfos, "'Until death does part us': Male friendship, intimacy and violence in late colonial Melbourne," in *Intimacy, Violence and Activism: Gay and Lesbian Perspectives on Australasian History and Society*, ed. Graham Willett and Yorick Smaal (Melbourne: Monash University Publishing, 2013), 39–55.

which women enacted their same-sex desires and the violence and controlling behaviours which some women encountered in lesbian subcultures and in same-sex relationships. In considering these forms of violence alongside each other, it may be possible to elucidate both the impact of anti-lesbian violence on women themselves and the factors that precipitated violent behaviour within lesbian communities.

Peer and familial violence

Throughout much of the twentieth century, a powerful social disapproval of homosexuality impacted the lives of women who desired other women in Australia. Female homosexuality was subject to social taboos that restricted discussion and created a culture of silence. Cultural representations of desire between women in literature, film and television were prohibited under strict censorship laws; with the exception of very occasional salacious reports in the tabloid press, newspapers also avoided the subject. Social norms emphasised women's expected roles as wives and mothers. Women who recognised their desires for other women and chose to act on them typically lived double lives, hiding their emotional and sexual experiences and relationships from family, friends and society at large.[11]

In this context, women who were suspected of being lesbian or whose relationships with other women were discovered faced severe and often violent penalties. Girls and young women were particularly vulnerable in these circumstances. Although the lack of cultural recognition of same-sex desire between women meant the adolescents of the 1950s and 1960s typically did not articulate a lesbian identity until they reached adulthood, some experienced difficulties in performing the conventional heterosexual identities expected by family and peers. This could result in bullying at school and conflict within familial and social networks. Laurene, who was at school in Sydney in the 1960s, recalled:

> It definitely made me different from other people because particularly in my teenage years at high school and stuff, when we started the whole heterosexual game, I just couldn't play it very well…

11 Rebecca Jennings, *Unnamed Desires: A Sydney lesbian history* (Melbourne: Monash University Publishing, 2015).

> They used to call me a dyke, witch, lesbian, all that sort of stuff and everything like that... But luckily I had a really good sense of humour and I was a very good fighter so I could actually withstand the blows.[12]

Girls who acted on their same-sex desires, kissing other girls or forming same-sex relationships, were often at risk of familial conflict and violence if their activities were discovered. The social expectation that unmarried women would remain living with family into adulthood meant that both teenage girls and young women could find themselves facing a choice between domestic violence or homelessness. Carolyn, who grew up in Petersham, Sydney, in the late 1960s, recalled her parents' initially hostile reaction to the discovery that she was in a relationship with another girl:

> I came up against a lot of rejection from my parents and a very, very tough stage of my life actually... They chose to read my personal diary ... It was wide open when I got home that evening from TAFE ... So it was a pretty rough night... [My parents became] very intimidating, very intrusive and very aggressive.

Carolyn remained living at home while she completed her studies. The situation escalated when her parents were again confronted with an awareness of her sexuality. She explained:

> Another time my father used my car ... and there was a gay paper in the car. We'd been to the Centennial Park Hotel ... and picked up the general papers... On the cover it had a very explicit swathing of sexual description ... It was under the seat of the car ... But my car was borrowed and my father took my brother to Sunday school and immediately he came back and just almost kicked the bedroom door in and I was immediately flung from one side of the room to the other, just because – he thumped and bashed and he gave me a hard time.[13]

Other women left home entirely to escape difficult domestic environments or attempted to minimise the risk of conflict by spending as much time as possible outside the home. However, the streets carried their own dangers and young women in these circumstances were at potential risk of random violent or sexual assaults. Explaining her experience of sexual assault as a teenager, Alex reflected: "I think because I didn't want to be at home, I

12 Interview with Laurene Kelly, 19 February 2013.

13 Interview with Carolyn Bloye by Sandra Mackay, 9 November 2007, Pride History Group Collection.

was hanging around the local park too much which actually did lead to me being pack raped."[14]

The streets could be particularly dangerous for women whose appearance or behaviour did not conform to conventional notions of appropriate femininity. Laurie described being the focus of repeated acts of verbal abuse and physical assault on the streets of Sydney in the 1960s and 1970s:

> If I was just walking up the street holding my girlfriend's hand, a car load of guys would go past and yell out lezzo, you know and all that sort of shit. Then they'd pull round the corner and come back and they'd always pick on the butch one. Because you want to look like a bloke, you fight like a bloke, hence they'd have bricks in their hands … and the more I retaliated, the worse it got … because one bloke would start on me and if I retaliated, there'd be another two.[15]

According to Mason, "Verbal hostility, the violence it insinuates, and actual physical assault constitute a warning or intimidating mechanism against breaking the wall of silence surrounding lesbianism."[16] Its aim is to police visible expressions of lesbian sexuality and render women fearful of openly expressing affection for other women or presenting an identifiable lesbian identity. Butch lesbians were particularly vulnerable to harassment when in the company of their girlfriends, as erotic statements such as holding a woman's hand were interpreted as an encroachment on male territory.[17] Women's accounts of their experiences of verbal abuse and physical assault on the streets also highlight the extent to which gender non-conformity was interpreted as a signifier of lesbianism, rendering butch lesbians particularly vulnerable to random acts of violence in public.

The authorities and social control

In a social context in which expressions of lesbian identity or sexuality were silenced, exposure as a potential lesbian could result in the intervention of the authorities, including medical professionals, social workers and even the police. Medical approaches to lesbianism varied widely in post-war

---

14 Interview with Alex Kaufman, 23 August 2014, National Library of Australia, ORAL TRC 6510/48.

15 Interview with Laurie van Camp by Sandra Mackay, 18 February 2008, Pride History Group Collection.

16 Mason, "Heterosexed violence," 27.

17 Ford, "Filthy, Obscene and Mad," 96.

Australia, where the issue had not been the subject of any published research and was not on the medical school curriculum. Australian medical journals reviewed some of the key literature on homosexuality from Britain and the United States, which in the 1950s and 1960s typically adopted psychoanalytic models to explain homosexuality as a form of arrested development and advocated a range of therapies including psychotherapy, behavioural therapies, or psychosurgery. As a result, girls and women who were referred to doctors in this period described a variety of medical responses, depending on the level of knowledge and opinions of the individual practitioner.[18]

Helen was referred to a psychiatrist in Perth in the mid-1960s when she attempted suicide due to the emotional pressure of experiencing same-sex attractions in a hostile society. The psychiatrist advised her that she must suppress her desires and keep silent in order to avoid being confined to a mental hospital. Helen tried to follow this advice by marrying and having a child, before the emotional strain again rendered her suicidal in the early 1980s.[19] Laurie, who grew up on a farm in Western Australia in the 1950s, was sent by her father to see a doctor at the age of 10 or 11. Laurie had her first sexual experience with another girl at the age of 11, but had no clear sense of sexual identity at that age. However, she recalled that her behaviour and self-presentation had caused her father to have some concerns about her sexuality:

> He'd figured there was something wrong with me and now I've learnt that that's what it was, that I was a lesbian... He was going to have me cured and I thought the doctor was giving me – at that age, I was about 10, 11 – at the time I thought it was hot needles I was having but it wasn't, it was electric shock treatment.[20]

This hope that doctors would be able to "cure" daughters of lesbianism reflected the attitude of a number of medical professionals who aimed to redirect lesbians' sexual desires toward men. A number of other women described being non-consensually confined in mental hospitals and subjected to intrusive treatments as juveniles and young women.

---

18 Jennings, *Unnamed Desires*; Emily Wilson, "'Someone who is sick and in need of help': Medical attitudes to homosexuality in Australia, 1960–1979," in *Homophobia*, 148–171.

19 Interview with Helen [pseudonym], 23 April 2008.

20 Interview, Laurie van Camp.

Despite the lack of any explicit legislation prohibiting sexual acts between women, a number of girls and young women were subject to intervention by the police and social welfare authorities as a result of their same-sex desires. Sandra received a police caution as a teenager in 1950s Sydney when her attempt to explain her attraction to a young woman who lived nearby ended in conflict. A few years later, when, at 16, she was discovered by police to be living with a girlfriend in a flat in Bondi, both girls were charged with "Being exposed to moral danger" and Sandra was sent to a girls' home for several months.[21] Alex similarly endured a number of periods of incarceration in Sydney girls' homes in the late 1960s and early 1970s after her parents reported her to the police as "uncontrollable" and "exposed to moral danger."[22] Both described the girls' homes as frightening and violent environments in which inmates were subjected to bullying and violence from staff and other girls. Sandra described the initial medical examination to which she was subjected upon her arrest as "a fearfully intrusive and painful experience, handled so impersonally by the Shelter's medical staff".[23] Laurie similarly recalled the internal examination she received on entering prison in 1975: "They hurt me, I fought it and four screws held me down and this bloke made me bleed, he took my virginity basically, in that sense, for lack of a better word."[24]

Violence within lesbian communities

Acts of violence or attempts to control women who were attracted to other women did not solely originate from hostile families or figures of authority: they were frequently endemic in these women's lives. Although many lived in isolation or alone with a partner in the 1950s and 1960s due to the constraints imposed by social taboos on homosexuality, some were able to form social networks through work or leisure activities. A small number frequented the camp social scene which existed in Australian cities from the early 1960s onwards.

This was a largely mixed scene, in which lesbians socialised alongside camp men, prostitutes and drug users. Although many women had positive memories of friendship, love and support in such spaces, most also

21 Sandra Willson, unpublished memoir. The author is grateful to Rev Peter Strong, beneficiary of Sandra Willson's estate, for a copy of this memoir, which is in the author's possession.

22 Interview, Alex Kaufman.

23 Willson, unpublished memoir, 46.

24 Interview, Laurie van Camp.

characterised the camp scene as violent and unstable. Historians of lesbian bar scenes in the United States and Canada have similarly noted the connections between bar subcultures and violent and criminal behaviour in the post-war period. In her work on the Toronto lesbian bar scene in the 1950s and 1960s, Elise Chenier has demonstrated that many of the (particularly butch) women who centred their lives and social networks on downtown lesbian bars had limited job options and were frequently drawn into criminal activities such as petty theft or into the drug and sex trades.[25] As Colette, who socialised on the camp bar scene in Sydney in the late 1960s, recalled:

> Look there wasn't any social life per se: it was the same thing as I found in Melbourne a few years later. Is that you would get the word that some back room in a pub was amenable to these groups of women...
>
> Often times ... there was trouble and girls were beaten up or the police would come. But anyway after three weeks you knew that there would be another place that you would go to and you'd get the word on the grapevine and then you'd meet there. So it was very nebulous.[26]

Tensions around women's criminal activities could lead to violence in these venues, while their location in less affluent areas of the city meant that women were also vulnerable to abuse and assault from men on surrounding streets or from hostile locals in the pub's main bar. The vulnerability of bars to police harassment and closure, as well as the involvement of some bar owners in contravening licensing and other regulations, meant that some camp venues were hostile to perceived outsiders and could use violence or threats to deter women who were not regulars.[27]

Police harassment was a common occurrence for women who socialised in camp bars and the hippie scene in Australia. As in the Toronto bar scene documented by Chenier, police often used petty drugs offences and other minor misdemeanours as a means of harassing lesbians. Laurie was sentenced to 12 months' imprisonment with hard labour in 1975 after being caught with a group of women who were passing a joint around in

25 Elise Chenier, "Rethinking class in lesbian bar culture: Living 'the gay life' in Toronto, 1955–1965," *Left History* 9, no. 2 (2004): 85–118.

26 Interview with Colette Parr by Digby Duncan, 1 December 2008, Pride History Group Collection.

27 For example, see: Interview with Jan McInnies and Margaret Cummins, Pride History Group Collection.

Sydney's Kings Cross. After ten years of verbal harassment from the police because of her self-presentation as a butch lesbian and her association with drug-users, she explained, the police were looking for an opportunity to charge her with an offence.[28] Colette recalled an incident in which police in Melbourne threatened to charge her with soliciting a woman:

> One night I had a fight with my girlfriend in the street ... and the police came because they were around hotels anyway. They separated us and let her go and took me off in the police car at 18 telling me they were going to charge me with soliciting women... It went on all night it was terrible.[29]

Other women described frequent police raids on camp bars, resulting in the intimidation and harassment of the clientele.

In the 1970s, when the emergence of lesbian and gay politics and the women's movement enabled the silence around homosexuality to be confronted, police violence against lesbians shifted onto the streets. Activists began to challenge some of the negative social attitudes toward same-sex desire. But levels of police brutality varied from state to state and between different police stations. Sandra, a Sydney lesbian feminist, recalled that she and her friends frequently travelled interstate to Brisbane to support demonstrations organised by local feminists and lesbians as the Queensland police were perceived as particularly brutal.[30] However, accounts of Sydney's first Mardi Gras in 1978 also highlight the high levels of police violence which women received from plain clothes officers based at Darlinghurst station. As Robyn, who participated in the march, commented: "Darlinghurst cop station ... was well known in that era to be totally corrupt and very violent." On the night of the first Mardi Gras, she herself was "grabbed" and "pulled" by police attempting to "throw [her] into the paddy wagon"; she recalled that she "had never seen so much violence, that the cops were meting out on people who were trying to get onto the pavement and go as they were asked to."[31]

Although police and hostile locals were regular sources of violence on the lesbian bar scene, trouble also frequently emerged from groups of women themselves. Ivy Richter, the proprietor of popular camp bars Chez Ivy and the Birdcage in 1960s Sydney, commented that, although she didn't recall

28 Interview, Laurie van Camp.

29 Interview, Colette Parr.

30 Interview with Sandra Mackay, 2 July 2007.

31 Interview with Robyn Plaister, 20 December 2007.

any problems with violence in the surrounding streets, "my only problems were with these girls ... And I used to have a couple of them barred even."[32] Margaret also recalled the camp scene in the 1960s as "rough", while Kris gave a graphic description of the violence endemic in the Sydney scene she was a part of in the same period, commenting that: "a lot of the women were thugs and ... you had to fight ... This one woman I had to fight and then the others left me alone you know, in that scene."[33] Conflict often arose because of jealousy and fights were fuelled by heavy use of alcohol and drugs. Colette, who socialised on the Sydney camp scene in the 1960s, explained:

> But with the early drag days and things it was quite a scary time. Because the butches were really jealous and there were lots of knives and broken bottles and things involved. It was quite dangerous times.[34]

Sidney Abbott and Barbara Love made a connection between lesbian violence and negative societal attitudes toward desire between women. Their classic book, *Sappho Was a Right-On Woman* (1972), argued: "violence, internally or externally directed, is a predictable human response to intolerable, unrelieved suffering. Lesbian violence has often been noted but has not been understood in relation to the overwhelming forces in the Lesbian's life running contrary to any affirmation of self or possible self-respect."[35] In her work on the lesbian scene in Canada from the mid 1960s to the mid 1980s, Liz Millward has similarly documented the impact of alcohol and drugs on women's violent behaviour, linking these self-destructive behaviours with the material environment of the bars themselves. Arguing that the nature of the space in which lesbians were able to socialise impacted on the self-perceptions and behaviour of the women who frequented them, she claims that women's low self-esteem was fuelled by the hidden and neglected condition of bars.[36]

---

32 Interview with Ivy Richter by John Witte, 22 May 2006, Pride History Group Collection.

33 Interview with Margaret Jones, 12 September 2007; Interview with Kris Melmouth, 25 August 2011.

34 Interview, Colette Parr.

35 Sidney Abbott and Barbara Love, *Sappho was a Right-On Woman: A liberated view of lesbianism* (New York: Stein and Day, 1972), 43.

36 Liz Millward, *Making a Scene: Lesbians and Community Across Canada, 1964–84* (Vancouver: University of British Columbia Press, 2015), 32.

Such connections were apparent in Sandra Willson's unpublished memoir of her life in Sydney in the 1950s. During a troubled childhood, Sandra was harassed and assaulted by men on the streets. By the age of 16, she had already been incarcerated in a girls' home and a mental hospital, where she had both experienced and perpetrated violence. On her release, she obtained a job as a salesgirl and found herself attracted to a colleague. Reflecting on her approach to the girl, Sandra described her behaviour at that time in aggressive terms, explicitly linking her own experience of harassment from men with her behaviour towards women:

> If I thought men had been harassing and preying on me, I should have taken a look at my own behaviour towards women. There was a nice young girl working at Woolworths. Trying to get to talk to her, I joked about dragging her off by force. I thought the meaning of what I was saying was obvious, despite the fact that she also knew I was carrying a knife. The obvious interpretation was that one does not harm someone one likes by carrying her off. I just wanted to be able to indicate [my] feelings to her (with a caveman-like bravado) without having to do anything. But she took me literally at my word and reported me to the manager.[37]

This tendency to use violence and aggressive language as a form of communication resurfaced in future relationships.

The following year, Sandra was given permission to live at a Salvation Army hostel, where she met and began a relationship with another girl, Barbara. The pair set up home together and Sandra recalled their domestic relationship as one in which she sought to impose her will upon Barbara:

> I also thought all real love involved sex and that sex-love made us husband and wife, tying us irrevocably together. My body's reactions to being with Barbara made this very easy for me to believe. I thus got into every role-playing game in any book. I expected Barbara to prepare the breakfast porridge and was surprisingly impatient when she burnt it.[38]

Describing her behaviour toward Barbara in her memoir, Sandra linked her desire to control Barbara with her own experience of having her desires silenced by social disapproval. When the pair were taken by police

37 Willson, unpublished memoir, 16.

38 Willson, unpublished memoir, 29.

to a girls' shelter and charged with "being exposed to moral danger", both were subjected to a medical examination. Bursting into the room during Barbara's exam, Sandra was confronted with the consequences of her behaviour toward Barbara. Before being removed from the room, she:

> had a glimpse of Barbara lying there, totally naked and exposed to the doctor... Although I had touched her and kissed her, I had never exposed her to gawk and gape at her like this fellow was doing! So I had never actually seen the extent of the blue bruising that I'd left upon her. If I had ever known that this was to happen to her, that the love bites would experience such public exposure, I would never have given them to her.[39]

The cycle Sandra described of responding to societal constraints by attempting to exert control over others was also apparent in other women's accounts. Personal testimonies record several women's experience of domestic violence and rape from lovers throughout this period. As in public spaces, domestic violence was often enabled or excused by alcohol and interpreted by the women who experienced it as an expression of frustration related to issues of control. Jan described her experience of domestic violence from a lover in the early 1980s as connected both to alcohol and depression, as well as a desire to exert some control in the relationship. She recalled:

> I suppose in most of my relationships up to a point I've been the dominant one and – it probably shows. Anyway, and the more stable one. I've certainly had a number of girlfriends who are alcoholic or had other issues... [One of my girlfriends] had a depression problem essentially which she medicated with alcohol and she lived here with me and the whole thing became completely impossible because her son committed suicide and that was obviously just completely traumatic and we had a really, really bad time. She did start to drink very early indeed and she was pretty violent. In fact she was definitely violent. In fact to the point that I had to get the police once... After she drank, yeah, she tried to strangle me.[40]

The dominance of lesbian feminist idealisations of lesbian relationships as egalitarian and nurturing during the 1970s and 1980s presented obstacles for lesbians to acknowledge or discuss these problems. Jennie, who

39 Willson, unpublished memoir, 33.

40 Interview with Jan Aitkin, 5 June 2012.

experienced ongoing domestic violence for several years in the context of a committed relationship in the late 1980s and early 1990s, also recalled:

> [she] used to drink a lot of alcohol and get very physically aggressive and hit me quite a lot, yes … It was sort of punches and waking me up in the middle of the night and hitting me around the head. Punching me on my body where bruises were left and other people couldn't see and it was just frustration.[41]

In her American study of partner abuse in lesbian relationships, Claire Renzetti argued that, in addition to substance abuse and intergenerational violence, domestic violence in lesbian relationships was typically linked to three major sources of relationship strain: dependency versus autonomy, jealousy, and the balance of power in relationships.[42]

On reflection, Jennie felt that the domestic abuse she had received was related to her partner's successful career and her fears of exposure as a lesbian in that context. Jennie's account of her partner's behaviour focused on a range of controlling behaviour:

> At one point she took my purse with my credit cards and everything, all my bank cards, everything. She took them away and said 'I'm [not] giving you these back.' So I couldn't get any money, I couldn't get any food, I couldn't get anything, any fuel… And she kept withdrawing from our joint account until there was nothing left.[43]

Although aware that her partner's behaviour was abusive, Jennie felt unable to explain it or seek help in the context of dominant perceptions of lesbian relationships being based on equality. She explained:

> I thought 'Oh, this is not normal, this doesn't happen in what I've known as lesbian relationships … this doesn't happen, this must be me. What have I done, to sort of ask for this? And I think maybe I didn't talk to people, one, because I was dismissed with that one person that I talked to, dismissed as a liar virtually: 'Oh, you're exaggerating, can't possibly happen.' But yeah, I think I didn't tell

41 Interview with Jennie Partington, 30 April 2012.

42 Claire M. Renzetti, *Violent Betrayal: Partner Abuse in Lesbian Relationships* (London: Sage, 1992).

43 Interview, Jennie Partington.

> anybody else because it was a lesbian relationship, and because nobody would empathise anyway.[44]

Jennie's account suggests that, while issues of power imbalance within the relationship were certainly a factor, the domestic violence she experienced was also fuelled by the broader context of social attitudes toward lesbianism. This generated negative associations with the relationship itself and prevented either partner from seeking support to deal with relationship problems.

Conclusion

Women's accounts of their lives in post-war Australia indicate that violence was a common experience for women who were attracted to other women. Negative social attitudes toward female same-sex desire could be given expression through a variety of forms of violence and control. This could come from a range of sources, including familial violence, medicalised violence and controlling and abusive behaviour from the police, in addition to random acts of anti-lesbian violence from strangers on the streets. The women who experienced these forms of violence frequently understood them as attempts to prevent them from articulating or acting on their same-sex desires. In consequence, these women connected their experiences of violence with wider systems of gendered social control.

However, violence and controlling behaviour were also widespread within lesbian communities and relationships in this period. Women drew upon similar tropes of control and frustration in making sense of these experiences, linking them to negative social attitudes toward lesbianism. While individual instances of community and domestic violence had specific immediate causes, they can also be understood within the context of a wider culture in which women who desired other women experienced ongoing hostility and discrimination and faced the constant threat of violence from multiple sources.

44 Ibid.

Chapter 11

"LAYING SIEGE AND STORMING CITADELS"

Hostility and marginalisation in higher education

Tanya Fitzgerald

Historically, there have been sharp challenges to women's access to and presence on university campuses, as both students and academic staff.[1] Their histories are marked with stories of exclusion, hostility, control and marginalisation. Although women's entry into the masculine environment of higher education dismantled a number of barriers, historical and contemporary testimonies attest to the exclusionary and gendered culture women experienced.[2] Their widespread entrance into higher education served as a basis for a more egalitarian social order. And yet, the troubling presence of women evoked a particular response that – though historical in its origins – still reverberates today.[3]

---

1 For example, see: Bettina Cass, *Why So Few? Women Academics in Australian* Universities (Sydney: University of Sydney Press, 1983); Patricia Crawford and Myrna Tonkinson, *The Missing Chapters: Women Staff at the University of Western Australia 1963*–1987 (Perth: Centre for Western Australian History, 1988); Christine D. Myers, *University Co–Education in the Victorian Era: Inclusion in the United States and United Kingdom* (New York: Palgrave Macmillan, 2010).

2 For example, see: Ann Mari May, *The "Woman Question" and Higher Education: Perspectives on Gender and Knowledge Production in America* (Cheltenham: Edward Elgar, 2008); E. Lisa Panayotidis and Paul Storz, ed. *Women in Higher Education, 1850–1970: International Perspectives* (London: Routledge, 2016); Patrick Dilley, *The Transformation of Women's Collegiate Education* (New York: Palgrave Macmillan, 2017).

3 Jill Blackmore, *Feminism, Leadership and Educational Change* (Buckingham: Open University Press, 1999).

Histories of women's entrance into higher education overflow with stories of riots, resistance, misogyny, hostility, harassment and exclusion. Historian Carol Dyhouse neatly sums this up:

> [T]he discursive narratives of both the history of women's entry into higher education in Britain since the mid nineteenth century, and indeed accounts of more recent history, are replete with the tropes of battlement.[4]

This chapter interrogates such discursive narratives by bringing together historical and contemporary examples which demonstrate troubling continuities in gendered social and institutional responses to women's presence in higher education. Methodologically, this approach fuses women's historical and contemporary voices to further underscore the alienation and marginalisation that many women experience. It begins by analysing an historical case study of women's lived experiences as students and staff in one colonial university to illustrate the overlapping expectations, perceptions and experiences between the past and present – to interrogate the antecedents of exposure to gendered assumptions and gendered cultures in universities. It then analyses narratives shared by women leaders in contemporary universities to illuminate the persistence of gendered forms of marginalisation, aggression and hostility. These barriers to women's full and equitable participation in higher education have not crumbled but, in fact, mark both historical and contemporary accounts.

Bastions falling

The movement of women into higher education, either as students or academic staff, has been a glacially slow process. For almost eight centuries, men wholly dominated universities in the western world. It was not until the nineteenth century that women's historical exclusion from universities was challenged.[5] In England, for example, Emily Davies and Barbara Bodichon worked to establish Girton College at the University of Cambridge in 1870; it was the first university college for women, although not overtly recognised or acknowledged by the university. Women could be

4 Carol Dyhouse, *Students: A Gendered History* (London: Routledge, 2006), 121.

5 See: Alison Mackinnon, *The New Women: Adelaide's Early Women Graduates* (Adelaide: Wakefield Press, 1986); Geraldine Jonçich Clifford, ed. *Lone Voyagers: Academic Women in Co-Educational Institutions 1870–1937* (New York: Feminist Press, 1989); Tanya Fitzgerald, *Outsiders or Equals: Women Professors at the University of New Zealand 1911–1961* (Oxford: Peter Lang, 2009).

admitted to the University of Cambridge but were not awarded full degrees until 1948. Similarly, the University of Oxford did not permit women to take degrees until 1920. In the United States, the 1870s saw women-only colleges such as the Seven Sisters – Mount Holyoake, Smith, Wellesley, Radcliffe, Barnard, Vasser and Bryn Mawr – established, initially to offer an appropriate education for middle-class women. Although women were admitted to the University of New Zealand as early as 1871 it was not until 1874 that they could be enrolled in degree courses.[6]

Similar patterns were repeated across Australia. Established in 1852, the University of Sydney did not admit women for three decades.[7] Although numbers were initially small,[8] women students began to outnumber men in Arts degrees by 1930. In 1881, the four women to enrol at the University of Melbourne experienced a less than enthusiastic reception.[9] Opening its doors in 1911, the University of Queensland admitted both women and men. Chancellor Sir William Macgregor's inaugural speech explicitly referred to the importance of a university education to "prepare men and women for the highest duties in the social, political, and industrial life of the State".[10] In colonial environments such as Australia and New Zealand, local circumstances as well as middle class settler desires for equality and opportunity created the necessary social and political conditions for the admission of their daughters to newly established universities.[11]

---

6 Kay Morris Matthews, *In Their Own Right: Women and Higher Education in New Zealand before 1945* (Wellington: New Zealand Council for Educational Research, 2008).

7 Senate voted to admit women in 1881. The first woman students were Mary Brown and Isola Thompson. Both graduated with a Bachelor of Arts degree in 1885; in 1887, Thompson was awarded a Master of Arts.

8 In 1890, there were 43 female undergraduates enrolled in Arts alongside 241 male undergraduate students. See: Julia Horne and Geoff Sherington, *Sydney: The Making of a Public University* (Sydney: The Miegunyah Press, 2012).

9 Ailsa Zainu'ddin, "The admission of women to the University of Melbourne, 1869–1903," *Melbourne Studies in Education* 15, no. 1 (1973): 50–106; Patricia Grimshaw and Lynne Strahan, ed. *The Half-Open Door: Sixteen Modern Australian Women Look at Professional Life and Achievement* (Sydney: Hale & Iremonger, 1982); Kelly Farley, *Degrees of Liberation: A Short History of Women in the University of Melbourne* (Parkville: The Women Graduates Centenary Committee, 1985).

10 The University of Queensland, *University of Queensland 1910–1911* (Brisbane: Government Printer, 1923), 12.

11 Marjorie Theobald, *Knowing Women: Origins of Women's Education in Nineteenth Century Australia* (Cambridge: Cambridge University Press, 1996); Morris Matthews, *In Their Own Right;* Julia Horne, "The final barrier? Australian women and the nineteenth century public university," in *Women in Higher Education*, 79–96.

Despite the numbers of women gaining degrees, universities remained the privileged enclave of male students and staff. Although it appears that women were admitted to a number of colonial universities in Australia, Canada and New Zealand with relative ease and without the same level of public hostility as elsewhere, women students nonetheless experienced a chilly climate of hostility and marginalisation.[12] Women students were not permitted to enrol in some subjects and departments for fear of impacting their health; certain courses were deemed neither appropriate nor feminine.[13] In addition, their movements were limited by contemporary social conventions, meaning women students were subject to intense public scrutiny.[14] Lecture halls and corridors remained intensely lonely places for women students; there were seldom more than a handful in any one lecture and women rarely occupied the library or walked the campus paths alone. As G.M. O'Rorke asserted:

> I think the timetable should be similar to those of other collegiate institutions and not spread over the whole day and far into the night. It should be adapted to the attendance of women; and I consider night hours, or any hour after dusk, quite unsuitable for any woman in this country. There is no protection afforded by the police at this end of town, and females walking out at night alone are liable to insult. Indecent exposure of the person has not been uncommon here of late, and there have been several convictions for that offence, which has in most cases been committed during or after the hours of twilight.[15]

---

12 Roberta Hall and Bernice Sandler, *The Classroom Climate: A Chilly One for Women?* (Washington, D.C.: Association of American Colleges, 1982). See also: Fitzgerald, *Outsiders or Equals;* Katie Pickles, "Colonial counterparts: The first academic women in Anglo–Canada, New Zealand and Australia," *Women's History Review* 10, no. 2 (2001): 273–297.

13 Maresi Nerad, *The Academic Kitchen: A Social History of Gender Stratification at the University of California Berkley* (Albany: State University of New York Press, 1999); Kay Whitehead, "Higher education, work and 'overstrain of the brain': Amy Marion Elliott MSC, University of Tasmania 1900," *History of Education Review* 29, no 1 (2000): 16–31; Marianne Gosztonyi–Ainley, *Creating Complicated Lives: Women and Science at English–Canadian Universities, 1880–1980*, ed. Marelene Rayner-Canham and Geoff Rayner-Canham (Quebec: McGill-Queen's University Press, 2012); Catriona Beaumont, *Housewives and Citizens: Domesticity and the Women's Movement in England, 1928–1964* (Manchester: Manchester University Press, 2013).

14 Morris Matthews, *In Their Own Right.*

15 G.M. O'Rorke, *Appendices to the Journals of the House of Representatives*, Vol. II, H–1, 15 April 1879, 182.

Irrespective of the espoused rhetoric of "no distinction of sex", there was a level of evident hostility from male students and staff when, for example, timetables had to be adjusted to accommodate "ladies",[16] who were deemed in need of social and moral protection in public places.

Admission to university did not guarantee an equitable experience for women students. In the academic world of settler societies, male university staff recruited from British and North American institutions had little or no previous experience of women students.[17] Consequently, the "woman student" was an unfamiliar and unknown – yet highly visible – body. An administrative remedy was to appoint women to academic positions – ostensibly to teach female students, model appropriate social and moral behaviour, and prepare them to be the future wives of educated middle class men. Thus, by the turn of the twentieth century, universities had started to employ graduate women, although such women staff were frequently appointed to more junior and precarious roles as assistants and demonstrators to male professors.[18]

Employed in small numbers and scattered across a number of departments, women struggled to claim a presence in the scholarly world of men.[19] The University of New Zealand (1871–1961) employed a woman professor as early as 1911.[20] Winifred Boys–Smith was appointed to a full professorial

---

16 *Appendices to the Journals of the House of Representatives*, vol II H–1, xiv.

17 For the circulation of academics across the British academic world, see: Tamson Pietsch, *Empire of Scholars: Universities, Networks and the British Academic World, 1850–1939* (Manchester: Manchester University Press, 2013).

18 Tanya Fitzgerald and Jenny Collins, *Historical Portraits of Women Home Scientists: The University of New Zealand, 1911–1947* (New York: Cambria Press, 2011). One of the first female professors was Sofia Kovalevskaya, a Swedish woman appointed as Chair in Mathematics at Stockholm University in 1884; Maria Sklodowska–Curie (also known as Marie Curie), a Polish woman, was awarded a professorship in general physics in 1908 at the Académie de Paris. See: Barbara Czarniawska and Guje Sevón, "The thin edge of the wedge: Foreign women professors as double strangers in academia," *Gender, Work and Organization* 15, no. 3 (2008): 235–287.

19 Margaret Rossiter, *Women Scientists in America: Struggles and Strategies* (Baltimore: The John Hopkins University Press, 1982); Alison Prentice, "Bluestockings, feminists, or women workers?: A preliminary look at women's early employment at the University of Toronto," *Journal of the Canadian Historical Association* 2, no 1 (1991): 231–262.

20 Historical commentary has noted that New Zealand was a social laboratory. Pakeha (white/European) women gained suffrage in 1893 and a raft of social welfare legislation (such as old age pensions) was introduced in the late nineteenth century. For example, see: James Belich, *Paradise Reforged: A History of the New Zealanders from the 1880s to the Year 2000* (Auckland: Allen Lane, 2000); Philippa Mein Smith, *A Concise History of New Zealand* (Cambridge: Cambridge University Press, 2005);

chair in Home Science.[21] Following Boys-Smith's resignation in 1921, Helen Rawson was appointed Dean and Professor of Home Science. Rawson's was to be a short tenure as she was required to resign prior to her marriage in 1923.[22] Although it was "pointed out that a man may marry without jeopardising his position so long as he otherwise fulfils his contract with the University",[23] women's careers were significantly "thwarted"[24] due to the marriage bar. Rawson's successor was Ann Munroe Gilchrist Strong, an American with strong links to the American Home Economics movement.[25] After Strong's retirement in 1941, New Zealand graduate Elizabeth Gregory was appointed. Located at the vanguard of women's higher education, across four decades each of these woman professors worked tirelessly to establish a new academic subject and department, prepare women for professional careers in scientific fields, foster a scholarly community and networks across New Zealand, England and the United States, and pursue their own intellectual interests.[26]

From the outset, women academics were required to conform to gendered expectations. For example, the following characteristics were deemed necessary:

> But she must have considerable force of character, the power of organization and initiation, a temperament that will be braced rather than depressed by opposition, a pleasing personality, a considerable

---

Jenny Collins, "Beyond the domestic sphere? A home science education at the University of New Zealand, 1911–1936," *Journal of Educational Administration and History* 41, no. 2 (2008):115–130.

21 Also known as Domestic Science, Household Arts, Home Economics. See: Sarah Stage and Virginia Vincenti, ed. *Rethinking Home Economics: Women and the History of a Profession* (Ithaca: Cornell University Press, 1997).

22 Helen Rawson married William Noel Benson, Professor of Geology. He continued to be employed after the marriage.

23 Ann Strong to Registrar, 19 February 1937, University of Otago: Records of Registry and Central Administration 1936–1937, AG–180–31/0250, Hocken Collection, University of Otago, Dunedin, New Zealand (hereafter DU).

24 Ann Strong to Registrar, 28 November 1927, University of Otago: Records of Registry and Central Administration 1936–1937, AG–180–31/0116, DU.

25 Ellen F. Fitzpatrick, *Endless Crusade: Women Social Scientists and Progressive Social Reform* (New York: Oxford University Press, 1990); Fitzgerald, *Outsiders or Equals*; Fitzgerald and Collins, *Historical Portraits.*

26 The story of Phyllis Rountree, an Australian research scientist, illustrates the struggles women faced in the mid-twentieth century to secure employment and be recognised for their work. See: Julia Horne, "Looking from the inside out: Rethinking university history," *Journal of Educational Administration and History* 46, no. 2 (2014): 174–189.

> amount of tact, and adaptability, facility in public speaking, and lastly if she is to convince others of the value of her work she must herself have vision and enthusiasm and an intense conviction of its value. The possession of the majority of the latter qualifications cannot be taken for granted but must be proved and the first professor must therefore be drawn from those few women who have already proved successful in difficult and responsible positions.[27]

This passage highlights both the explicit and implicit hurdles that women faced. The necessary qualifications were not sufficient: women had to demonstrate their worth and success as well as exhibit a range of predetermined characteristics. At all times, women were required to be "reliable, systematic and dignified".[28] Entering the citadel created an explicit obligation that women manage their appearance, dispositions and interactions as dictated by their male colleagues. Put simply, women's outward appearance and observed behaviour had to be both constrained and restrained as their very presence on the campus was a reminder of their status as outsiders.[29] Since "Home Science in the universities" was a "comparatively new innovation in New Zealand", the passage alluded to an implicit danger: the discipline might not continue to garner support if women were unable to convince "others" of the "value of her work".[30]

Despite being well-qualified and with careers that spanned decades, it remained difficult for women academics to be acclaimed or recognised. Their bodies, appearance and character were the object of comments by male colleagues. For example, Strong was described as having "a nature of great sweetness and sensibility", being of "ladylike deportment" with "her moral and religious character … above reproach".[31] In her response to a request for testimonials, Strong tellingly commented: "of late years I have not collected testimonials, feeling my work and experience should speak

---

27 Report to Chancellor by John Studholme, 19 May 1909, University of Otago: Records of Registry and Central Administration, Papers of John Studholme, AG–180–73/026, DU.

28 Ann Strong to Registrar, 9 January 1927, University of Otago: Records of Registry and Central Administration, AG–180–31/0110, DU.

29 Fitzgerald, *Outsiders or Equals?*

30 Helen Rawson to Registrar, 12 November 1921, University of Otago: Records of Registry and Central Administration, Papers of John Studholme, AG–180–31/0045, DU.

31 John Studholme to Chancellor 24 June 1920, University of Otago: Records of Registry and Central Administration, AG 180 31/0036, DU.

more clearly and definitely than words".[32] In their employment-related correspondence, both women focused on past successes, range of work experiences and qualifications to highlight their professional suitability. Each sought to stress her credentials and emphasise the importance of "securing the best person we possibly can for the work to be done and not concern ourselves with their personal life".[33] Yet despite their credentials and professorial positions, recognition was not immediately forthcoming from their male peers. For example, Strong admonished Professor Malcom (Chair of Physiology) when he constantly referred to her as "Mrs Strong".[34] This reluctance to acknowledge his colleague's status as a peer and equal was a deeply disrespectful form of misrecognition. In contemporary terms this example might be labelled a form of workplace incivility and micro aggression. This lack of civility further indicates that the marginalisation of women is part of their historical legacy in universities and that the repetition of these patterns of behaviour continues, albeit in more subtle forms in the twenty-first century.

Stepping out of their conventional roles as wives, mothers and housewives was risky for these early women professors. Each risked censure and their behaviour was regulated from the point of entry to university and throughout their studies. Although matriculation to university had become possible, women students were restricted in terms of the classes they could attend, the activities they could undertake and the places they could occupy.[35] These discriminatory practices worked to further marginalise women on the basis of their sex, despite a proclaimed commitment to equality by universities such as the University of New Zealand.[36] Establishing a new academic field and department was also risky work. Each of the woman professors had to negotiate the terrain of masculine power in the university and assuage public anxieties about the higher education of young women.

---

32 Ann Strong to John Studholme, 25 October 1906, University of Otago: Records of Registry and Central Administration, AG–180–31/0036, DU.

33 Ann Strong to Acting Registrar, 18 November 1932, University of Otago: Records of Registry and Central Administration, AG–180–31/0118, DU.

34 Ann Strong to Professor Malcolm, 19 September 1924, Malcom Papers, MS-2640/036, DU.

35 Dyhouse, *Students*; Morris Matthews, *In their Own Right.*

36 This was a term that was widely extorted in British universities and equally promoted by the University of New Zealand from 1877 onwards. See: *The University of New Zealand: Its History and Its System* (National Archives, Wellington: New Zealand, 1897).

In many ways, their presence in the university was conditional on "playing a straight game".[37]

In many ways, these early women professors trod an unknown path and ventured into a world in which they encountered male advantage, resistance, moral outrage, unwelcome hostility and resentment, and bureaucratic invisibility. What change, if any, has occurred in 100 years? I have a scholarly curiosity as to whether contemporary discursive narratives about women and higher education have altered.

The tropes of battlement

Despite the introduction of gender equity policies, affirmative action practices and equal employment legislation, the historical underrepresentation of women at higher levels in the university sector continues.[38] Although countries such as Sweden, Finland, Iceland, Norway and Israel have higher numbers of women vice chancellors, the global trend indicates that women are not equitably present in senior leadership roles.[39] The stark reality is that women in academia continue to face a level of hostility and aggression. The stories that women recount in the twenty-first century are simultaneously revealing and desultory. These stories do not offer the promise that much has changed.

While women students now graduate at higher levels than their male counterparts, this has not translated into successful career patterns at senior levels in professional settings.[40] Thus, the gendered patterns evident in the late nineteenth century remained in place in the early decades of the twenty-first century. Women are perceived as interlopers in a predominantly male world. As the institutional "Other," in order to succeed women must

37 Helen Rawson to Dr Malcolm, 17 September 1923, Malcom Papers, MS-2640/036, DU.

38 Tanya Fitzgerald, *Women Leaders in Higher Education: Shattering the Myths* (Abingdon: Routledge, 2014); Louise Morley, "Lost leaders: Women in the global academy," *Higher Education Research & Development* 33 no. 1 (2014): 114–128.

39 Tanya Fitzgerald and Jane Wilkinson *Travelling Towards a Mirage? Gender, Leadership and Higher Education* (Brisbane: Post Pressed, 2010); Barbara Bagilhole and Kate White, ed. *Gender, Power and Management: A Cross Cultural Analysis of Higher Education* (New York: Palgrave Macmillan, 2011); Fitzgerald, *Women Leaders in Higher Education*.

40 Deborah Kerfoot and David Knights, *Management, Organisation and Masculinity* (London: Sage, 2004); Kat Banyard, *The Equality Illusion: The Truth about Men and Women Today* (London: Faber and Faber, 2010).

manage their otherness.[41] This requires women to know and understand what is culturally appropriate and acceptable and engage in self-regulatory practices to demonstrate that they know the "way things are."[42]

My interest in the historical and contemporary experiences of women academics has prompted me to assemble the rich stories buried in archives as well as to compile oral narratives. This has been a two-stage process. The archival work began in 2008 and continues to this day as I encounter more names and venture into the records of international academic organisations such as the International Federation for Graduate Women. Over the past five years, I have chronicled the successes and challenges of (pseudonymous) women academics in higher education in Australia and New Zealand. To date, this project has drawn on the life and career histories of 55 women: 30 identify as senior leaders; and 25 women whose roles range from research assistants (2), associate lecturers (3), lecturers (11), and senior lecturers (9). In terms of demographic profile, the women's ages range from 35 to 67 and they worked in fields such as Humanities, Social Sciences, Education, Management and Public Health. All but 7 had doctoral degrees. These semi-structured interviews were recorded and transcribed. Using procedures common to interpretive analysis, transcripts were analysed and tentative categories formulated. Each interview was abstracted and indexed according to themes developed through extensive literature reviews. The interview data were then shared with participants to assist with accuracy and, more importantly, to engage in a collaborative process of curating these stories.[43]

In similar ways to the historic experiences of Boys-Smith, Rawson and Strong at the University of New Zealand, the women interviewed in Australia spoke of experiencing social isolation and marginalisation. Remembering her first management meeting, one commented:

> I recall my first senior management meeting. Yeah, how scary was that. I introduced myself but all I got back was "who do you barrack for?" I had no idea what this meant and so I could only stare back.

41 Silvia Gherardi and Barbara Poggio, *Gendertelling in Organisations: Narratives from Male-Dominated Environments* (Liber: Copenhagen Business School Press, 2007); Miriam David, *Feminism, Gender and Universities: Politics, Passion and Pedagogies* (Farnham, Surrey: Ashgate, 2014).

42 Debra E. Meyerson and Megan Tompkins, "Tempered radicals as institutional change agents: The case of advancing gender equity at the University of Michigan," *Harvard Journal of Law and Gender* 30, no. 2 (2007): 308.

43 For a fuller description of the project, see: Fitzgerald, *Women Leaders in Higher Education*.

> How was I to know it was a football team they were asking me about. Anyway, I do remember that someone in the room offered a name, can't remember what it was, but then the others all laughed. I think whatever was called out was a derogatory name for the team and that this was supposed to be my team. I just hate Monday and Friday meetings. Monday is all about the footy, Friday is all about tipping. I think that's a football term but I don't want to ask (Sheryl).

The language and imagery about the game directly speaks to stereotypically male interests. Sheryl, unable to contribute, was thereby isolated from the discussion. In order to "fit in", however, women must modify their behaviour to become more like their male colleagues.[44] Like the women professors at the University of New Zealand, the contemporary women leaders were engaged in risky work. Leadership, at times, is risky because it involves being the sole woman in the room. Sheryl felt under pressure to learn the game so that she would be able to engage in the conversation.

Evident in both the historical and contemporary examples is that women are not instigators of either the "games" or the "rules". As another participant observed:

> I've been in this place too long to not know the rules, you know, the rules of engagement. It may take longer than I expect but I get things done eventually. I don't get offside with my [male] colleagues. There's no point. They will just wear me down and win in the end. It's about knowing what will work and what will not, playing to your strengths and keeping your cool (Alana).

However Sheryl and Alana might "read" the rules, their interpretations and subsequent actions might not rebound to their advantage. They could, like Rawson, be accused of "not … playing a straight game".[45] The imagery evident here is the importance of adherence to the "rules" and not transgressing. Alana "plays the game" and she is acutely aware of the need to speak and act when required – or be deprived of male patronage. While Alana has learned to be a "good" girl and not rattle any patriarchal cages, Rawson was verbally sanctioned and was accused of having "deviated from the line of action" and therefore not "played a straight game".[46]

---

44 Patricia Bryans and Sharon Mavin, "Women learning to be managers: Learning to fit in or to play a different game?" *Management Learning* 34, no. 1 (2003): 111–134.

45 Rawson to Dr Malcolm, 17 September 1923, Malcom Papers, MS-2640/036, DU.

46 Ibid.

Another way in which women were marginalised was through the implicit expectation that they dress and act in gender appropriate ways. Being present in men's scholarly worlds was an act of transgression for the first generation of women professors. The contemporary transgression is to enter the male enclave of leadership. Accordingly, women felt the pressure to manage their bodies and appearance:

> I experience a high degree of angst before I even get to some of the meetings. Sure, I read the meeting papers, sure I canvas colleagues' views, but what troubles me most is what to wear. I need to look formal, I need to look like I know what I am doing. I am the only woman in the room. I always wear a suit. Sometimes I use a little colour, like a scarf, it helps me feel brighter but then when I see all the men in sombre suits I feel frivolous. It reminded me I was not one of them and never could be (Kathleen).

Again, links exist between the historical and contemporary. Over a century later women's appearance, dress and language is moderated to temper their visibility. The above account speaks to the level of re-imaging, re-packaging and re-presentation of the self.[47] Careful posture, neat and subdued clothing, minimal make-up and conservative hairstyles denote an individual woman's capacity to exert a level of self-control and self-management. This external management of self is ostensibly for the male gaze that ultimately has the permissible power of seeing how women present and project themselves.

How women perceive themselves and their dress, their body and their appearance is symbolically experienced as violence. Whether in historical or contemporary settings, women's bodies are expected to be contained, not visible, and overtly linked with prevailing social norms.[48] Wearing a scarf, for example, was an outward (and colourful) sign that Kathleen was not "one of them". Yet that she always wore a suit was a marker of her own willingness to be "one of them". For Kathleen, her anxiety and ambivalence about what to wear created a level of uncertainty about how she would be perceived. Read another way, her female bodily presence at the meeting was

47 Joan Eveline, *Ivory Basement Leadership* (Crawley: University of Western Australia Press, 2004); Sharon Mavin and Gina Grandy, "Women elite leaders doing respectable business femininity: How privilege is conferred, contested and defended through the body," *Gender, Work and Organization* 23, no. 4 (2016): 379–396.

48 Marianna Fotaki, "The sublime object of desire (for knowledge): Sexuality at work in business and management schools in England," *British Journal of Management* 22, no. 1 (2011): 42–53; Mavin and Grandy, "Women elite leaders."

an overt threat to the dominant masculinity in the room. Similarly, Julia was told by a senior male colleague to dress in "understated colours … black or dark blue … because too much colour makes me look too casual". For Kathleen and Julia, the logic of performativity and the management of their bodies and appearances reminded them they were out of place and therefore had to be both restrained and constrained.[49]

The workplace incivility and disrespectful communication that both Strong and Rawson recounted was also evident in these contemporary narratives. As one participant described:

> I continue to be agitated by the big boys at the table and their reluctance to hear what I have to say. They don't listen. I can tell. You know, shrug of the shoulders, facial expressions. In fact, I see them put their heads down, check emails when I am talking and sometimes there is even a murmur of another conversation. I thought I had the support of a few male colleagues but they seem to side with the other blokes. I feel like I am always in competition for the space to be heard. I just can't get on with my job some days (Sue).

This example highlights the constant interruptions and ignoring of contributions that women experience. Belinda also reported the outright hostility and aggression she faced:

> There is a senior male colleague that takes every opportunity to put me down. Actually, it's more than that. It's outright bullying. He said to me the other day … I can't deal with you when you go all feminist on me. I was shocked. What does that mean? What did he mean? Such a put down. I think he was telling me that I had "overstepped". Another of his favourite words. I don't answer his emails anymore, they are so aggressive. Maybe I don't fit in. Sometimes I am the only woman at the table. But this does not even begin to explain or excuse his behaviour. But why is it that I have to call him out? His [male] colleagues remain silent.

Belinda's narrative underscores the impact of symbolic violence and the misrecognition of her own stance as being "feminist", which is read as being aggressive and threatening. Her senior male colleague attempted to dominate and silence her through subtle marginalisation (put downs). The aggressive language used is a graphic example of his own expression of

---

49 Fitzgerald, *Women Leaders in Higher Education.*

aggressive masculinity and need to reinforce the status quo. The language co-opted for this exchange is illustrative of the use of labels, for example "feminist", to establish his dominance at the same time as intimidating his female colleague and reinforcing her subordinate position.

Historical considerations of the experiences of the first generations of women academics offer a timely reminder that changing an institution and its cultural mores is no easy task. Despite challenges to their presence, whether in historical or contemporary settings, women continue to lay siege, storm citadels, and work to dismantle bastions of power.

Conclusion

For women, as for people from minority backgrounds, walking into corridors of power was a daunting experience. As the snapshots presented here attest, although universities have been opened up to women, their struggles and challenges have abated. Critical questions remain about the under-representation of women in higher education – and, importantly, about the significant under-representation of women of colour in senior management.[50] Despite attention to this widely acknowledged and complex issue, gender barriers remain firmly in place. The historical and contemporary narratives presented in this chapter illustrate the challenges and difficulties women have faced. The historical legacy of discrimination, contestation, hostility and marginalisation has not changed. The implications of gender in the university still cannot be avoided.

Women's presence in the scholarly world of men is conditional on their willingness to "fit in", adapt to the prevailing culture and modify their behaviour to become more like men. Curiously, universities trumpet their roles as critics and conscience of society yet continue to legitimise gendered structures and processes. It seems to be that universities are incapable of self-scrutiny and institutional logics reinforce visible masculinist practices and beliefs as "the way things are".[51]

The rise of new managerialist values and practices do offer an alternative starting point to interrogate and potentially shift cultures that reinscribe "the way things are". In calls for accountability and transparency, judgements and actions (such as academic recruitment and promotions) as well as institutional policies (such as salary) can be more fully scrutinised. It is

50 Tanya Fitzgerald, "Spaces in–between: Indigenous women leaders speak back," *International Journal of Leadership in Education* 13, no. 1 (2010): 93–105.

51 Meyerson and Tompkins, "Tempered radicals as institutional change agents," 308.

precisely these entrenched and gendered systems, processes and decisions that have historically favoured men and continue to mark women's experiences in higher education. Critical historical inquiry and interpretation offers an important lens through which to view contemporary issues and their antecedents. Universities, historically predicated on their role as the critics and conscience of society, are uniquely placed to identify and shatter these imbalances of power. Histories of universities ought to be more than a chronicle of identity, growth and influence, but instead present a narrative of being at the vanguard of social, intellectual and cultural change. This would indeed be a historical legacy to narrate and celebrate.

Section III

Activism against Gender Violence

Chapter 12

FROM PAGE TO MEME

The print and digital revolutions against gender violence

Ana Stevenson and Brigitte Lewis

Gender violence has never been far from the public imagination or private realities of Australian women. Women's rights reformers and suffragists began to consider the issue of violence against women in the last decades of the nineteenth century. From the 1970s onwards, it formed a core issue for feminist activists. In the process, changing technologies have proven central to how activist women have approach gender violence, with print then digital media providing a platform where women can communicate in a public sphere otherwise dominated by men. As Stine Eckert and Linda Steiner emphasise, "Feminists have always been eager to experiment with new media."[1] This chapter considers how Australian women's movements of different eras used the most cutting-edge technologies available to approach and respond to the question of gender violence in its various forms.

Gender violence has not, historically, been vitally concerning for the mainstream media. Between the 1870s and the 1970s, many Australian newspapers published a section aimed at women readers and edited by a female journalist to capture a woman's – but not necessarily a feminist

---

1 Stine Eckert and Linda Steiner, "Feminist uses of social media: Facebook, Twitter, Tumblr, Pinterest, and Instagram," in *Defining Identity and the Changing Scope of Culture in the Digital Age*, ed. Alison Novak and Imaani Jamillah El-Burki (Hershey: IGI Global, 2016), 211.

– perspective.[2] A reliance on gender stereotypes meant the newspapers of the 1980s and 1990s perpetuated common myths about domestic violence.[3] An Australian government public education campaign – "Violence Against Women: Australia Says No," now familiar to so many – did acknowledge the severity of family violence, yet it inhibited "meaningful and transformative change" by decentralising gender in downplaying the predominance of male violence.[4]

In contrast, women's rights reformers, suffragists, and feminists gradually developed a print culture deeply concerned with the social questions surrounding gender violence. As Louise Poland observes, feminist cultural production has long generated a platform in the public sphere for "creating and sanctioning a feminist cultural space" through newsletters, journals, and books, as well as ephemera such as pamphlets, placards, posters, badges, and banners.[5] Activist women, less inhibited by moderating editorial directives, have consistently produced subversive responses to gender violence by seeking to humanise the experiences of violated women. Since activists have repeatedly developed perspectives antithetical to the mainstream media, tracing feminist responses to gender violence through different media formats offers insight into the changing preoccupations of the activists themselves.

A *long durée* feminist media history reveals gender violence to have been an enduring though vacillating concern in Australia. Activist women have, at times, been more preoccupied with other questions, while feminist print and then digital culture only gradually captured the important connections between different forms of gendered violence. Today, the digital revolution against gender violence emphasises how physical violence exists alongside factors such as economic, emotional, and sexual abuse, for women as well as men. While male violence towards white women figured at the centre of such discussions historically, feminists have gradually broadened their critique to recognise how gender violence disproportionately affects women of colour and gender non-binary people. By tracing the history of feminist responses to gender violence from page to meme, this chapter analyses

2 Justine Lloyd, "Women's pages in Australian print media from the 1850s," *Media International Australia* 150, no. 1 (2014): 61–65.

3 Ilsa Evans, "Desperate lovers and wanton women: Press representations of domestic violence," *Hecate* 27, no. 2 (2001): 148.

4 Ruth Phillips, "Undoing an activist response: Feminism and the Australian government's domestic violence policy," *Critical Social Policy* 26, no. 1 (2006): 212–213.

5 Louise Poland, "Printing presses and protest banners: Feminist presses in Australia," *Lilith: A Feminist History Journal* 10 (2001): 121.

how feminist print and digital culture sought to expose the depth of such violence in the public sphere.

"Poor little sister": The print revolution

The violence of husbands against wives was paramount in women's rights discussions of gender violence during the nineteenth century. However, as Jo Aitken argues, in comparison to their British counterparts, Australian suffragists seemed more reticent to focus on examples of working-class husbands' violence against wives. After voting rights were extended to women of European descent in the Commonwealth Franchise Act of 1902, wife beating came to be seen as a brutal relic of a bygone era.[6] The question of violence against women appeared only infrequently in turn-of-the-century women's rights and suffragist print culture. Vida Goldstein's *Australian Woman's Sphere* idealised marriage and domesticity by promoting an ideal of the "Australian girl."[7] Even the Australian branches of the World's Woman's Christian Temperance Union (WTCU), an organisation which acknowledged connections between alcohol and male violence, sometimes elided the more specific issue of violence against women.[8]

A notable exception was Louisa Lawson's *Dawn*, described by Sharyn Pearce as "an unpretentious but feisty departure from the superficial journals which Lawson loathed."[9] Periodically, Lawson concerned herself with publishing "protests against drunken wife beaters," specifically in the context of reforming divorce laws.[10] An 1890 editorial, for example, argued that the drunkard "may do violence to the best feelings of [his wife's] nature," and further asked, "can there be anything sacred in the bond which binds a good woman to a sot, felon, or brute?"[11] Other articles detailed the injustice of irresponsible, drunken, violent men having the legal and political

6 Jo Aitken, "'The horrors of matrimony among the masses': Feminist representations of wife beating in England and Australia, 1870–1914," *Journal of Women's History* 19, no. 4 (2007): 107–131.

7 Sharyn Pearce, "'The best career is matrimony': First-wave journalism and the 'Australian girl'," *Hecate* 18, no. 2 (1992): 64–78.

8 Jo Aitken, "Home protection," in *Alcohol and Temperance in Modern History: An International Encyclopedia*, ed. Jack S. Blocker Jr., David M. Fahey and Ian Tyrrell (Santa Barbara: ABC-Clio, 2003), 298–299.

9 Sharyn Pearce, "From bush battler to city editor: Louisa Lawson and the *Dawn*," *Journal of Australian Studies* 21, no. 54–55 (1997): 12.

10 Aitken, "'The horrors of matrimony'," 109.

11 "The Divorce Extension Bill, or, the drunkard's wife," *Dawn*, March 5, 1890.

rights and privileges upright women did not.[12] Lawson's transgressive practice of employing only women in the journal's print production led to her employees themselves facing violence, to the point of seeking police protection.[13]

Newspapers were not the only realm where discussions about gender violence were beginning to take place. Early-twentieth-century Australian romance novels, Hsu-Ming Teo illustrates, made connections between gender violence and the masculine culture of the frontier. Miles Franklin's *My Brilliant Career* (1901) was suspicious of the gendered implications of marriage, while Mary Bryant's *Dave's Sweetheart* (1894) viewed the institution as leading to physical violence, verbal abuse, abandonment, and untimely death. Novelists characterised daughters as reticent to marry because of their own experiences of family violence. The title character in Broda Reynolds's *The Selector's Girl* (1917) becomes suspicious of marriage after witnessing her father's violence toward her mother, while Mabel Forrest's *The Wild Moth* (1924) depicted a drunken father's violent rage against his daughter. These novelists did not necessarily see themselves as feminists, yet their concerns overlapped with anxieties about gender and the perceived dangers of the colonial frontier.[14]

Yet, when turn-of-the-century women's rights print culture did address gender violence, commentators largely overlooked settler colonial frontier violence and the exploitation of Indigenous women. Only in the 1920s and 1930s did some feminists begin to concern themselves with the situation of Indigenous women, especially in the WCTU's *White Ribbon Signal*.[15] Other campaigns emphasised maternal rights, especially in cases of separation or divorce, but connections were typically not drawn between such issues to the wider culture of gender violence.[16]

---

12 "The man question, or, the woman question re-stated," *Dawn*, September 2, 1889; Emma Platter Seabury, "Views of equal suffrage," *Dawn*, August 1, 1896; "Warra," "Queensland Women's Property Act," *Dawn*, October 1, 1897.

13 "Our anniversary," *Dawn*, May 1, 1895.

14 Hsu-Ming Teo, "'We have to learn to love imperially': Love in late colonial and federation Australian romance novels," *Journal of Popular Romance Studies* 4, no. 2 (2014): 5–7.

15 Patricia Grimshaw, "Gender, citizenship and race in the Woman's Christian Temperance Union of Australia, 1890 to the 1930s," *Australian Feminist Studies* 13, no. 28 (1998): 199–214.

16 Marilyn Lake, "Childbearers as rights-bearers: Feminist discourse on the rights of Aboriginal and non-Aboriginal mothers in Australia, 1920–50," *Women's History Review* 8, no. 2 (1999): 347–363; Wendy Michaels, "The final factor: What political action failed to do," *Lilith: A Feminist History Journal* 19 (2013): 18–31.

Beyond feminist print culture, mainstream newspapers were periodically concerned with instances of gender violence. After World War One, men's brutality towards women was mitigated by public sympathy towards ex-servicemen, with the trauma of war frequently used as a defence for such violence in court.[17] Arguments about whether or not women should be admitted as jurists also revealed competing attitudes, with women's rights reformers arguing that women jurors would ensure fairer hearings in sexual offense trials.[18] Yet, well into the 1950s, women's fitness as jurors was also questioned in relation to the potential for embarrassment in cases of sexual violence.[19]

The print culture of the women's liberation movement enabled new insights to be developed, with Australian feminists naming domestic violence as a social issue.[20] As Germaine Greer famously stated in 1970, "Women have very little idea of how much men hate them."[21] The many feminist newsletters and periodicals which emerged discussed questions surrounding domestic and sexual violence, initially with respect to the developing women's refuge movement, while rape, especially in the context of the Vietnam War, also emerged as a key concern.[22] Important new works, such as Anne Summers' *Damned Whores and God's Police: The Colonisation of Women in Australia* (1975) and Miriam Dixson's *The Real Matilda: Woman and Identity in Australia, 1788 to the Present* (1976), brought insights from the emerging field of women's history to inform these developing feminist interventions. New academic journals – including *Refractory Girl* and *Hecate* in the 1970s, then *Australian Feminist Studies* and *Lilith: A Feminist History Journal* in the 1980s – would become intellectual mainstays for feminist studies and women's history in Australia. Often discussing similar questions as activists, these journals even facilitated dialogue between activists and academics.[23]

---

17 Elizabeth Nelson, "The First World War, returned soldiers and understandings of domestic violence in Australia," *Journal of Women's History* 19, no. 4 (2007), 83–106.

18 "Reforms," *Daily Examiner*, 18 October 1929, 4; "Women on juries," *Gilgandra Weekly*, 31 October 1929, 1.

19 Sonia Walker, "Battle-axes and sticky-beaks: Women and jury service in Western Australia 1898–1957," *Murdoch University Electronic Journal of Law* 11, no. 4 (2004).

20 See Zora Simic's chapter in this volume.

21 Germaine Greer, *The Female Eunuch* (London: MacGibbon & Kee, 1970).

22 *Sydney Women's Liberation Newsletter*, August 1977 and May 1984, State Library of Queensland; *Scarlet Woman*, Autumn 1986, State Library of Victoria.

23 For example, see: Dianne Otto and Eileen Haley, "Health shelter: A history of Adelaide women's shelter," *Refractory Girl* Winter (1975): 11–16; Rosemary Pringle, "Rape: The other side of Anzac Day," *Refractory Girl*, no. 26 (1983): 31–35; Ludo

Unlike the sensationalistic approach of the mainstream media, feminist print culture enabled heartrending emotional perspectives to be shared through individualised responses to gender violence. A detached *Times on Sunday* account of a young woman's murder in 1987, entitled "She Must Be Someone's Daughter, Sister, Wife … Killed," prompted a letter to the *Sydney Women's Liberation Newsletter*:

> They found your discarded body thrown over a rocky embankment … and as I read about you (a stranger) it is three weeks since you were murdered and still nobody knows who you are.
>
> We know that you are female, blond, with green eyes, that you were mid-way through your menstrual cycle. You have short well-kept nails and shaved legs. We also know you recently had your hair cut and streaked and that you have a small scar on the lower right side of your torso. We even know that you were a light smoker or a heavy coffee drinker.
>
> All those strangers, handling and inspecting your body and all those millions of strangers who have read the above personal and private details about you in the newspaper.
>
> What we also know is this –
>
> > A MAN STRANGLED AND SEXUALLY ABUSED YOU BEFORE AND POSSIBLY AFTER YOUR DEATH.
>
> Poor little sister, I hope you have loved ones who will ache for you as I do.[24]

Feminist print culture thus sought to humanise violated women in a way that the mainstream media did not. Anticipating many twenty-first-century digital initiatives, this letter presented the unidentified female victim in terms of herself, rather than as an extension of or in relation to the men around her.

More women emerged in positions of political, professional, and cultural power and influence by the early 1990s. But the election of Prime Minister John Howard in 1996 precipitated the gradual dismantling and de-funding

---

McFerren [sic], "Can men change? What to do with batterers," *Refractory Girl* 33 (1989): 3–4; Ludo McFerrin [sic], "Domestic violence: Stories, scandals and serious analysis," *Refractory Girl* 44–45 (1993): 152–159.

24 Phyl Elmiger, "To a sister," *Sydney Women's Liberation Newsletter*, April 1987, State Library of Queensland.

of those government agencies that had been a product of the "agitation, activism, and agency" of 1970s women's liberation and remained dedicated to protecting women's interests.[25] When Howard introduced the "Violence Against Women: Australia Says No" campaign under a cloud of controversy between 2003 and 2004, its individualistic approach diluted the strategies of earlier feminist anti-violence campaigns and, in spite of the campaign's name, embraced gender-neutral language.[26] Moving away from "domestic violence" and men's violence against women, the Howard government prioritised "family violence". Unlike the graphic imagery used in government campaigns dedicated to alcohol and smoking awareness, the "Violence Against Women" campaign depicted calm, well-presented women physically unaffected by violence.[27]

The early print culture associated with the Australian women's movement rejected women's disenfranchisement and, to a certain extent, issues relating to gender violence, especially against wives. Such concerns were developed with far more vehemence by women's liberationists and their academic feminist counterparts, an intervention all the more evident when placed alongside mainstream media and governmental approaches to gender violence. For these activists, women's rights were articulated in print and then fought and won on the streets (figure 1).

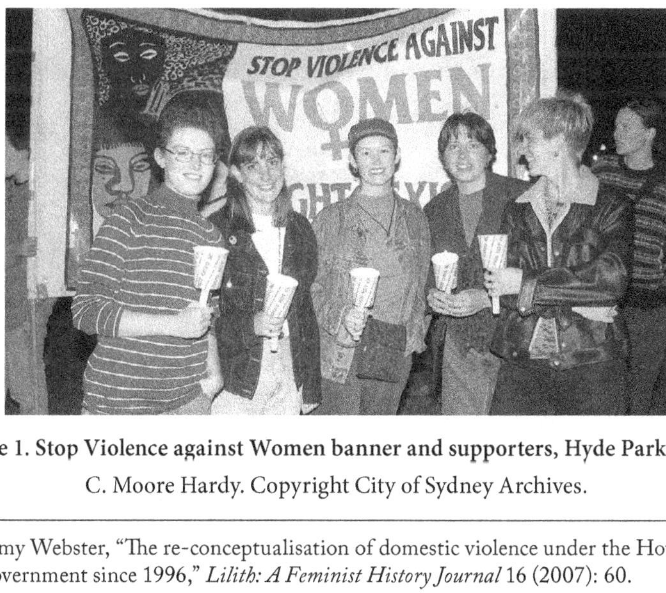

Figure 1. Stop Violence against Women banner and supporters, Hyde Park, 1995.
C. Moore Hardy. Copyright City of Sydney Archives.

25 Amy Webster, "The re-conceptualisation of domestic violence under the Howard government since 1996," *Lilith: A Feminist History Journal* 16 (2007): 60.

26 Phillips, "Undoing an activist response," 192–219. For women's refuges, see Jacqui Theobald and Suellen Murray's chapter in this volume.

27 Webster, "The re-conceptualisation of domestic violence," 61–64.

"Joint Destroyers": The digital revolution

Since the early 2000s, the internet and associated technologies have become a new site of activism for Australian feminists. Digital activism has enabled the rearticulation of a feminist and female-led revolution which is streamed, photographed, tweeted, and then turned into a meme somewhere online. A mechanism for centralising feminist concerns, both locally and globally, social media can highlight the "intellectual strength and the political edge of intersectionality."[28] Social media users worldwide embrace hashtags to promote feminist causes in response to contemporary events, although trending hashtags become most visible when invoked by mainstream media outlets.[29] But digital mediums have also become vehicles for backlash and, consequently, different forms of gender violence.

A meme is a neat encapsulation of a broader, more complex idea which becomes easily and widely reproducible. For women, platforms like Twitter have become a powerful way to speak back to power, allowing for greater self-expression and information distribution among diverse individuals, organisations, and communities.[30] When feminist hashtags come to signify more than that which initially provided inspiration, they can become what is described as a "feminist meme event."[31] Feminist meme propagation represents the "social practices of cultural production that create and transform memes as small units of culture; a social, rather than genetic, mode of cultural reproduction."[32] Social media platforms can, in turn, participate in meme creation. A key example is the Twitter emoticon associated with #MeToo, undoubtedly the loudest call to action in recent times. Coined in the United States by activist Tarana Burke in 2006 but first used on Twitter in 2017 by actress Alyssa Milano, #MeToo encouraged women to share personal stories of sexual assault and harassment online.[33] In this spirit, Twitter created an emoticon that literally turns the hashtag into a cartoon

28 Eckert and Steiner, "Feminist uses," 222.

29 Laura Portwood-Stacer and Susan Berridge, "Introduction: The year in feminist hashtags," *Feminist Media Studies* 14, no. 6 (2014): 1090.

30 Eckert and Steiner, "Feminist uses," 222.

31 Samantha C. Thrift, "#Yesallwomen as feminist meme event," *Feminist Media Studies* 14, no. 6 (2014): 1091.

32 Carrie A. Rentschler and Samantha C. Thrift, "Doing feminism in the network: Networked laughter and the 'binders full of women' meme," *Feminist Theory* 16, no. 3 (2015): 331.

33 Christen A. Johnson and K.T. Hawbaker, "#MeToo: A timeline of events," *Chicago Tribune*, 25 May 2018, accessed 30 April 2018, http://www.chicagotribune.com/lifestyles/ct-me-too-timeline-20171208-htmlstory.html.

featuring three multiracial hands in the air, symbolising the movement of women and men speaking about their experiences.

Despite the global possibilities and connections the internet facilitates, the particularities of local and national contexts must be emphasised. In Australia, feminist activists and the mainstream media continue to produce divergent responses to gender violence. In 2008, only two years after Twitter was founded, the Eliminating Violence Against Women Media Awards (EVAs) were established to honour "excellence in the reporting of violence against women" in the state of Victoria.[34] The EVAs ultimately proved so influential that, in 2013, the Australian government expanded the initiative nationwide to become the Our Watch Awards.[35] And yet, the harassment of Australia's first female prime minister gained significant media attention between 2010 and 2013. Prime Minister Julia Gillard, who was beleaguered by the media and (now infamously) called a "witch" and "JuLIAR" by her political opponents, only reluctantly delivered her famous "sexism and misogyny" speech in parliament during October 2012.[36] Embraced with scepticism in the national media though celebrated internationally, this speech later inspired a song recorded by young adult choral ensemble Australian Voices, which later went viral on Youtube.[37]

Using hashtags on Twitter has been a particularly powerful way for women to spark media attention around gender violence. Some flourish nationally, while others interact with feminist digital activism globally. In August 2012, radio commentator Alan Jones claimed that women such as Gillard, Chief Commissioner of the Victoria Police Christine Nixon, and Lord Mayor of the City of Sydney Clover Moore were "destroying the joint" by daring to occupy positions of power and influence.[38] The digital platform Destroy the Joint (followed by #destroythejoint) was formed in the aftermath. Addressing its adherents as "Joint Destroyers" on social media

34 "About the EVAs Media Awards," *the evas*, n.d., accessed 31 May 2018, http://www.evas.org.au/index.php/what-are-the-evas/about-the-evas-media-awards.

35 "Our Watch Awards," *The Walkley Foundation*, 2016, accessed 31 May 2018, http://www.walkleys.com/awards/our-watch-awards/.

36 Ana Stevenson, "Making gender divisive: 'Post-feminism,' sexism and media representations of Julia Gillard," *Burgmann Journal* 2 (2013): 55 and 60.

37 Robert Davidson, "Not now, not ever!" (Gillard Misogyny Speech), *Australian Music Centre*, accessed 1 June 2018, https://www.australianmusiccentre.com.au/work/davidson-robert-not-now-not-ever.

38 Jessamy Gleeson, "'Destroying the joint?': Challenging and changing representations of women in mainstream media via online feminist campaigns," in *Creating Space in the Fifth Estate*, ed. Janet Fulton and Phillip McIntyre (Newcastle upon Tyne: Cambridge Scholars Publishing, 2017), 61–62.

enabled activists to invert the original slur and facilitate a positive digital community identity. In May 2014, Destroy the Joint launched its Counting Dead Women campaign.[39] The hashtag #CountingDeadWomen literally illustrates the extent of femicide in Australia by circulating memes featuring an ever-increasing death toll alongside, a weeping female statue. Destroy the Joint reveals how feminist campaigns can actively challenge the mainstream media's dominant discourses by using social media to "assert a form of power."[40] It therefore represents "one part of the resistance" to the public sexism experienced by women leaders, which has the potential to "encourage substantive change with respect to persistent gender inequality."[41]

Despite these possibilities, "the visibility, community, and access that are often touted as the boons of social media are by no means uniform nor do they hold the same meaning or value for everyone."[42] Such disparities became clear during the two-day "Sydney siege" of December 2014. When Man Haron Monis took hostages in a Lindt Café in Sydney CBD's Martin Place while displaying an Islamic flag, Muslim women were targeted and attacked on public transport. In response, writer Tessa Kum began #illridewithyou on Twitter. As the hashtag spread, white Australians offered to ride with *hijab*-, *niqab*-, and *burka*-wearing women to show solidarity. These actions gained widespread media acclaim.[43] But the hashtag simultaneously highlighted the privileges whiteness affords when moving through public space. Some commentators also critiqued the "bad Muslim" versus "good white person" frame of reference from which it emerged.[44]

Similarly, Indigenous digital activism does not always receive the same degree of media attention as other movements, yet it can be envisaged as a "'new frontier'" where communities are creating "a cultural and

---

39 *Destroy The Joint: Submission to the Senate Inquiry into Domestic Violence in Australia* (Destroy The Joint Ltd., 2014), 15–17.

40 Gleeson, "'Destroying the joint?'" 65.

41 Jessica McLean and Sophia Maalsen, "'We don't want it to be like that for her again': Gendered leadership and online feminism in Australian politics and planning," *Australian Planner* 54, no. 1 (2017): 24.

42 Portwood-Stacer and Berridge, "Introduction," 1090.

43 John Falzon, "#illridewithyou shows the kind of world that is possible," *Eureka Street* 24, no. 24 (2014): 7; Jordan Valinsky, "Australians just showed the world exactly how to respond to terrorism with #IllRideWithYou," *Mic*, 15 December 2014, accessed 1 November 2017, https://mic.com/articles/106442/australians-show-the-world-exactly-how-to-respond-to-terrorism-with-ill-ride-with-you#.gY6oIwkuJ.

44 Nazri Bahrawi, "Why #illridewithyou is an ill ride," *Al Jazeera*, 18 December 2014, accessed 1 November 2017 http://www.aljazeera.com/indepth/opinion/2014/12/why-illridewithyou-an-ill-ride-20141217124023253335.html.

political reterritorialisation of social media spaces."[45] In a March 2015 radio interview with ABC Goldfields, Western Australia, Prime Minister Tony Abbott said of the state's remote Aboriginal communities: "It's not the job of the taxpayer to subsidise lifestyle choices."[46] Digital conversations generated an #SOSBLAKAUSTRALIA social media campaign in response.[47] This led to a rally in conjunction with Closing the Gap Day, a government initiative claiming to "deliver sound service and results for Aboriginal participation into the broader Australian social fabric."[48] Through collective action, #SOSBLAKAUSTRALIA mobilised in every state and territory and saw 30,000 people march.[49] The *Herald Sun*, which largely ignored activists' efforts, instead ran a hostile headline – "Selfish Rabble Shut City" – to denounce these actions.[50] When the community responded by initiating #SelfishRabble, in less than an hour the hashtag overtook national sports events to trend to the top of Australia's Twitter.[51]

Perhaps the most famous female-led hashtag of the 2010s, #BlackLivesMatter has also offered inspiration in Australia, just as the predecessors of contemporary Indigenous activists identified with the Black Power movement in the United States during the 1960s and 1970s.[52] Established in 2013 after policeman George Zimmerman was acquitted for the murder of Trayvon Martin, an unarmed African American teenager, the hashtag

45 Alex Wilson, Bronwyn Lee Carlson, and Acushla Sciascia, "Reterritorialising social media: Indigenous people rise up," *Australasian Journal of Information Systems* 21 (2017): 1.

46 Australian Government, "Interview with Kirstyn March, ABC Goldfields, Western Australia," *PM Transcripts: Transcripts from the Prime Ministers of Australia*, 10 March 2015, accessed 19 December 2017, http://pmtranscripts.pmc.gov.au/prime-minister/abbott-tony?page=102.

47 Alan Clarke, "How a single facebook post Inspired thousands to stand up for Indigenous rights," *BuzzFeed*, 13 May 2015, accessed 1 November 2017, https://www.buzzfeed.com/allanclarke/how-a-single-facebook-post-inspired-thousands-to-stand-up-fo.

48 Sam Cook, "SOSBLAKUSTRALIA: Stop the forced closure of Aboriginal communities," *Cultural Survival Quarterly Magazine* 39, no. 2 (2015), https://www.culturalsurvival.org/publications/cultural-survival-quarterly/sosblakaustralia-stop-forced-closure-aboriginal.

49 "The #SOSBLAKAUSTRALIA story," *Stop the Forced Closure of Aboriginal Communities in Australia @sosblakaustralia*, Facebook, 19 March 2016, accessed 1 November 2017, https://www.facebook.com/sosblakaustralia/photos/a.1042299689120174.1073741828.1042255972457879/1269093729774101/?type=3&theater.

50 David Hurley and Ellen Whinnett, "Selfish rabble shut down city," *Herald Sun*, 11 April 2015.

51 Cook, "SOSBLAKUSTRALIA," 15.

52 Jon Piccini, *Transnational Protest, Australia and the 1960s: Global Radicals* (London: Palgrave Macmillan, 2016), Chapter 6.

precipitated a movement led by Patrisse Cullors, Opal Tometi, and Alicia Garza, three queer African American women. In the United States, Black Lives Matter "advocates for dignity, justice, and respect."[53] In Australia, Indigenous activists have come to see this hashtag as exemplifying how "a movement can maintain its focus on the people impacted by discriminatory policing, while engaging all parts of the progressive movement to build political influence."[54]

Amid these expanding feminist and Indigenous digital cultures, family violence campaigner Rosie Batty's appointment as 2015 Australian of the Year brought even greater attention to gender violence in mainstream and social media alike. In spite of the increased social awareness that resulted, even effective campaigns had their limitations. Significantly, by focusing its activism around statistics scrutinised only by gender, Destroy the Joint's Counting Dead Women campaign fails to account for how gender violence disproportionately affects women of colour. Indigenous women, according to Aileen Moreton-Robinson, perceive all white Australian feminists as the beneficiaries of colonialism, both historically and in the present.[55] What is changing, however, is the democratised digital space the internet offers Indigenous women to occupy and engage in self-representation. "Social media, particularly Twitter and the feminist blogosphere," Patricia Hill Collins and Sirma Bilge observe, provide "platforms for feminists of colour who hitherto rarely had access to larger audiences."[56] To this end, Aboriginal activist Celeste Liddle, whose blog *Rantings of an Aboriginal Feminist* facilitates particularly influential discussions about gender violence and intersectionality, intervened in the #CountingDeadWomen initiative. In 2015 and again in 2016, Liddle began "Counting Dead Aboriginal Women" via her blog and popular Twitter account, @Utopiana.[57]

Australian feminist print culture now coexists alongside this diverse feminist digital culture. Books such as Emily Maguire's *Princesses and*

---

53 *Black Lives Matter*, 2013–, accessed 1 November 2017, https://blacklivesmatter.com/.

54 Tamar Hopkins, "#Blacklivesmatter: The crisis of being Black in America (and Australia)," *New Matilda*, 13 March 2016, accessed 19 December 2017, https://newmatilda.com/2016/03/13/blacklivesmatter-the-crisis-of-being-black-in-america-and-australia/.

55 Aileen Moreton-Robinson, *Talkin' Up to the White Woman: Aboriginal Women and Feminism* (St Lucia: University of Queensland Press, 2000), xxv.

56 Patricia Hill Collins and Sirma Bilge, *Intersectionality* (Cambridge: Polity Press, 2016), 85.

57 Celeste Liddle, *Rantings of an Aboriginal Feminist*, 2012–, accessed 22 October 2017, http://blackfeministranter.blogspot.com.au/.

Pornstars: Sex, Power, Identity (2008) and Rosie Waterland's *The Anti-Cool Girl* (2015) continue to engage with questions of gender violence, often semi-autobiographically. In such books, gender violence is conceived less in terms of alcoholism and coverture, but more as a product of systemic oppressions. Another key example is Clementine Ford's *Fight Like a Girl* (2016), the celebrated autobiography of the outspoken feminist journalist and former *Daily Life* columnist. Echoing Greer, Ford asks, rhetorically, "*why do so many men seem to hate women so fiercely, so aggressively, so violently and so passionately?*" Their awareness of the connections between gender, class, and (to a lesser extent) race means these authors now present reasonably intersectional rationales which detail contemporary feminist perspectives towards gender violence. For Ford, the violence inflicted by men has "more physical, cultural and economic power behind it than women subjugated by a patriarchal system could ever hope to replicate."[58]

But the converse to the consciousness-raising successes of feminist digital cultures is the harassment many activist women face online. The accessibility and cultural prevalence of social media has precipitated unprecedented levels of online sexual harassment – for politicians and activists alike. For example, Ford's journalistic writing, which often explores women's lived experiences of controversial feminist issues such as abortion and body image, has repeatedly provoked vicious responses. On White Ribbon Day 2015, an initiative which seeks to raise public awareness about men's violence against women, Ford shared some of the online harassment she had experienced, an action which only precipitated further online abuse.[59] Ford's autobiography details the countless violent rape threats she has received as a result of voicing her stridently feminist opinions.[60] While digital feminist campaigners often donate their time willingly, they are simultaneously "subject to troll attacks, harassment and are at risk of burnout."[61] But this phenomenon goes beyond high-profile women. Digital harassment and abuse is a problem for both men and women, with three in five

58 Clementine Ford, *Fight Like a Girl* (Sydney: Allen & Unwin, 2016), Chapter 9, 152, and 159. Emphasis in original.

59 Anthony Caggiano, "Many shamed for trolling Clementine Ford apologies for online attack," *Sydney Morning Herald*, 26 June 2015, accessed 1 November 2017, http://www.smh.com.au/national/man-shamed-for-trolling-clementine-ford-apologises-for-online-attack-20150625-ghxz24.html.

60 Ford, *Fight Like a Girl*, 146–147, 163–165, and Chapter 10.

61 Jessamy Gleeson, "'(Not) working 9–5': The consequences of contemporary Australian-based online feminist campaigns as digital labour," *Media International Australia* 161, no. 1 (2016): 79.

Australians reporting such experiences; but women are more likely to feel "very or extremely upset" in consequence.[62]

There are now more mobile phones in the world than people.[63] This means digital activists have the potential, and perhaps even the responsibility, to reach larger communities of women than ever before. The internet – once considered the realm of the unreal – has now become an instrument for change-makers and Joint Destroyers in Australia and across the world, and their face is overwhelmingly female identified.

Reflections

Some key threads can be identified in the print and digital culture responses to gender violence that emerged at the highpoints in Australian women's movements from the late nineteenth to the twenty-first century. Each era sought to humanise women and their experiences, emphasising their personhood in the face of an antagonistic mainstream media. Increasingly, print culture enabled women to develop connections between violence and other forms of gendered experience, from marriage and family to culture and economics. The digital realm has emerged as a clear site for intervention into the discussion about gender violence, yet it also constitutes another avenue wherein new and different forms of gender violence can flourish.

Every technological development and method of communication has its limitations, even in the digital realm. Social media only constitutes what is described as "selective exposure": users are exposed to a "relatively narrow cluster" which develops only "fragmented interactions" and forms "divided groups."[64] Hence the internet, while allowing for new kinds of revolutionary action, can also reinscribe some existing forms of exclusion. Only those who have access to electricity, are technologically literate, and can afford to be connected – for example, via an internet-enabled phone or a laptop – can partake in the digital history-making that happens on social media. And only those who have these things and are situated outside technologically restrictive authoritarian regimes can easily and safely participate. "Even feminisms highly conscious of and committed to intersectionality," scholars rightly note, "cannot eliminate these differences."[65]

62 Anastasia Powell and Nicola Henry, *Digital Harassment and Abuse of Adult Australians: A Summary Report* (Melbourne: RMIT, 2015), 1–4.

63 "Definitive data and analysis for the mobile industry," *GSMA Intelligence*, 2004–2017, accessed 1 November 2017, https://www.gsmaintelligence.com/.

64 Eckert and Steiner, "Feminist uses," 223.

65 Ibid.

It is important to recognise the growth of online feminism and its "substantive interventions," in spite of the critique that online campaigns do not create "'real world' change" or are merely "limited to clicktivism."[66] Digital campaigns can – and do – prompt real-world action far more rapidly than earlier print technologies. In comparison to the technological limitations of earlier women's movements when printing presses and a far larger labour force was necessary, the speed and ease of digital publishing is an important factor in the rapid dissemination of content with relatively low production costs. Women from diverse backgrounds can now be connected with other women to an unprecedented degree. Indigenous social media traction, in turn, is directly related to the extent that the "Indigenous public sphere" as a "counter public" both contests and is heard in the mainstream.[67] Digital feminisms, Hester Baer argues, can be seen to be "redoing feminism for a neoliberal age by working through, making visible, and re-signifying central tensions in contemporary feminism ... beyond the realm of the self-styled individual" to create the space for a collective feminism.[68]

Feminism is not dead; new media platforms, facilitated by new technologies, have consistently brought about its reinvigoration. Together, women are standing, scrolling, and shouting to denounce gender violence. Digital text and image are the old born anew. Feminist activists are embracing new technologies to mobilise online as well as on the streets, where the revolution began.

---

66 McLean and Maalsen, "'We don't want it to be like that'," 31.

67 Jack Latimore, David Nolan, Margaret Simons, and Elyas Khan, "Reassembling the Indigenous public sphere," *Australasian Journal of Information Systems* 21 (2017): 2.

68 Hester Baer, "Redoing feminism: Digital activism, body politics, and neoliberalism," *Feminist Media Studies* 16, no. 1 (2016): 19.

Chapter 13

FEMINIST FILMS ON WOMEN'S EXPERIENCES OF VIOLENCE[1]

Mary Tomsic

Since October 2017, #MeToo has gained prominence in public declarations and conversations about sexual harassment, assault and violence.[2] *Time Magazine* identified those speaking out as "The Silence Breakers" and collectively named them *Time*'s 2017 "Person of the Year".[3] The women actors in Hollywood who publicly spoke of experiences of sexual harassment in their workplace were the catalyst for this use of #MeToo, but it has expanded to provide "an umbrella of solidarity for millions of people to come forward with their stories".[4] Writer and scholar Anne Helen Petersen has said #MeToo is "all about reckoning: about declaring that things can no longer be how they were before, about calling out bullshit, about indicting the mechanisms within industries at large that allow abuse to continue,

---

1 My thanks to Ana Stevenson, Alana Piper, Meighen Katz, Jessica Freame, Sarah Pinto and the reviewers for their insightful and generous feedback.

2 Joyce Chen, "Alyssa Milano wants her 'me too' campaign to elevate Harvey Weinstein discussion," *Rolling Stone* 17 October 2017, accessed 15 November 2017, https://www.rollingstone.com/movies/news/alyssa-milano-on-her-me-too-campaign-weinstein-conversation-w509345. #MeToo follows others campaigns, including #YesAllWomen and #YouOkSis? See: Jessalynn Keller, "#MeToo campaign brings conversation of rape to the mainstream," *The Conversation*, 25 October 2017, accessed 15 November 2017, https://theconversation.com/metoo-campaign-brings-conversation-of-rape-to-the-mainstream-85875/.

3 Stephanie Zacharek, Eliana Dockterman and Haley Sweetland Edwards, "'TIME person of the year 2017: The silence breakers'," *Time*, 18 December 2017, accessed 9 May 2018, http://time.com/time-person-of-the-year-2017-silence-breakers/.

4 Ibid.

and allow subjects of abuse to be further victimized."[5] Commentators have also noted the potential political limitations of the #MeToo protest, in the form of social media disclosure. What concerns Australian poet and critic Melody Paloma "about #MeToo is that it requires a performance of trauma, that we're peddling victims as affective labourers in the vain hope of revolution."[6]

Without valorising this current moment, the ideas inherent to #MeToo are part of a longer history of feminist activism and responses to sexual harassment and gender violence. #MeToo is a form of political action primarily focused around women's voices, social inequalities and working towards change. Using different means of expression, Australian filmmakers and feminist activists called similar issues to attention during the 1970s. These women particularly focused on the place of women's stories and experiences, thinking about how narratives can be used in hopeful ways for social change.

Many of the themes evident in the history of Australian feminist activism around gender violence, as expressed in cultural texts, can also be connected to this current moment: the demand for individual women's experiences to be known and understood in a broader context, and for women's lives to be taken seriously and openly discussed. Obvious though these links may be, I want to highlight them because feminism is a diverse political project and feminist protest takes different forms at different times. The methods of social protest, action and expression may have changed but these themes remain present, demonstrating the extent to which such concerns remain unresolved.

As early as the late 1960s, feminist filmmaking was a form of cultural activism and political expression linked to the Australian women's liberation movement.[7] The histories of feminist filmmaking and other forms of expression have recently reinvigorated histories of Australian feminism,

---

5 Anne Helen Petersen, "Uma deserves better," *the collected ahp*, 4 February 2018, accessed 19 April 2018, https://tinyletter.com/annehelenpetersen/letters/uma-deserves-better.

6 Melody Paloma, "Bodies in trouble: On sexual violence and the problem with hashtags," *Overland*, 25 October 2017, accessed 15 November 2017, https://overland.org.au/2017/10/from-hashtag-to-action/. See also: Jessica Megarry, "Why #metoo is an impoverished form of feminist activism, unlikely to spark social change," *The Conversation*, 30 October 2017, accessed 15 November 2017, https://theconversation.com/why-metoo-is-an-impoverished-form-of-feminist-activism-unlikely-to-spark-social-change-86455.

7 Mary Tomsic, "'We will invent ourselves, the age of the new image is at hand': Creating, learning and talking with Australian feminist filmmaking," *Australian Feminist Studies* 22, no. 53 (2007): 287-306.

placing particular attention on material culture and feminist remembering.[8] The violence women experienced, particularly sexual violence in its many forms, was a concern addressed by feminist filmmakers. This chapter focuses on five films which explored women's experiences of gender violence during the 1970s and 1980s. Film scholar Felicity Collins has comprehensively examined the larger body of Australian feminist filmmaking from the late 1960s to the late 1980s by focusing on the psyche of independent feminist filmmaking in Sydney, revealing how politics, film culture and political activism were both experienced and expressed.[9] This chapter focuses on key films which explore gender-based violence. To develop a sense of how violence was culturally represented in the 1970s and 1980s, it highlights the use of humour and sound as well as the representation of women as active subjects, alongside filmmakers' work in expanding forms of creative expression.

Chronologically, the films this chapter analyses are: *We Aim to Please* (As If Productions, 1976), *Size 10* (Red Heart Pictures, 1978), *Behind Closed Doors* (Red Heart Pictures, 1980), *This Woman is Not a Car* (Arid Zone Productions, 1982), and *Nice Coloured Girls* (Ronin Films, 1987).[10] The women who made these films have varied creative work lives which continue today, making any categorisation of their work limiting. Collectively, their work includes art, film (in many forms), activism, theatre, photography and performance. The Sydney Filmmakers Co-operative distributed *We Aim to Please, Size 10* and *Behind Closed Doors.* Released when this Co-op was in decline, *This Woman is Not a Car* and *Nice Coloured Girls* were distributed

---

8 For example, see: Alison Bartlett and Margaret Henderson, "What is a feminist object? Feminist material culture and the making of the activist object," *Journal of Australian Studies* 40, no. 2 (2016): 156–171; Alison Bartlett and Margaret Henderson, "The Australian Women's Movement goes to the museum: The 'Cultures of Australian Feminist Activism, 1970–1990' project," *Women's Studies International Forum* 37 (2013): 85–94; Catherine Kevin, "Creative work: Feminist representations of domestic violence in 1970s Australia," in *Everyday Revolutions: Gender, sexuality and society in 1970s Australia* ed. Michelle Arrow and Angela Woollacott (Canberra: ANU Press, forthcoming 2019). Petra Mosmann, "Encountering feminist things: Generations, interpretations and encountering Adelaide's 'scrap heap'," *Journal of Australian Studies* 40, no. 2 (2016): 172–189.

9 Felicity Collins, "Ties that bind: The psyche of feminist filmmaking: Sydney, 1969–1989" (PhD diss., University of Technology Sydney, 1995); Felicity Collins, "Film," in *Australian feminism: a companion* ed. Barbara Caine (Melbourne: Oxford University Press, 1998), 111–112.

10 *We Aim to Please.* Film. Robin Laurie and Margot Nash (Australia: 1976); *Size 10.* Film. Susan Lambert and Sarah Gibson (Australia: 1978); *Behind Closed Doors.* Film. Martha Ansara, Pat Fiske, Sarah Gibson, and Susan Lambert (Australia: 1980); *This woman is not a car.* Film. Margaret Dodd (Australia: 1982); *Nice Coloured Girls.* Film. Tracey Moffatt (Australia: 1987).

through the Australian Film Institute and were closely linked to art practices.[11] All the films had some government support in their production through the Experimental Film Fund, the Creative Development Branch and/or the Women's Film Fund of the Australian Film Commission.

Together, these films are part of the vibrant and creative history of women's liberation and feminism in Australia during the 1970s and 1980s.[12] To use historian Susan Magarey's terms, these activities can be understood as a cultural renaissance, cultural transformation and cultural disruption.[13] Additionally, talking and discussion were important within the women's liberation movement, particularly in consciousness-raising groups where personal politics were addressed and many participants felt, for the first time, "as if their lives *counted*".[14] Feminist films were created to inspire and encourage political discussions, and film screenings were about framing and enabling conversations. The women making and distributing these films were described in 1980 as "among the most active, purposeful, creative and productive" feminists working in the area of media and culture.[15] What these works collectively show is a recognition and examination of gender violence alongside a desire to share these creative works with others to broaden cultural and social action. These historical artefacts can readily be screened for new audiences, in different times and places, in a way that speaks to significant issues both past and present.

We Aim to Please

This 13-minute experimental film was made in 1976 by Margot Nash and Robin Laurie. The film explores sex, desire and violence while also questioning the operation of cinematic spectatorship. Laurie has recently spoken about the insurrectionary nature of the late 1970s, telling of her

---

11 John Hughes, "Work in progress: The rise and fall of the Australian filmmakers cooperatives, 1966–86," *Senses of Cinema*, no. 77 (2015), http://sensesofcinema.com/2015/australian-film-history/australian-filmmakers-co-operatives/#fn-25650-9.

12 For example, see: Bartlett and Henderson, "The Australian women's movement"; Catriona Moore, "The more things change… Feminist aesthetics, then and now," *Artlink* 33, no. 3 (2013): 22; Catriona Moore, *Indecent Exposures: Twenty Years of Australian Feminist Photography* (Sydney: Allen & Unwin, 1994).

13 Susan Magarey, "Feminism as cultural renaissance," *Hecate* 30, no. 1 (2004): 231–246.

14 Kristin Henry and Marlene Derlet, *Talking Up a Storm, Nine Women and Consciousness-Raising* (Sydney: Hale and Iremonger, 1993), x.

15 Barbara Hall, "How will be lean to remember tomorrow? A catalogue of independent women's films," *Lip: A Feminist Journal of Women in the Visual and Performing Arts* (1980): 128.

interest in feminism, history and surrealism. At that time, she and Nash could be fearless and unafraid in their political activism.[16] This sense of confidence and assertiveness is evident throughout their short film.

The film opens with the question "is the camera rolling?" Nash and Laurie stand naked in front of the camera, initially laughing. They directly address the viewer, saying the "ideal spectator is always assumed to be male and the image of woman designed to flatter him" (figure 1). Audio and visual are purposefully disjointed, with fragmented images presented throughout the film. Nash and Laurie put on makeup in an exaggerated manner, rendering them like unkempt clowns rather than "pretty" or "feminine" women. Sequences such as this are at times playful, yet also have serious consequences. The audience hears one of the filmmakers making increasingly aggressive demands for the women onscreen to smile.[17]

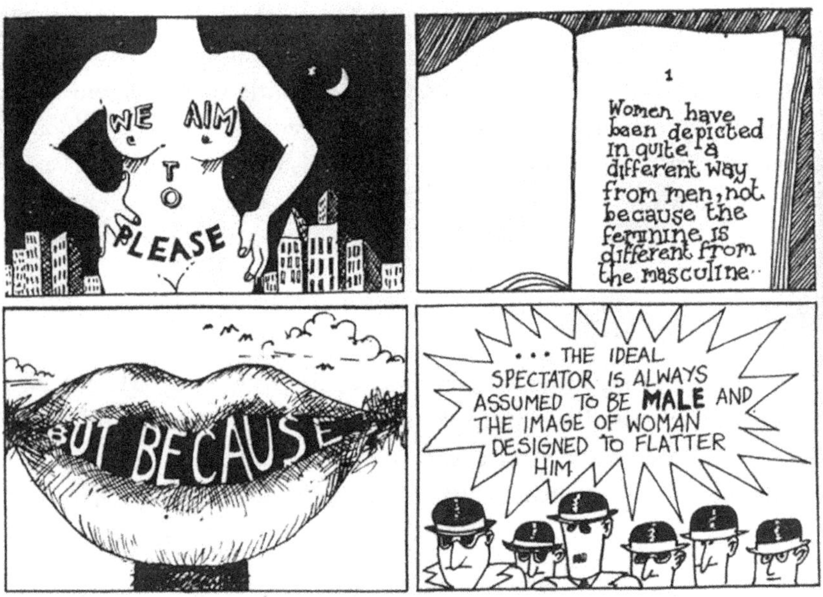

Figure 1. Graphic explaining the gendered nature of spectatorship presented in *We Aim to Please* (1976).
Graphic by Carol Porter.
Reproduced with permission from Margot Nash and Robin Laurie.

16 Robin Laurie, "'We Aim To Please' at a 'The Form That Accommodates The Mess': A series of film screenings at Institute of Modern Art, Brisbane, November 2014," *Margot Nash: As If Productions,* accessed 11 June 2018, http://www.margotnash.com/we-aim-to-please.

17 See: "We Aim to Please (1976)," *Australian Screen*, National Film and Sound Archive, https://aso.gov.au/titles/shorts/we-aim-to-please/.

Vulnerability and violence are themes which are present throughout the film. In one particularly brutal representation, an unseen person wielding a beer bottle viciously attacks and destroys a watermelon inscribed with the words "FUCK ME". The accompanying audio is not clearly decipherable: it seems to be, in part, a scratchy CB radio exchange in which male voices, as well as references to the "Royal Melbourne Hospital" and "police will be there as soon as possible," are heard. This is a stark representation of violence in which the obscured sound is disconcerting. But as fellow filmmaker Susan Lambert notes, viewers are not left "feeling frightened and powerless". Instead, Nash and Laurie shout "that they won't be intimidated and are determined to change the power relationships inherent in capitalism and sexual politics".[18] The film's response to the violence captures the energy and excitement of the era (figure 2).

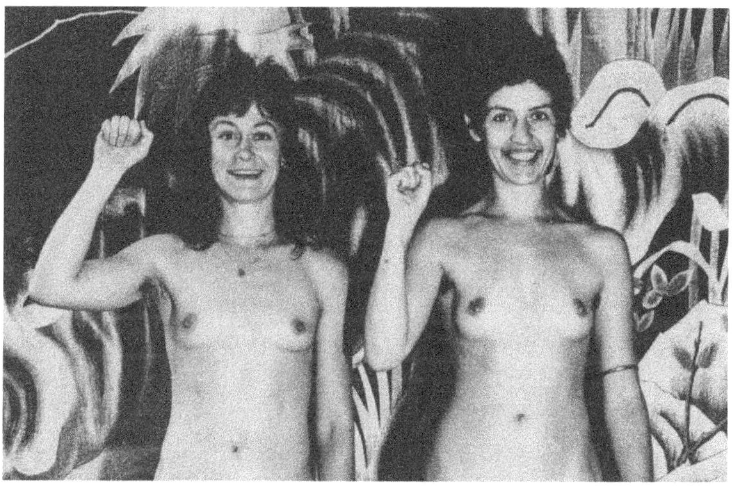

Figure 2. Robin Laurie and Margot Nash in *We Aim to Please*.
Reproduced with permission from Margot Nash and Robin Laurie.

Towards the film's end, the audience sees closeups of the filmmakers' body parts – breasts and genitals – surrounded by plants. There is laughter as well as concern in their voices. As Collins suggests, this is a key scene that is aware of its creation as a performance; the filmmakers are performers and the film is part of answering back to the cinematic male gaze.[19] Viewers are positioned to see the humour and creativity in this response to female objectification, as well as to the violence women experience.

18 Susan Lambert, "Curator's notes," in "We Aim to Please."

19 Collins, "Ties that bind," 74–75.

Size 10

Susan Lambert and Sarah Gibson's 1978 film focuses on four women's understandings, feelings and experiences of their bodies in relation to a socially idealised size 10.[20] The film depicts the women's naked bodies, sometimes as a whole but also with attention towards specific body parts. The women discuss how they feel and understand these parts of their bodies. The audience sees and hears these naked women smiling, laughing *and* using their bodies. Made in a consciousness-raising form as a purposeful prompt for viewer discussion, *Size 10* became one of the most-rented films from the Sydney Filmmakers' Cooperative and the Australian Film Institute.[21]

A specific discussion of gender violence is part of one of the women's stories. She describes her understanding of her body, and her thoughts in observing a group of men and women at the beach: the men were active and the women were sitting passively. She felt the women did not know how to inhabit and use their seemingly weak bodies. This is related to her own sense of feeling "very powerless" as her body does not "have [the] muscles I should have". She recounts an experience from "the other night" when, walking down the street, a man stuck his hand around her bum and pinched it. She described being "completely powerless". Partly, she says, it was about being pregnant and concerned about being hit, but "I couldn't do anything because I just didn't have that sense of strength in myself". She links this sense of powerlessness to a lack of strength in her teenage years, saying: "when I could have been building muscles, instead [laughs] I was worried about my face and what I looked like".

This discussion of recent but non-spectacular violence, the final story recounted in the film, is accompanied by visuals of women having fun. It is placed next to joyous naked swimming in a pool, followed by the women, fully clothed, laughing and making faces in front of mirrors which distort their reflections. This is seen with the film's soundtrack of Australian singer Robyn Archer's country and western song about the idealised "Size 10" body.[22] The powerlessness the woman laments is articulated against visual representations of women enjoying their bodies. An experience of sexual violence in this context is presented as common, and framed alongside women using their bodies on their own terms.

---

20 See: "Size 10 (1978)," *Australian Screen*, National Film and Sound Archive, https://aso.gov.au/titles/documentaries/size-10/notes/.

21 Collins, "Film", 112; Pat Fiske, "Curator's notes," in "Size 10".

22 Fiske, "Curator's notes".

Behind Closed Doors

Released in 1980, this six-and-a-half-minute film explicitly deals with women's experiences of domestic violence. Viewers hear from women telling their experiences of men's violence. Historian Catherine Kevin has noted the film's significance as one feminist representation of domestic violence at a time when domestic violence had been newly cemented in feminist language, understandings and activism.[23]

The film is visually confined to one place: a bedroom. Initially in full colour, the room is well ordered and immaculate. Throughout, viewers are drawn towards particular aspects of the room – for example, handles on cupboards, the corner of a table, an ashtray, lamps, chairs, magazines and a neatly-made bed. During the course of the film, however, viewers begin to see the room very differently. It is disordered; objects, once in place, are strewn around the room. Images are no longer in full colour, but black and white, and then with blue and red tones. The movement and focus on parts of the room and furniture continues, yet the film ends with the room being shown as it was at the beginning, in full colour and with order restored.

The film's soundtrack begins with popular love songs but then shifts to what was described at the time as "mournful sax", as well as to the sounds of violence.[24] In contrast to *Size 10*, where the audience hears and sees the women tell their stories, in *Behind Closed Doors* the audience only hears the women narrate their experiences of violence. The filmmakers said that this "non-literal fusion of sound and image" was to "force attention away from women as victims".[25]

Filmmakers Martha Ansara, Pat Fiske, Sarah Gibson and Susan Lambert made *Behind Closed Doors* with the purpose of opening conversations.[26] A flyer for the film articulated the importance of discussion, calling it "a discussion starter about domestic violence. It questions the romanticised image of love and marriage and raises discussion of rape within marriage."[27] The

23 Kevin, "Creative work".

24 Jeni Thornley, "Age Before Beauty/Behind Closed Doors Red Heart Pictures," *Filmnews* (December 1980): 8.

25 Sarah Gibson and Susan Lambert from Application to Australian Film Commission (1984), in Annette Blonski, Barbara Creed and Freda Freiberg, ed. *Don't Shoot Darling! Women's Independent Filmmaking in Australia* (Melbourne: Greenhouse Publications, 1987), 199; Jane Madsen, "Listening at closed doors: A consideration of the use of sound in *Behind Closed Doors*," in *Don't Shoot Darling!*, 323–327.

26 "Behind Closed Doors," *Filmnews* (November 1980): 13.

27 Rouge Papers, Accession no. 2003/218, film folder, box 2 Victorian Women's Liberation and Lesbian Feminist Archive, University of Melbourne Archives.

film was also part of a screening and discussion day about domestic violence and rape at the Sydney Filmmakers Co-op in 1980. The event was for feminists working in these areas or interested in using films for discussion as well as women filmmakers who were "struggling with the problems of portraying these issues in film".[28] A report in *Filmnews* focused on the significance of the film dispelling myths around class and domestic violence alongside the depiction of domestic isolation. *Behind Closed Doors* was seen as having made a "positive contribution" circumventing "exploitation and voyeurism that often comes with seeing the victims of domestic violence on screen".[29]

Such an exploration of a then "taboo [subject]" constituted a significant creative and public intervention, and through this viewers were encouraged to consider the gendered nature of domestic violence.[30] The back of the film's publicity flier provided a list of "discussion points" for groups viewing the film.[31] These questions placed domestic violence in a complex web of relationships of power and influence, which are also constructed cinematically. As fellow feminist filmmaker Jeni Thornley wrote in 1980, in addition to generating discussion, the film "exists on its own merits and is a superb cinematic piece".[32]

A key moment in the film centres on violence and sex. The women explicitly discuss experiences of extreme violence, after which their male partners want to have sex. One woman understands the men as thinking sex "makes everything better". Another says, "If you don't give in, like they end up raping you, [quickly] oh you can't really call it rape because [pause] you **can** because you've been bashed beforehand and they're taking what they want." Murmurs of agreement can be heard; the conversation continues, relating what the women see men as thinking. "Sex comes with marriage," one suggests, "so I demand my rights and you've got to give it to me, it doesn't matter how you feel". This is followed by a closeup of the end of a belt and the lattice of the bed head, looking more like the walls of a cage or fence.

The dangers of what can happen within this marital bedroom are revealed through these women's stories, together with the aftermath of violence depicted by fragmented shots of the bedroom. Throughout the film as well as the upbeat love songs, viewers hear (in the background) glass smashing

---

28 "What's on where," *Filmnews* (November 1980): 4.

29 Joy Toma, "On the offensive," *Filmnews* (January 1981): 6.

30 Janet Merewether, "Fuck the mainstream," in *WomenVision: Women and the Moving Image in Australia*, ed. Lisa French (Melbourne: Damned Publishing, 2003), 135.

31 Rouge Papers, Accession no. 2003/218, film folder, box 2.

32 Thornley, "Age before beauty," 8.

and what sounds like someone banging on a door. In words, sounds and images, women's experiences of domestic violence are not only represented and discussed, but action is also taken. The audience knows that these women left their partners and the homes where violence occurred. In this historical creative artefact, past conversations and interpretations of how feminists understood gender violence and presented it to the broader community are preserved.[33]

A utopian vision for the creation, distribution and influence of feminist films such as these is illustrated in Lee Whitmore's 1986 cartoon.[34] It shows Sydney redrawn with filmmaking at the city's foundation. The Feminist Film Workers house is on one side, while the Sydney Women's Film Group at the Sydney Filmmakers Co-op is on the other. Filmmakers including Ansara, Fiske, Gibson and Lambert were members of the former. Later, Ansara, Gibson and Lambert became members of the Feminist Film Workers, a closed group established in 1978 which wanted to foster closer links to the women's liberation movement.[35] From both of these buildings, cans of film are emerging and being delivered around Australia and the world. The city is populated almost entirely by active women, in a community centered around a women's liberation banner and surrounded by feminist organisations. The place of women's active responses to gender violence is clearly present. A women's refuge both acknowledges the existence of and feminist-led responses to domestic violence.[36]

This Woman is Not a Car

Artist Margaret Dodd's 1982 film features her "funk ceramic" FX Holden car series in a short, surreal, suburban horror film. It was made over the course of seven years (beginning in 1976) and explores the isolated place of a woman, who is a mother, in outer suburban Adelaide. The film follows the woman's day, as she takes a seemingly ever-increasing number of children to activities and shopping and then for a picnic at the beach. Domestic and maternal work is represented as depressing, and existing within an Australian masculine car-worshiping culture that sexualises women (and

33 Considering these sources as 'creative artefacts' is derived from Catherine Kevin, "Creative work".

34 Collins, "Ties that bind," 139.

35 Mary Tomsic, *Beyond the Silver Screen, A history of women, filmmaking and film culture in Australia 1920–1990* (Melbourne: Melbourne University Press, 2017), 177–207.

36 For women's refuges, see Jacqui Theobald and Suellen Murray's chapter in this volume.

cars) in violent ways.[37] Violence and women's dehumanisation is central to the narrative. Dodd described one of her car sculptures, which feature in the film, as "very smart" but with its "bottom ripped out … very destroyed … and attacked – raped".[38]

The film moves between reality and imagination. It includes a sexual fantasy at a petrol station where one of the mechanics, who is filling the woman's car with petrol, is having sex with the car (and/or the woman, who earlier revealed a breast to be a car part). The sex becomes violent, with a woman's voice saying "stop" and screaming a number of times, while men's voices are heard laughing while cars are revving. This sexual violence is linked to a wedding scene, where a knife repeatedly stabs at a wedding cake and a red blood filter overlays a wedding photograph. The film concludes with the woman in a hospital delivery suite where she gives birth to a ceramic Holden sculpture. The intertitle reminds viewers, "This woman is not a car".

"The woman character is trapped inside this male-dominated culture," Lambert writes. "But the filmmaker is not."[39] As Collins suggests, this "surreal journey into sexual desire" is seen through "hilarious, violent and fantastic manifestations".[40] Such a representation was not welcomed by all. It was reported that a 1984 screening in England at the Tyneside Film Festival had the audience "somewhat scandalised" and "some thought it should be banned!"[41] From a historical perspective, however, Dodd's use of fantasy effectively explores the position of women in Australian life as one that includes sexual violence at its core. *This Woman is Not a Car*, like *We Aim to Please*, provides space for viewers to consider how violence is linked to the demands placed on women within the white suburban Australian dream.

Nice Coloured Girls

Tracey Moffatt's 17-minute film, released in 1987, depicts the contemporary urban action of three Indigenous women in Kings Cross, Sydney. Two of the women "pick up" a Captain, a white man that Moffatt descried as "just a sucker, a slob" rather than a stereotypical white baddie intent on

37 Collins, "Ties that bind," 261.

38 "Margaret Dodd talking with Julie Ewington," *Lip: A Feminist Journal of Women in the Visual and Performing Arts* (1978-9): 37.

39 "This woman is not a car (1982)," *Australian Screen*, National Film and Sound Archives, https://aso.gov.au/titles/shorts/this-woman-is-not-a-car/notes/.

40 Collins, "Ties that bind," 261; Jennifer Stott, "Celluloid maidens: All teched-up and nowhere to go," *Don't Shoot Darling!*, 17.

41 "Making waves new currents in world cinema," *Filmnews* (March 1984): 4.

exploiting black women.[42] The women guide the Captain to finance their night out, ultimately stealing his wallet and making their escape. This narrative is interspersed with aural excerpts from men's colonial diaries and writings about Indigenous women. The aural excerpts accompany stark and dramatically staged visual representations featuring Indigenous women.

Nice Coloured Girls disputes conventional historical narratives. Moffatt's film vividly challenges both historical and contemporary understandings of Indigenous women's personal autonomy and sexual activities.[43] Its advertising flyer described it as "one of the first films to actively confront sex and racism". Upon release, it was noted that the film was not commensurate with demands from some parts of Indigenous communities to portray Black women "positively", as it depicted Indigenous women using their desirability to exploit a white man.[44] Moffatt responded by saying this "demand annoys me ... because we're not little angels".[45]

Indigenous studies scholar Marcia Langton argues that a concern about "negative" portrayals has acted as a "conservative restraint on Aboriginal creativity".[46] Representing Indigenous women "negatively" was also seen as threatening in the feminist and academic communities, including for readers of the women's liberation and academic journal *Hecate*. A *Hecate* film review, which was glowing overall, came with a lengthy concluding "disclaimer" that *Nice Coloured Girls* is "not an easy film to watch".[47] The possible problems it may cause for viewers included potential alienation by an endorsement of exploitation. It was also seen as a revenge story or a

---

42 Moffatt quoted in Lyndell Fairleigh, "Challenging images of Aboriginal women," *Tribune*, no. 2 (September 1987): 13.

43 E. Ann Kaplan, "Aborigines, film and Moffatt's *'Night Cries: A Rural Tragedy'*: An outsider's perspectives," *Bulletin of the Olive Pink Society* 1, no. 2 (1989): 15. This is also seen in relation to Moffatt's *Night Cries: A Rural Tragedy* (1990), see: Meagan Morris, "Beyond assimilation: Aboriginality, media history and public memory," *Aedon: Melbourne University Literary Arts Review* 4, no. 1 (1996): 15.

44 Fairleigh, "Challenging images of Aboriginal women"; Kaplan, "Aborigines, film and Moffatt's *'Night Cries'*," 15. Lisa French suggests this political climate was applicable to all women. Lisa French, "An analysis of *Nice Coloured Girls*," *Senses of Cinema*, no. 5 (2000), http://sensesofcinema.com/2000/australian-cinema-5/nice/.

45 Fairleigh, "Challenging images of Aboriginal women".

46 Marcia Langton, *"Well, I Heard it on the Radio and I saw it on the Television... ": An essay for the AFC on the Politics and Aesthetics of Filmmaking by and about Aboriginal People and Things* (Sydney: Australian Film Commission, 1993), 43.

47 Karen Jennings and David Hollinsworth, "Ways of seeing and speaking about Aboriginal women: II. Shy maids and wanton strumpets," *Hecate* 13, no. 2 (1987/88): 133.

tale of "urban terrorism" which reinforced negative stereotypes of "amoral" Aboriginal women, and its anti-realist techniques could be difficult and confusing.[48]

As with other feminist films, here Moffatt presented women onscreen as active, not passive. *Nice Coloured Girls* "doesn't portray black women as victims, for once," she emphasised, "it portrays them as survivors".[49] This is particularly salient in relation to how the film presents women's past and present experiences of gender violence. In the contemporary narrative, the women explain through the intertitles, the Captains "usually like to drink a lot and we like to encourage them." The women's repulsion at such behaviour is clear – they look at the Captain with disgust when he is drunkenly slumped on the dinner table. The Italian restaurant is a bustling venue and Dean Martin's signature 1953 song "That's A'more" completes the scene. Their narration via the written intertitle emphasises the importance of ensuring the Captain is drunk: "This way they're more helpless and less likely to get nasty with us. If you know what we mean."

The next scene features an Indigenous woman leaning across the screen. Viewers see her head, neck and parts of her shoulders. Her hair covers her face. A white man's hands, dug into her head, hold her down. The previous scenes, with narrative intertitles, are mostly jovial despite the Captain's drunken state; the image of the woman being held down is presented in silence. This provides a clear space to stop and take in this photographic-like image of violence, so that viewers know exactly what the women mean. The Indigenous women's active management of violence is clear. They steal the captain's wallet and make a fast getaway, first on foot and then by taxi. They are the heroines of this successful heist, but the threat of violence is ever-present, and one they manage effectively.

Conclusion

In different ways, all of these films were part of feminist-led public conversations about gender violence during the 1970s and 1980s. As creative responses to the forms of sexual violence women experienced, these films are interesting to consider in relation to the current online spaces that are being used to speak out about and protest against sexual violence. For this first generation of feminist filmmakers, as well as those using social media

48 Ibid.

49 Peter Hackett, "Tracey wants to picture blacks in right light," *Adelaide Advertiser*, in March 1988, *Nice Coloured Girls* file, AFI Research Collection, RMIT University.

today, one objective is to generate conversations. While these take different forms for film and online, each is nonetheless about talking, understanding and creating action for change. The places and spaces for such conversations, however, are starkly different. Previously, audiences physically attended film screenings and the program was intentionally curated. The feminist control of form, content and distribution was significant. This is in stark contrast to social media platforms today which, although relatively accessible, are commercial spaces where misogyny and violence towards women are commonplace.[50]

The creative feminist storytelling in the films considered in this chapter effectively use sound, visual imagery and imagination to develop hopeful depictions of women's experiences of and responses to violence. Violence is a force linked to understandings of nation, beauty, self, relationships and autonomy. Many of the women's stories, whether real or imagined, render them victims of gender violence. And yet, in no way could it be said that they contain a "vain hope of revolution".[51] The desire and plan for feminist rebellion is clear. This woman-centred revolution, at times humourous and irreverent, understood that violence was a reality women faced and showed their active role working against it. Many feminist films have been publicly screened recently in Sydney at the Future Feminist Archive in March 2015 and during the 2017 Sydney Film Festival.[52] Through events such as these, it is possible to see new audiences forming to engage with the hopeful cultural activism and political expression created in the past, and from this vital conversations can continue.

---

50 For example, see: Emma Alice Jane, "'Back to the kitchen, cunt': Speaking the unspeakable about online misogyny," *Continuum* 28, no. 4 (2014): 558–570; Sarah Banet-Weiser and Kate M Miltner, "#MasculinitySoFragile: Culture, structure, and networked misogyny," *Feminist Media Studies* 16, no. 1 (2016): 171–174; Ana Stevenson and Brigitte Lewis's chapter in this volume.

51 Paloma, "Bodies in trouble".

52 "Future feminist archive," March 2017, *Sydney College of the Arts: The University of Sydney*, accessed 11 June 2018, http://sydney.edu.au/sca/galleries-events/future-feminist-archive/index.shtml; "Feminism & film: Sydney women filmmakers, 1970s & 1980s," June 2017, *Sydney Film Festival*, accessed 13 June 2018, https://web.archive.org/web/20170601061312/http://www.sff.org.au/2017-film-guide/feminism-film-sydney-women-filmmakers-1970s-1980s/.

Chapter 14

DOMESTIC VIOLENCE ACTIVISM IN VICTORIA, 1974–2016

Jacqui Theobald and Suellen Murray

During the 1970s, feminists and women's liberationists in the state of Victoria and across Australia established women's refuges to pursue the eradication of domestic violence. The refuge movement politicised domestic violence by drawing attention to the women and children seeking emergency accommodation and the difficulties they faced in consequence.[1] This chapter focuses on the movement's shifting advocacy strategies between the 1970s and 2010s. It considers how the movement influenced social policy and political processes concerning domestic violence, paying particular attention to the contemporary context from the 1990s onwards. Over time, this chapter reveals, the Victorian women's refuge movement has developed to embrace a degree of sophistication and diversity of advocacy strategy akin to that outlined by sociologist Claire Reinelt, in that it incorporates "participatory and bureaucratic elements, outside and

---

1 The Australian women's refuge movement adopted the phrase "domestic violence" from the late 1970s. This chapter primarily uses "domestic violence" to describe intimate partner violence. More recently, "family violence" has become the Victorian state government's preferred terminology to acknowledge that perpetrators can be other family and community members. Typically, "women's refuges" are now talked about in terms of domestic and family violence services (rather than "refuges" or "shelters" as they are known in some Australian states), reflecting the much greater diversity in services now available. This chapter employs the phrase "Victorian women's refuge movement" when referring to earlier periods and "domestic violence services movement" to reflect the sector's changes over time.

inside political strategies, grassroots mobilisation and organising within institutions".[2]

Scholars have documented the effects of diversity on feminist women's services, including domestic violence organisations, from their experiences of internal division to working together to achieve change despite considerable external pressures, such as the impact of economic rationalism.[3] But such analyses largely pertain to the movement's earlier years.[4] This chapter demonstrates the enduring nature of the collaborative advocacy of the domestic violence services movement and contributes further to understandings of these processes in the contemporary context.[5] While domestic violence activism has been largely collaborative in these later years, a

2 Claire Reinelt, "Moving onto the terrain of the state: The battered women's movement and the politics of engagement," in *Feminist Organisations: Harvest of the New Women's Movement*, ed. Myra Marx Ferree and Patricia Yancey Martin (Philadelphia: Temple University Press, 1995), 90.

3 Wendy Weeks, ed. *Women Working Together: Lessons from Feminist Women's Services* (Melbourne: Longman Cheshire, 1994); Roselyn Melville, "The external organisational environment and organisational survival and change," *Third Sector Review* 1 (1995): 65–77; Ronnie Egan and Lesley Hoatson, "Desperate to survive: Contracting women's services in Melbourne," *Australian Feminist Studies* 14, no. 30 (1999): 405–414; Marian Sawer, "Governing for the mainstream: Implications for community representation," *Australian Journal of Public Administration* 61, no. 1 (2002): 39–49; John McDonald, "Neo-liberalism and the pathologising of public issues: The displacement of feminist service models in domestic violence support services," *Australian Social Work* 58, no. 3 (2005): 275–284; Merrindahl Andrew and Kirsty McLaren, "Damaged but determined: The Australian women's movement, 1996–2007," *Social Movement Studies* 9, no. 2 (2010) 171–185; Jacqui Theobald, Suellen Murray with Judith Smart, *From the Margins to the Mainstream: The Domestic Violence Services Movement in Victoria, Australia, 1974–2016* (Melbourne: Melbourne University Press, 2017), 86–100, 120–128, 203–229.

4 Liz Orr, "The women's refuge movement in Victoria," in *Women Working Together: Lessons from Feminist Women's Services*, ed. Wendy Weeks (Melbourne: Longman Cheshire, 1994); Suellen Murray, *More than Refuge: Changing Responses to Domestic Violence* (Perth: University of Western Australia Press, 2002); Adele Murdolo, "Safe homes for immigrant and refugee women: Narrating alternative histories of the women's refuge movement in Australia," *Frontiers: A Journal of Women Studies* 35, no. 3 (2014): 126–153; Theobald et al, *From the Margins*.

5 Ludo McFerran, "Interpretation of a frontline State: Australian women's refuges and the State," in *Playing the State: Australian Feminist Interventions*, ed. Sophie Watson (Sydney: Allen & Unwin 1990); Heather McGregor and Andrew Hopkins, *Working for Change: The Movement Against Domestic Violence* (Sydney: Allen & Unwin 1991); Jacqui Theobald, "Women's refuges and the State in Victoria, Australia: A campaign for secrecy of address," *Women's History Review* 23, no. 1 (2014) 60–81.

particular shift in tactics was used as "a last resort" to achieve change in the 2010s, in part through the adoption of confrontational advocacy strategies.[6]

This chapter canvasses the key opportunities and challenges that emerged from the Victorian movement's state engagement. Historian Ann Curthoys has noted how much of the literature on the Australian women's movement "concentrates on ... its close relationship with the government as a means of achieving its ends".[7] A close relationship with "the state" has certainly characterised the domestic violence services movement for much of its existence, while feminist scholars have analysed the "risks" for feminist organisations which enter into funding and contractual arrangements with governments.[8] However, the assumption that state engagement will necessarily be detrimental and is anti-feminist assumes the state is "a coherent unity" and lacks reflection on the "dynamics of power", such as the preparedness of bureaucrats to support the refuge movement's social change agenda.[9] Indeed, Carol Bacchi has argued against seeing "the state as a body operating either for or against claimant groups".[10]

We agree with Reinelt's view: involvement with state institutions has political risks, but can also "create political opportunities for transforming institutional practices and furthering a feminist agenda".[11] Collaborative advocacy strategies — particularly those directed at the state — have been enduring and productive, resulting in considerable benefits for domestic violence services. Key achievements have included: the enshrinement of feminist principles in state government programs and policy; funding for services; cross-government and community sector collaboration and coalition building, resulting in integrated approaches to tackling domestic violence and changing public perceptions.

---

6 Although refuges were sometimes understood by women experiencing domestic violence to be "the last resort", this chapter utilises a different meaning of this term—the nature of the political activities of the domestic violence activists. See: Vivien Johnson, *The Last Resort: A Women's Refuge* (Melbourne: Penguin, 1981).

7 Ann Curthoys, "Doing it for themselves: The women's movement since 1970," in *Gender Relations in Australia: Domination and Negotiation*, ed. Kay Saunders and Raymond Evans (Sydney: Harcourt Brace Jovanovich, 1992), 425–445.

8 Anna Yeatman, *Bureaucrats, Technocrats, Femocrats: Essays on the Contemporary Australian State* (Sydney: Allen & Unwin, 1990); Marian Sawer and Gwendolyn G. Jamieson, "The women's movement and government: Feminist fading," *Australian Feminist Studies* 29, no. 82 (2014): 403–418.

9 Rosemary Pringle and Sophie Watson, "Fathers, brothers, mates: The fraternal state in Australia," in *Playing the State*, 229; Reinelt, "Moving onto the terrain," 99.

10 Carol Bacchi, "Rolling back the state: Feminism, theory and policy," in *Women, Public Policy and the State*, ed. Linda Hancock (Melbourne: Macmillan, 1999), 57.

11 Reinelt, "Moving onto the terrain," 100.

Background and context

Women's refuges in Victoria formed part of an Australian and international movement that began within the women's liberation movement and identified domestic violence as gendered.[12] Similar movements also developed in Britain, the United States and Canada during the 1970s.[13] Significantly, these movements argued for a powerful re-framing of the causes of domestic violence. Dominant understandings interpreted such violence as arising from the nature of individual men and women, whereas feminists emphasised unequal gender relations in society. In Victoria, as well as nationally, Australia's radical feminist refuges played a significant role in this conceptual reframing process.[14]

The refuge movement, like the broader women's movement, incorporated activists of differing ideological persuasions. Not all organisations were necessarily feminist. However, in 1974, Victoria's first refuge emerged from the women's liberation movement with a radical feminist plan for social revolution.[15] Committed to empowerment and special rights for women, this refuge sought to create social change. Their ideas influenced other refuges and, by the end of 1979, there were sixteen throughout Victoria. The state's refuges united under the auspice of the Victorian Women's Refuge Group (VWRG). By 1976, however, radical feminist refuges were often in conflict with ideologically different organisations, such as religious groups and government funding bodies, which also provided refuges and therefore appeared as a threat to their autonomy.[16] Like other radical feminist organisations, the Victorian refuge movement favoured autonomous institutions outside the mainstream during the 1970s and the 1980s. Radical feminists were suspicious of government or other conservative organisations and viewed any work in partnership as depoliticising their

---

12 Theobald et al, *From the Margins*, 16–52; Murray, *More than Refuge*; Orr, "The women's refuge movement in Victoria."

13 Erin Pizzey, *Scream Quietly or the Neighbours will Hear* (Harmondsworth: Penguin, 1974); Gillian Walker, *Family Violence and the Women's Movement: The Conceptual Politics of Struggle* (Toronto: University of Toronto Press, 1990), 21–35; Reinelt, "Moving onto the terrain of the state," 83.

14 Jacqui Theobald, "The beginnings of the Victorian women's refuge movement: Difference, equality and protectionism, 1974–1979," *Lilith: A Feminist History Journal* 21 (2015): 48–62.

15 Ibid., 53–56.

16 Theobald, "Women's refuges and the State in Victoria," 60–81.

social change agenda.[17] The issue of government control over feminist organisations more broadly was a contentious public debate.[18]

The women's refuge movement undertook political activity publicly, with the aim of redressing the lack of resources available to women. Radical feminist refuges argued that this should be the main objective for the refuge movement.[19] Confrontational direct action tactics were fundamental to the VWRG, which undertook street marches, street theatre, sit-ins and squatting in order to raise awareness.[20] Collaborative tactics, such as direct lobbying of government, was also adopted as a core advocacy strategy. This enabled feminist principles to be enshrined in the state government program and policy development pertaining to women's refuges.[21]

By the end of the 1970s, the divide between those who argued for and against state involvement was less obvious because refuges desperately needed financial assistance. However, throughout the 1980s, radical feminists maintained their reluctance to engage with the state and were committed to confrontational direct action tactics. Such tactics were designed to influence public perceptions of domestic violence as well as to address the inadequacy of government funding. Refuges more aligned with conservative or liberal feminist values saw engagement with the state as critical to achieving political equality, as well as their capacity to obtain funding to provide a good quality service to support women individually. These groups prioritised policy change over campaigning for political and social change and, by the mid-1980s, began adopting collaborative advocacy strategies that involved participating in government steering committees and research projects designed to inform social policy and program development in relation to domestic violence.[22]

Ideological differences among Victorian refuges were negotiated internally through the development of two groups — a radical Caucus and a

---

17 Kaye Hargreaves, interviewed by Jacqui Theobald, 7 May 2008; Theobald, "Women's refuges".

18 Victorian Women's Refuges Group, "A paper on women's refuges in Victoria," Victorian Women's Refuges Group State Conference, Melbourne, October 1979, Maggie Burrows papers, 93/15, University of Melbourne Archives.

19 Ulla Svensson for the Women's Liberation Halfway House, "Women's refuges are no solution," Opening Address of National Women's Refuge Conference, Melbourne, 17–19 November 1982. Ulla Svensson private papers, in possession of Jacqui Theobald. Collection now held in Melbourne Women's Liberation and Lesbian Feminist Archives. AN2012.0002, no. 151.

20 Theobald et al, *From the Margins*, 37.

21 Theobald, "Women's refuges," 69–70.

22 Theobald et al, *From the Margins*, 61–63.

conservative Coalition — which allowed them to achieve compromise and present a unified position in negotiating with state bureaucrats.[23] As long-term domestic violence services worker Wendy Austin reflects, working together and sharing information also enhanced their capacity for advocacy:

> Bit by bit the work that was being done by both of them came together in quite a good way because you'd go off to government and they'd say "well show me … is this true? Give me the story", and we could.[24]

A key political opportunity harvested from collaborative strategies and state engagement included the development of reciprocal relationships with feminist bureaucrats who supported women's refuges. These bureaucrats incorporated feminist framings of domestic violence into policy and program development, and provided them a degree of autonomy in relation to their administration.[25] As former bureaucrat Marg D'Arcy recalled: "The people in the department … were actually quite committed to maintaining the refuge program and to being able to fund it properly. It wasn't a hostile bureaucracy".[26]

Surviving the 1990s

The economic rationalist environment of the 1990s produced enormous risks for feminist women's services as a consequence of their engagement with conservative governments. Services faced competitive tendering, techniques to enforce "accountable management", under-funding, and the promotion of individualised service responses. Domestic violence services also dealt with countless administrative and organisational demands from government, including expanding their service delivery — without additional financial support.[27] Victoria's new conservative government defunded non-government services at an alarming rate, which severely affected domestic violence services. As former refuge activist Hanna Kaiser pointed out:

> [S]o many people had lost their jobs and so many organisations lost their funding. That meant that for us working at Halfway House all the resources that we had used to tap women into and so on, were no

23 Wendy Austin, interviewed by Jacqui Theobald, 15 October 2007; Marg D'Arcy, interviewed by Jacqui Theobald, 6 October 2008.

24 Austin interview.

25 Tony Newman, interviewed by Jacqui Theobald, 9 February 2009; D'Arcy interview.

26 D'Arcy interview.

27 Theobald et al, *From the Margins*, 86–100.

> longer there. That made a huge difference in terms of how we were able to support women.[28]

Services necessarily focussed on survival. Their capacity to be openly critical of government, operate autonomously and undertake political protest was undermined. As such, confrontational tactics were not publicly adopted.

This period also saw the reduction of protest as characteristic of the Australian women's movement more broadly.[29] The lack of reciprocity with the state meant domestic violence services survived by adopting "outsider" advocacy strategies that included lobbying government directly for funding. This resulted in continued funding of women's refuges because of their sustained engagement with members of parliament. This included women from the Victorian Liberal-National Party Coalition government, the main conservative political party from whom they received support.[30] In a more confrontational style — albeit behind closed doors — refuge services refused to sign service agreements because the government declined to fund the community development component of their work.[31] In this sense, services stood up against attempts to change the nature of their work – from dealing with both the individual and structural factors underpinning domestic violence to an approach that increasingly focused on the individual – a goal that was characteristic of women's services more broadly.[32] More commonly though, and in keeping with the now-dominant liberal feminist approach, they implored government to work in partnership in a manner that was conducive to developing trust.[33]

The growth in diversity of domestic violence organisations combined with demands from government led to a growing need for increased cooperation. The incorporation of a new peak body in 1992 — the Victorian Women's Refuges and Associated Domestic Violence Services (VWRADVS) — and its constitution was an internal strategy designed to reduce division among members and promote a unified voice.[34] The influence of liberal feminists

28 Hanna Kaiser, interviewed by Jacqui Theobald, 28 August 2008.

29 Andrew and McLaren, "Damaged but determined," 173; Sawer and Andrew, "Hiding in plain sight," 70.

30 Vig Geddes, interviewed by Jacqui Theobald, 24 October 2007; Natalie Tomas, interviewed by Jacqui Theobald, 26 September 2008.

31 Theobald et al, *From the Margins*, 95.

32 Sawer and Jamieson, "The women's movement and government," 406.

33 Theobald et al, *From the Margins*, 108.

34 Julie Oberin for Victorian Women's Refuges and Associated Domestic Violence Services, "The future of VWRADVS as an effective peak-body for women's domestic violence services in Victoria," October 1997, Brenda House papers, University of Melbourne Archives, AN 2012.0238.

in the formation of VWRADVS was evident through their leadership of affiliated subgroups and commitment to lobbying for legal reform.

Throughout the decade, various other collaborative advocacy strategies were adopted in response to the immediate threat posed to the survival of women's services. The domestic violence services movement, like the Australian women's movement more broadly, continued to operate "via submerged networks ... within and between groups" and undertook numerous coalition-building activities.[35] For example, alliances were forged between domestic violence services and other feminist women's services with the aim of promoting collaborative ways of working together. A growing willingness to build coalitions with organisations outside women's services — particularly those in the legal system —characterised the movement's increasing recognition of the benefits of achieving reform within the system through awareness raising and education via participation in countless committees and taskforces.[36]

More generally, the women's movement organisations of the 1990s are considered to have become "less effective as a political base for feminist initiatives in government".[37] While this is true of the Victorian domestic violence services movement, it did not — as some would suggest — give up confronting the government and politicising the issues. Despite the threatening and competitive environment, the women's services opposed when they could and challenged where possible, particularly in relation to funding threats. Over time, they began to work in greater cooperation in order to survive.[38] Marian Sawer and Merrindahl Andrew similarly contend that active coalition building among Australian women's non-government organisations challenges the widely held view that the women's movement was necessarily weaker during this period.[39]

"Partnering" the State in the 2000s

Under the state's social democratic Australian Labor Party government, progressive policy development during the 2000s saw a range of public policy initiatives specifically designed to tackle inequality and promote the

35 Andrew and McLaren, "Damaged but determined," 175; Sawer and Andrew, "Hiding in plain sight," 83.

36 Theobald et al, *From the Margins*, 109–110.

37 Sawer and Jamieson, "The women's movement and government," 405.

38 Theobald et al, *From the Margins*, 82–112.

39 Sawer and Andrew, "Hiding in plain sight," 83.

safety of Victorian women. Strategies to tackle domestic violence became part of a broader agenda to improve the status and equality of women. This period was also characterised by an approach to public administration that reflected the Labor government's commitment to "partnering" non-government organisations.

The strategies and actions of the domestic violence services movement throughout the 2000s reflected the co-operative status of their relationship with government. Domestic violence activists began working in close collaboration with a wide range of government institutions in the context of an emerging integrated policy response. Liberal feminist methods characterised their work as they focussed attention on influencing public policy and mainstream organisations. Reflecting this "partnership" approach, VWRADVS accepted government funding for their newly constituted peak body, Domestic Violence Victoria (DVVic), in 2004. It was the culmination of a long campaign. As bureaucrat Alison Fraser confirms, "the sector had lobbied for years to get a funded peak".[40] It stemmed from a recognition of the need to formalise relationships between the movement and government. Further, it reflected a social policy context where responses to domestic violence were institutionalised — particularly through the allocation of funding for direct service provision. The decision also meant hierarchical decision-making processes were adopted, which signalled a further shift from radical feminist values regarding collective organisational structures.[41] However, like other women's advocacy organisations, consultative techniques under DVVic became enshrined in policy and practice.[42]

More generally, this marked a significant point of departure from the uncertain environment generated by the former conservative government of the 1990s. Opportunities emerged following the formalisation of a partnership with government and the adoption of "insider" strategies, including participation in the State-Wide Steering Committee to Reduce Family Violence (SSCRFV). Established by the Chief Commissioner of the Victoria Police Christine Nixon early in the decade, the SSCRFV progressed a whole-of-government integrated policy response to domestic violence through the development of a best-practice framework. While the movement's advocacy had resulted in many achievements, a proactive response from the police was something new. As former Victorian Labor MP Kay Setches observes: "You dreamt … [that] there'd be a police

40 Alison Fraser, interviewed by Jacqui Theobald, 22 April 2009.

41 Theobald et al, *From the Margins*, 126–127.

42 Sawer and Jamieson, "The women's movement and government," 407.

commissioner that would say, 'this is serious, and we're going to do something about it, and we're going to put resources into it, and I'm going to measure it'".[43]

The SSCRFV committee members included representatives from a range of government and non-government organisations, including various domestic violence organisations in addition to DVVic. By the middle of the decade, an important achievement stemming from the SSCRFV was a successful whole-of-government bid to improve funding for existing domestic violence services by $30 million.[44] Cross-government and community sector collaboration facilitated by SSCRFV was also critical to ensuring feminist framings of domestic violence continued to inform policy, including their incorporation in a government-funded risk assessment framework later rolled out across the community services sector and beyond.[45]

Alongside a partnership approach to working with government, the movement continued to adopt "outsider strategies" to achieve their goal of improved funding. A key tactic was the direct lobbying of ministers. When combined with "insider" strategies such as participating in the SSCRFV, the achievement of increased funding was enabled. There were other opportunities stemming from engaging the state and adopting "insider" tactics. For example, DVVic began strategically cultivating informal relationships with bureaucrats, who could safely seek advice and consultation while trusting that such information was not going to be circulated more broadly.[46] These kinds of non-participatory advocacy strategies enabled DVVic to promote "capacity building within government" and educate bureaucrats who sought advice about program and policy development.[47]

But engaging the state was not without challenges and risks. Indeed, throughout the 2000s, domestic violence services continued to receive inadequate funding, combined with growing demands for accountability, self-regulation and output-based funding measures.[48] The question of how to deal with these issues generated a degree of discord among member services. Some were wary of DVVic's engagement with the state and criticised their unwillingness to adopt militant protest tactics during negotiations with

43 Kay Setches, interviewed by Jacqui Theobald, 2 April 2009.

44 Theobald et al, *From the Margins*, 134–137.

45 Ibid., 143–144.

46 Fiona McCormack, interviewed by Jacqui Theobald and Suellen Murray, 23 June 2016.

47 McCormack interview.

48 Theobald et al, *From the Margins*, 120–125.

government.[49] Comparable challenges and criticisms faced domestic violence advocacy bodies internationally, as state engagement progressed similarly.[50]

However, DVVic's approach to advocacy reflected an increased level of sophistication that took account of the political context to inform decision-making. Radical confrontational advocacy tactics were likely to have undermined their capacity to influence social policy processes given the provision of support and leadership to tackle domestic violence across various arms of government.[51] "At that time, we had leadership from a range of ministers, the chief commissioner, and the department that coordinated the whole of government reform," CEO of DVVic Fiona McCormack explains. "We had a voice at the table and a committed partner in the Office of Women's Policy – if we had continued 'radical' approaches to advocacy in that context we would have been dismissed as a risk to government."[52]

Even so, DVVic was not averse to adopting radical-inspired protest tactics – but only when they considered the risks of not doing so outweighed the benefits of collaboration. For example, a decision by the Department of Human Services in 2005 to distribute new funding through a form of competitive tendering was widely seen to put domestic violence services under threat.[53] After attempts to prevent it failed, DVVic invited non-government members of the SSCRFV to step down alongside them in protest. However, such a decision was considered too risky by other non-government members of the committee. Consequently, McCormack recalls, DVVic was constrained in their ability "to advocate for member services".[54] Their status as a fledgling organisation with a limited profile and relationships across government further impeded this action. In response, DVVic adapted by altering their tactics and worked strategically in collaboration with other non-government organisations to ensure they influenced "criteria against which [government] decisions would be made" so that funded services were required to "demonstrate expertise in family violence services".[55] This advocacy process demonstrates how DVVic challenged normative institutional practices concerning the public management of human service organisations. The end result meant that

---

49 McCormack interview.

50 Reinelt, "Moving onto the terrain," 100.

51 Fiona McCormack, personal correspondence to Jacqui Theobald, 27 June 2017.

52 Ibid.

53 Ibid.

54 Ibid.

55 Ibid.

long-standing services — most of which incorporated feminist frameworks in relation to service delivery and practice — were re-funded and the family violence sector "didn't lose a service".[56]

By the middle of the decade, the movement began to pursue "outsider" strategies designed to extend their political reach and influence to the widest audience possible. Significantly, they sought to influence public perceptions of domestic violence and generate social change by working collaboratively with a coalition of organisations to influence the quality and extent of media reporting through a range of innovative strategies. This included: the development of resources to inform the media about family violence and the sector about working with the media; the establishment of the Eliminating Violence Against Women Media Awards (EVAs) in 2008, to celebrate reporting on violence against women; and training for women who had experienced domestic violence to be media advocates.[57]

While differences exist, there are some noteworthy similarities between the refuge movement of the 1970s and contemporary approaches to advocacy. Significantly, both pursued direct lobbying to ensure feminist principles were embedded and maintained in state government policy and programs. However, the criticism of DVVic reflected a widely-held view that contemporary advocacy strategies are "less radical than the early feminist organising efforts of the 1970s".[58] However, we contend that DVVic's achievement of transcending institutional norms reflected a radical agenda. This is particularly noteworthy, given the managerialist context in which it was achieved does not require "direct action" to be radical. It also meant that, when a significant political opportunity emerged in the form of a Royal Commission into Family Violence in the 2010s, their specialist knowledge and expertise was critical to informing its recommendations. Ultimately, this included nearly half a billion dollars' worth of investment to tackle domestic violence.

The achievements of the 2000s meant that, across the decade, DVVic developed into an organisation that gained the trust and respect of its members, coalition partners and government representatives. This positioned them to work in a manner which was both consultative and also "assumed a position of authority" on its members' behalf – an approach representing a significant "cultural shift" from past collective processes.[59]

56 McCormack interview.

57 Theobald et al, *From the Margins*, 165–168.

58 Reinelt, "Moving onto the terrain," 101.

59 McCormack interview.

Confrontation and collaboration in the 2010s

A change of government in 2010 occasioned some continued positive developments, together with significant challenges for engaging Victoria's new conservative coalition. The family violence sector, according to McCormack, was "very practised at working with government, [had] much better understanding about how government operates and [was] much more savvy in their political approach".[60] Yet the relationship between DVVic and the Victorian government, which had been based on partnership, was to change dramatically. It was in this context that the tactics of "last resort" were enacted in the lead up to the 2014 state election.

In the early 2010s, the loss of "partnership" with government was immediately apparent. In stark contrast to practice under the previous administration, it was many months before DVVic met regularly with some departmental staff and ministers. In response, DVVic and its alliance partners initially continued collaborative endeavours and, with some success, directly lobbied ministers and departmental staff for increased funding. They achieved outcomes for women and children with disabilities, as well as the implementation of new responses in circumstances where women and children were at high risk of injury or death. Despite these important developments, there was a strong concern that the government's socially conservative agenda would undermine progressive policy developments and that the reforms of the 2000s had stalled. Three key issues were of particular concern: the inadequate funding of family violence services; the enactment of failure to protect laws that were likely to impact unjustly on women in circumstances of family violence; and the defunding of the systemic review of family violence deaths.

No More Deaths, an alliance of community-sector organisations led by DVVic and the Federation of Community Legal Centres, conducted a sophisticated campaign to make domestic violence an issue in the 2014 state election, revealing serious clashes between the movement and the government on key issues. "We got together with our partner agencies," policy and program manager at DVVic Alison Macdonald recalls. "We really organised, we pulled together and we got people to help us do the media and communications and the election strategising".[61] Adopting a more public and confrontational approach to advocacy, the alliance initiated

60 Ibid.

61 Alison Macdonald, interviewed by Jacqui Theobald and Suellen Murray, 13 July 2016.

tactics that included developing an election scorecard and publicly quizzing politicians on domestic violence. In an effort to further re-invigorate grassroots mobilisation — particularly in response to the government's steadfast refusal to refund a systemic review on family violence deaths — a public demonstration was held on the steps of Parliament House. One red rose was laid for each of the twenty-nine Victorian women killed by their partners in the previous year. Due to the lack of government action, the decision to proceed with this protest was made by assessing the current political context and potential risks. As the partnership approach was no longer working, such action occurred as a "last resort" and also garnered media interest.

In the lead up to the election, the No More Deaths Alliance lobbied leaders across the political spectrum, including Opposition Leader Daniel Andrews, who was to become the new Premier of Victoria in 2014. Andrews responded to their concerns by making a Royal Commission into Family Violence an election pledge, which was later honoured following a change of government in November that year. While state engagement has clearly presented a significant opportunity for the movement, the family violence sector had not lobbied explicitly for a royal commission, which was initially considered a risk due to concerns that funds would be spent unnecessarily on an inquiry. One of the key concerns was the desperate lack of funding for services, however this was addressed immediately after the conclusion of the inquiry. Indeed, the Victorian government agreed to fully support all 227 recommendations of the royal commission; it has, to date, committed a total of $1.9 billion to support the reforms.[62]

During the commission's consultations, DVVic and their allies continued advocacy via collaborative tactics that included extensive submissions and participation as expert witnesses. Their authority provided a platform through which to influence the recommendations of the Victorian royal commission, which reflected the advocacy concerns of the movement from the past 40 years. Key areas for reform included: upgrading and expanding crisis accommodation and support services; increasing social housing and services for children; prevention strategies; safe-at-home initiatives; legal services as well as improving police; and court responses and information sharing. The documents produced by the commission provide a blueprint for keeping women and children safer by "bringing specialist services together,

62 Sue Clifford, "The way forward in responding to domestic and family violence," *Parity* 31, no. 1 (2018): 6–8, esp. 6.

placing greater scrutiny on the perpetrator, making better use of universal services and placing a greater emphasis on safety and recovery".[63]

The commission thus marked a momentous juncture in the history of the domestic violence services movement. In part through the allocation of enormous resources, this juncture is generating "profound and long-lasting transformation".[64] Such a radical achievement is demonstrative of Sawer and Andrew's contention that "victories" for women's advocacy organisations "continue to happen, sometimes after very long campaigns".[65]

Following the release of the commission's report, there has since been a return to a partnership approach, with DVVic's Fiona McCormack co-chairing a committee overseeing the implementation of some of the recommendations with a senior government minister. As noted by DVVic's policy advisor Alison Birchall, implementing policy recommendations from the royal commission has required "ongoing" and "frequent" participation by DVVic in both "formal and informal" advocacy processes.[66] They are also collaborative in nature and include participation and consultation with a range of government and non-government partners on various "taskforces, reference groups and advisory committees directly or indirectly related to the family violence reforms, across portfolios that include systems design, health, justice, accommodation and housing, child protection, adolescent family violence, responses to men using violence, social responsibility, technology solutions and industry planning".[67] However, a perennial issue that continues to challenge the domestic services movement and stems from entering into partnership with the state is "protect[ing] its independence from government while facilitating opportunities for government to fulfil their responsibilities".[68]

Conclusion

From its inception in the 1970s, the domestic violence services movement has adopted a range of advocacy strategies to advance their social change agenda. The complexity and constraints that characterise their decision-making processes and strategies as well as the enduring nature of

63 Ibid, 6–8.

64 Reinelt, "Moving onto the terrain," 101.

65 Sawer and Andrew, "Hiding in plain sight," 85.

66 Alison Birchall, "Opinion," *Parity* 31, no. 1 (2018): 63–65, esp. 63.

67 Ibid, 63.

68 Ibid, 65.

collaborative advocacy are evident in this chapter's case study. The domestic violence services movement has altered their methods of advocacy over time, demonstrating a growing level of sophistication that is responsive to the political and institutional context through the adoption of collaborative and/or confrontational strategies. In recent years, "outsider" confrontational direct action approaches were adopted for the first time since the 1980s as "a last resort" due to inadequate responses from the government. These responses did not match the severity or significance of the impact and extent of men's violence against women and children.

More generally, collaborative approaches have characterised the movement's advocacy over time. Particularly since the 2000s, opportunities to work in partnership have emerged under progressive state governments. This is evidenced by years of strategic coalition building and direct government lobbying with the aim of influencing policy and program development pertaining to domestic violence and funding for services. While fraught with challenges, the achievement of incremental social change — what Sawer and Jamieson have described as "institutionalised incrementalism"[69] — has characterised how the domestic violence services movement has engaged with the state. This has resulted in feminist principles being enshrined in Victoria's state government program and policy, leading to funding priority for specialist domestic violence service providers and the gradual transformation of public perceptions towards domestic violence.

69 Sawer and Jamieson, "The women's movement and government," 52.

REFERENCES

Abbott, Sidney and Barbara Love. *Sappho was a Right-On Woman: A liberated view of lesbianism* (New York: Stein and Day, 1972).

Abrahams, Naeemah, Karen Devries, Charlotte Watts, Christina Pallitto, Max Petzold, Simukai Shamu and Claudia Garcia-Moreno. "Worldwide prevalence of non-partner sexual violence: a systematic review," *The Lancet* 383, no. 9929 (2014): 1684–1654.

Access Economics, *The Cost of Domestic Violence to the Australian Economy: Part I* (Australian Government Office for the Status of Women, Commonwealth of Australia, 2004).

Adler, Jeffrey S. "'It is his first offense. We might as well let him go': Homicide and criminal justice in Chicago, 1875–1920," *Journal of Social History* 40, no. 1 (2006): 5–24.

Aitken, Jo. "Home protection," in *Alcohol and Temperance in Modern History: An International Encyclopedia*, ed. Jack S. Blocker Jr., David M. Fahey and Ian Tyrrell (Santa Barbara: ABC-Clio, 2003).

Aitken, Jo. "'The horrors of matrimony among the masses': Feminist representations of wife beating in England and Australia, 1870–1914," *Journal of Women's History* 19, no. 4 (2007): 107–131.

Allen, Judith. "Desperately seeking solutions: Changing battered women's options since 1880," in *National Conference on Domestic Violence: Proceedings*, Vol. 1, ed. Suzanne E. Hatty (Canberra: Australian Institute of Criminology, 1986).

Allen, Judith. "Evidence and silence: Feminism and the limits of history," in *Feminist Challenges: Social and Political Theory*, ed. Carole Pateman and Elizabeth Gross (Sydney: Allen & Unwin, 1986).

Allen, Judith. "'Mundane' men: Historians, masculinity and masculinism," *Historical Studies* 22, no. 89 (1987): 617–628.

Allen, Judith. *Sex and Secrets: Crimes Involving Australian Women Since 1880* (Melbourne: Oxford University Press, 1990).

Allen, Judith. "The invention of the pathological family: A historical study of family violence in NSW," in *Family Violence in Australia*, ed. Carol O'Donnell and Jan Craney (Melbourne: Longman Cheshire, 1982).

Andrew, Merrindahl and Kirsty McLaren. "Damaged but determined: The Australian Women's Movement, 1996–2007," *Social Movement Studies* 9, no. 2 (2010) 171–185.

Angelides, Steven. "Sexual offences against 'children' and the question of judicial gender bias," *Australian Feminist Studies*, 23, no. 57 (2008): 359–373.

Arrow, Michelle. "Making family violence public in the Royal Commission on Human Relationships, 1974–1977," *Australian Feminist Studies* 33, no. 95 (2018): 81–96.

Ashton, Paul and Paula Hamilton. *Australians at the Crossroads: Australians and the Past* (Halstead: Sydney, 2013).

Ashton, Paul and Paula Hamilton. *History at the Crossroads: Australians and the Past* (Ultimo, NSW: Halstead Press, 2010).

Atkinson, Judy. "Intimate partner abuse and Indigenous peoples," in *Intimate partner abuse and health professionals: New approaches to domestic violence*, ed. Gwenneth Roberts, Kelsey Hegarty and Gene Feder (Edinburgh: Churchill Livingstone Elsevier, 2006).

Atkinson, Judy. "Violence in Aboriginal Australia: Colonisation and gender," *Aboriginal and Islander Health Worker Journal* 14, no. 2 (1990): 5–21.

Australian Human Rights Commission. *Change the Course: National Report on Sexual Assault and Sexual Harassment at Australian Universities* (Sydney: Australian Human Rights Commission, 2017).

Australian Senate Community Affairs References Committee. *Commonwealth Contribution to Former Forced Adoption Policies and Practices* (Canberra: Senate Printing Unit, Parliament House, 2012).

Australian Senate Community Affairs References Committee. *Forgotten Australians: A Report on Australians Who Experienced Institutional or out-of-Home Care as Children* (Canberra: Senate Printing Unit, 2004).

Australian Senate Community Affairs References Committee. *Lost Innocents: Righting the Record Report on Child Migration* (Canberra: Senate Printing Unit, 2001).

Azzopardi, Corry, Ramona Alaggia and Barbara Fallon. "From Freud to feminism: Gendered constructions of blame across theories of child sexual abuse," *Journal of Child Sexual Abuse* 27, no. 3 (2018): 254–275.

Bacchi, Carol. "Rolling back the state: Feminism, theory and policy," in *Women, Public Policy and the State*, ed. Linda Hancock (Melbourne: Macmillan, 1999).

Backhouse, Constance. "'Her protests were unavailing': Australian legal understandings of rape, consent and sexuality in the 'roaring twenties,'" *Journal of Australian Studies* 24, no. 64 (2000): 14–33.

Bacon, Wendy and Robyn Landsdowne. "Women who kill husbands: The battered wife on trial," in *Family Violence in Australia*, ed. Carol O'Donnell and Jan Craney (Melbourne: Longman Chesire, 1982).

Baer, Hester. "Redoing feminism: Digital activism, body politics, and neoliberalism," *Feminist Media Studies* 16, no. 1 (2016): 17–34.

Bagilhole, Barbara and Kate White, ed. *Gender, Power and Management: A Cross Cultural Analysis of Higher Education* (New York: Palgrave Macmillan, 2011).

Bailey, Victor and Sheila Blackburn. "The punishment of Incest Act 1908: A case study of law creation," *Criminal Law Review* (1979): 708–718.

Ball, Matthew. *Criminology and Queer Theory: Dangerous Bedfellows?* (Basingstoke: Palgrave Macmillan, 2016).

Banet-Weiser, Sarah and Kate M Miltner. "#MasculinitySoFragile: Culture, structure, and networked misogyny," *Feminist Media Studies* 16, no. 1 (2016): 171–174.

Banyard, Kat. *The Equality Illusion: The Truth about Men and Women Today* (London: Faber and Faber, 2010).

Barnard, Jill and Karen Twigg. *Holding onto Hope: A History of the Founding Agencies of Mackillop Family Services 1854–1997* (Melbourne: Australian Scholarly Publishing, 2004).

Barnwell, Ashley. "Convict shame to convict chic: Intergenerational memory and family histories," *Memory Studies* (published online first 24 May 2017): 1–14. DOI: 10.1177/1750698017709870

Bartlett, Alison and Margaret Henderson. "The Australian Women's Movement goes to the museum: The 'cultures of Australian feminist activism, 1970–1990' project," *Women's Studies International Forum* 37 (2013): 85–94.

Bartlett, Alison and Margaret Henderson. "What is a feminist object? Feminist material culture and the making of the activist *Report of the Commission of Inquiry* object," *Journal of Australian Studies* 40, no. 2 (2016): 156–171.

Barter, Christine. "Independent Investigations into Institutional Child Abuse: Developing Theory and Practice," in *Institutional Abuse: Perspectives across the Life Course*, ed. Nicky Stanley, Jill Manthorpe, and Bridget Penhale (London: Routledge, 1999).

Bavin-Mizzi, Jill. *Ravished: Sexual violence in Victorian Australia* (Sydney: University of New South Wales Press, 1995).

Beaumont, Catriona. *Housewives and Citizens: Domesticity and the Women's Movement in England, 1928–1964* (Manchester: Manchester University Press, 2013).

Behrendt, Larissa. "Consent in a (neo)colonial society: Aboriginal women as sexual and legal 'other'," *Australian Feminist Studies* 15, no. 33 (2000): 353–367.

Belich, James. *Paradise Reforged: A History of the New Zealanders from the 1880s to the Year 2000* (Auckland: Allen Lane, 2000).

Bell, Diane. *Daughters of the Dreaming* (North Sydney: McPhee Gribble, 1983).

Bennice, Jennifer A. and Patricia A. Resick. "Marital rape: History, research, and practice," *Trauma, Violence and Abuse* 4, no. 3 (2003): 228–246.

Birchall, Alison. "Opinion," *Parity* 31, no. 1 (2018): 63–65.

Blackmore, Jill. *Feminism, Leadership and Educational Change* (Buckingham: Open University Press, 1999).

Blonski, Annette, Barbara Creed and Freda Freiberg, ed. *Don't Shoot Darling! Women's Independent Filmmaking in Australia* (Melbourne: Greenhouse Publications, 1987).

Blue, Ethan. "Seeing Ms. Dhu: Inquest, conquest, and (in)visibility in black women's deaths in custody," *Settler Colonial Studies* 7, no. 3 (2017): 299–320.

Boots, Denise Paquette and Kathleen M. Heide. "Parricides in the media: A content analysis of available reports across cultures," *International Journal of Offender Therapy and Comparative Criminology* 50, no. 4 (2006): 418–445.

Bottero, Wendy. "Practising family history: 'Identity' as a category of social practice," *British Journal of Sociology* 66, no. 3 (2015): 534–556.

Bottero, Wendy. "Who do you think they were? How family historians make sense of social position and inequality in the past," *British Journal of Sociology* 63, no. 1 (2012): 54–74.

Bourke, Joanna. *Rape: A History from 1860 to the Present Day* (London: Virago, 2008).

Boyd, Nan Alamilla and Horacio N. Roque Ramírez, ed. *Bodies of evidence: The practice of queer oral history* (New York: Oxford University Press, 2012).

Bradfield, Rebecca. "Domestic homicide and the defence of provocation: A Tasmanian perspective on the jealous husband and the battered wife," *University of Tasmanian Law Review*, 19, no.1 (2000): 5–37.

Breines, Wini and Linda Gordon. "The new scholarship on family violence," *Signs: Journal of Women in Culture and Society* 8, no. 3 (1983): 490–531.

Bromfield, Leah, Craig Hirte, Olivia Octoman and Ilan Katz. *Child Sexual Abuse in Australian Institutional Contexts 2008–13: Findings from Administrative Data* (Sydney: Royal Commission into Institutional Responses to Child Sexual Abuse, 2017).

Bronitt, Simon and Wendy Kukulies-Smith. "Crime, punishment, family violence, and the cloak of legal invisibility," *Journal of Australian Studies* 37, no. 3 (2013): 390–401.

Bryans, Patricia and Sharon Mavin, "Women learning to be managers: Learning to fit in or to play a different game?" *Management Learning* 34, no. 1 (2003): 111–134.

Bryant, Willow and Tracy Cussen. *Homicide in Australia: 2010–11 to 2011–12: National homicide monitoring program report*, Monitoring Reports, no. 23 (Canberra: Australian Institute of Criminology, 2015).

Bumby, Kurt M. "Psycholegal considerations in abuse-motivated parricides: Children who kill their abusive parents," *The Journal of Psychiatry & Law*, 22 (1994): 51–90.

Burton, Mandy. "Sentencing domestic homicide upon provocation: Still getting away with murder," *Feminist Legal Studies* 11, no. 3 (2003): 279–289.

Butterworth, Lee Karen. "What good is a coroner?: The transformation of the Queensland office of coroner 1859–1959" (PhD diss., Griffith University, 2012).

Carmody, Moira. "Uniting all women: A historical look at attitudes to rape," in *Crimes of Violence: Australian Responses to Rape and Child Sexual Assault*, ed. Jan Breckenridge and Moira Carmody (Sydney: Allen & Unwin, 1992).
Cass, Bettina. *Why So Few? Women Academics in Australian* Universities (Sydney: University of Sydney Press, 1983).
Chenier, Elise. "Rethinking class in lesbian bar culture: Living 'the gay life' in Toronto, 1955–1965," *Left History* 9, no. 2 (Spring/Summer 2004): 85–118.
Chenoweth, Joelle. "Rape, and nothing else: Sex, violence and law reform in NSW," *Antithesis* 6 (1993): 34–38.
Chesser, Lucy. "'Woman in a Suit of Male': Sexuality, Race and the Women Worker in Male 'Disguise', 1890–1920," *Australian Feminist Studies* 23, no. 56 (2008): 175–194.
Clark, Manning. *A History of Australia* (Carlton: Melbourne University Press, 1962).
Clifford, Geraldine Jonçich. ed. *Lone Voyagers: Academic Women in Co–Educational Institutions 1870–1937* (New York: Feminist Press, 1989).
Clifford, Sue. "The way forward in responding to domestic and family violence," *Parity* 31, no. 1 (2018): 6–8.
Collins, Anne-Maree. "Testimonies of sex: Rape in Queensland, 1880–1919," *Journal of Australian Studies* 15, no. 29 (1991): 50–63.
Collins, Felicity. "Film," in *Australian feminism: a companion* ed. Barbara Caine (Melbourne: Oxford University Press, 1998).
Collins, Felicity. "Ties that bind: The psyche of feminist filmmaking: Sydney, 1969–1989" (PhD diss., University of Technology Sydney, 1995).
Collins, Jenny. "Beyond the domestic sphere? A home science education at the University of New Zealand, 1911–1936," *Journal of Educational Administration and History* 41, no. 2 (2008): 115–130.
Collins, Patricia Hill and Sirma Bilge. *Intersectionality* (Cambridge: Polity Press, 2016).
Colvin, Eric, Suzie Linden, and John McKechnie. *Criminal Law in Queensland and Western Australia*, 4th ed. (Chatswood, NSW: LexisNexis Butterworths, 2005).
Colvin, Eric, Suzie Linden, and John McKechnie. *National Action Plan to Combat Human Trafficking and Slavery 2015–19* (Barton: Attorney-General's Department, 2014).
Commonwealth of Australia Parliamentary Joint Committee on Law Enforcement, *An Inquiry into Human Trafficking, Slavery and Slavery-like Practices* (Canberra: Senate Printing Unit, Parliament House, July 2017).
Connors, Libby. "Uncovering the shameful: Sexual violence on an Australian colonial frontier," in *Legacies of Violence: Rendering the Unspeakable Past in Modern Australia*, ed. Robert Mason (New York: Berghan Books, 2017).
Conor, Liz. "Classification and its discontents," *Interventions: International Journal of Postcolonial Studies* 17, no. 2 (2015): 155–173
Conor, Liz. *Skin Deep: Settler Impressions of Aboriginal Women* (Crawley: UWA Publishing, 2016).
Conrad, Margaret, Kadriye Ercikan, Gerald Friesen, Jocelyn Létourneau, Delphin Muise, David Northrup, and Peter Seixas. *Canadians and their Pasts: The Pasts Collective* (Toronto: University of Toronto Press, 2013).
Corns, Christopher. "Liability of husbands for rape-in-marriage – the Victorian position," *Criminal Law Journal* 7 (1983): 104–106.
Cox, Peta. *Violence Against Women: Additional analysis of the Australian Bureau of Statistics' personal safety survey, 2012*, Horizons Research Report, no. 1 (Sydney: ANROWs Horizons, 2015).
Crawford, Patricia and Myrna Tonkinson. *The Missing Chapters: Women Staff at the*

University of Western Australia 1963–1987 (Perth: Centre for Western Australian History, 1988).
Crenshaw, Kimberlé. "Mapping the margins: Intersectionality, identity politics, and violence against women of color," *Stanford Law Review* 43, no. 6 (1991): 1241–1299.
Criminal Law and Penal Methods Reform Committee of South Australia, *Special Report* (1976).
Curthoys, Ann. "Doing it for themselves: The women's movement since 1970," in *Gender Relations in Australia: Domination and Negotiation*, ed. Kay Saunders and Raymond Evans (Sydney: Harcourt Brace Jovanovich, 1992).
Curthoys, Ann. "Race and gender in recent Australian historiography," *Journal of Interdisciplinary Gender Studies* 1, no. 1 (1995): 1–9.
Cussen, Tracy and Willow Bryant. "Domestic/family homicide in Australia," in *Research in Practice*, no. 38 (Canberra: Australian Institute of Criminology, 2015).
Czarniawska, Barbara and Guje Sevón. "The thin edge of the wedge: Foreign women professors as double strangers in academia," *Gender, Work and Organization* 15, no. 3 (2008): 235—287.
David, Miriam. *Feminism, Gender and Universities: Politics, Passion and Pedagogies* (Farnham, Surrey: Ashgate, 2014).
Davidson (now Frances), Raelene. "Prostitution in Perth and Fremantle and on the eastern goldfields, 1895–1939" (MA thesis, University of Western Australia, 1980).
Davies, Kerrie. *A Wife's Heart: The Untold Story of Bertha and Henry Lawson* (St Lucia, Qld: University of Queensland Press, 2017).
Davis, Madeline and Elizabeth Lapovsky Kennedy. "Oral history and the study of sexuality in the lesbian community: Buffalo, New York, 1940–1960," *Feminist Studies* 12, no. 1 (1986): 7–26.
Davis, Megan. "Aboriginal women: The right to self-determination," *Australian Indigenous Law Review* 16, no. 1 (2012): 78–88.
Department of State (USA), *Trafficking in Persons Report June 2016*, accessed 13 June 2018, https://2009-2017.state.gov/documents/organization/258876.pdf.
Destroy The Joint: Submission to the Senate Inquiry into Domestic Violence in Australia (Destroy The Joint Ltd., 2014).
Dilley, Patrick. *The Transformation of Women's Collegiate Education* (New York: Palgrave Macmillan, 2017).
Dixson, Miriam. *The Real Matilda: Woman and Identity in Australia 1788 to the Present* (Ringwood: Penguin, 1976).
Douglas, Heather. "Do we need a specific domestic violence offence?" *Melbourne University Law Review* 39, no. 2 (2015): 434–471.
Douglas, Heather, Francesca Bartlett, Trish Luker and Rosemary Hunter. *Australian Feminist Judgments: Righting and Rewriting Law* (Oxford: Hart Publishing, 2014).
Doyle, Sue. "The pyjama girl," *Journal of Australian Studies* 24, no. 64 (2000): 34–41.
Durkheim, Emile. *The Rules of Sociological Method*, ed. Vani Prakashan (New Delhi: Nine Books, 1895, 2015).
Dyhouse, Carol. *Students: A Gendered History* (London: Routledge, 2006).
Eckert, Stine and Linda Steiner. "Feminist uses of social media: Facebook, twitter, tumblr, pinterest, and instagram," in *Defining Identity and the Changing Scope of Culture in the Digital Age*, ed. Alison Novak and Imaani Jamillah El-Burki (Hershey: IGI Global, 2016),
Edmonds, Penelope and Amanda Nettelbeck, ed. *Intimacies of Violence in the Settler Colony: Economies of Dispossession Around the Pacific Rim* (Basingstoke: Palgrave Macmillan, 2018).

Egan, Ronnie and Lesley Hoatson. "Desperate to survive: Contracting women's services in Melbourne," *Australian Feminist Studies* 14, no. 30 (1999): 405–414.

Egan, Ted and Robert Ingpen. *The Drover's Boy* (Port Melbourne: Lothian, 1997).

Evans, Ilsa. "Desperate lovers and wanton women: Press representations of domestic violence," *Hecate* 27, no. 2 (2001): 147–173.

Evans, Raymond. "A gun in the oven: Masculinism and gendered violence," in *Gender Relations in Australia: Domination and Negotiation,* ed. Raymond Evans and Kay Saunders (Sydney: Harcourt Brace Jovanovich, 1992).

Evans, Raymond. "'Soiled Doves': Prostitution in Colonial Queensland," in *So Much Hard Work: Women and Prostitution in Australian History*, ed. Kay Daniels (Melbourne: Fontana/Collins, 1984).

Evans, Raymond and Kay Saunders, ed. *Gender Relations in Australia: Domination and Negotiation* (Sydney: Harcourt Brace Jovanovich, 1992).

Evans, Tanya. *Fractured Families: Life on the Margins in Colonial NSW* (Sydney: New South, 2015).

Evans, Tanya. "Love thy neighbour: Local and community history," in *What is Public History Globally?* ed. Paul Ashton and Alex Trapeznik (London: Bloomsbury, 2018).

Evans, Tanya. "Who do you think you are? Historical television consultancy," *Australian Historical Studies* 46, no. 3 (2015): 454–467.

Evans, Tanya and Anna Clark. "Family history and transnational historical consciousness," in *Transnationalism, Nationalism and Australian History*, ed. Anna Clark, Anne Rees and Alecia Simmonds (Singapore: Palgrave Macmillan, 2017).

Eveline, Joan. *Ivory Basement Leadership* (Crawley: University of Western Australia Press, 2004).

Fairleigh, Lyndell. "Challenging images of Aboriginal women," *Tribune*, no. 2 (September 1987): 13.

Falzon, John. "#illridewithyou shows the kind of world that is possible," *Eureka Street* 24, no. 24 (2014): 7–9.

Family and Community Development Committee Parliament of Victoria, *Betrayal of Trust: Inquiry into the Handling of Child Abuse by Religious and Other Non-Government Organisations* (Melbourne: Parliament of Victoria, 2013).

Farley, Kelly. *Degrees of Liberation: A Short History of Women in the University of Melbourne* (Parkville: The Women Graduates Centenary Committee, 1985).

Featherstone, Brid and Barbara Fawcett. "Feminism and child abuse: Opening up some possibilities," *Critical Social Policy* 14, no. 42 (1994): 61–80.

Featherstone, Lisa and Amanda Kaladelfos. "Hierarchies of harm and violence: Historicising familial sexual violence in Australia," *Australian Feminist Studies* 29, no. 81 (2014): 306–324.

Featherstone, Lisa and Amanda Kaladelfos. *Sex Crimes in the Fifties* (Melbourne: Melbourne University Publishing, 2016).

Featherstone, Lisa and Alexander George Winn. "Marital rape and the marital rapist: The 1976 South Australian rape law reforms," *Feminist Legal Studies*, (2018): 1-22. DOI:10.1007/s10691-018-9382-3.

Fedina, Lisa. "Use and misuse of research in books on trafficking: Implications for interdisciplinary researchers, practitioners, and advocates," *Trauma, Violence and Abuse* 16, no. 2 (2015): 188–198.

Ferguson, Harry. "Abused and looked after children as 'moral dirt': Child abuse and institutional care in historical perspective," *Journal of Social Policy* 36, no. 1 (2007): 123–139.

Finnane, Mark. "Guns and massacres: The politics of firearms control in Australia," in *Australian Violence: Crime, Criminal Justice and Beyond* ed. Julie Stubbs and Stephen Tomsen (Sydney: The Federation Press, 2016).

Finnane, Mark. *Punishment in Australian Society* (Melbourne: Oxford University Press, 1997).

Finnane, Mark and Andy Kaladelfos. "Race and justice in an Australian Court: Prosecuting homicide in Western Australia, 1830–1954," *Australian Historical Studies* 47, no. 3 (2016): 443–461.

Fitzgerald, Tanya. *Outsiders or Equals: Women Professors at the University of New Zealand 1911–1961* (Oxford: Peter Lang, 2009).

Fitzgerald, Tanya. "Spaces in–between: Indigenous women leaders speak back," *International Journal of Leadership in Education* 13, no. 1 (2010): 93–105.

Fitzgerald, Tanya. *Women Leaders in Higher Education: Shattering the Myths* (Abingdon: Routledge, 2014).

Fitzgerald, Tanya and Jenny Collins, *Historical Portraits of Women Home Scientists: The University of New Zealand, 1911–1947* (New York: Cambria Press, 2011).

Fitzgerald, Tanya and Jane Wilkinson *Travelling Towards a Mirage? Gender, Leadership and Higher Education* (Brisbane: Post Pressed, 2010).

Fitzpatrick, Ellen F. *Endless Crusade: Women Social Scientists and Progressive Social Reform* (New York: Oxford University Press, 1990).

Flood, Michael and Clive Hamilton. "Mapping homophobia in Australia," in *Homophobia: An Australian History*, ed. Shirleene Robinson (Sydney: The Federation Press, 2008).

Ford, Clementine. *Fight Like a Girl* (Sydney: Allen & Unwin, 2016).

Ford, Ruth. "'Filthy, obscene and mad': Engendering 'homophobia' in Australia, 1940s-1960s," in *Homophobia: An Australian History*, ed. Shirleene Robinson (Sydney: The Federation Press, 2008).

Forde, Leneen. *Report of the Commission of Inquiry into Abuse of Children in Queensland Institutions* (Brisbane: The Inquiry, 1999).

Forgotten Australians Submissions, *Parliament of Australia*, 2005, accessed 29 October 2017, https://www.aph.gov.au/Parliamentary_Business/Committees/Senate/Community_Affairs/Completed_inquiries/2004-07/inst_care/submissions/sublist.

Fotaki, Marianna. "The sublime object of desire (for knowledge): Sexuality at work in business and management schools in England," *British Journal of Management* 22, no. 1 (2011): 42–53.

Foucault, Michel. "The politics of health in the eighteenth century," in *The Foucault Reader*, ed. Paul Rabinow (London: Penguin, 1984).

Frances, Raelene. "Shifting barriers: Twentieth century women's labour patterns," in *Gender Relations in Australia: Domination and Negotiation*, ed. Kay Saunders and Raymond Evans (Marrickville: Harcourt Brace Jovanovich, 1992).

Frances, Raelene. *Selling Sex: A Hidden History of Prostitution* (Sydney: University of New South Wales Press, 2007).

French, Lisa. "An analysis of *Nice Coloured Girls*," *Senses of Cinema*, no. 5 (2000), http://sensesofcinema.com/2000/australian-cinema-5/nicc/.

Furniss, Elizabeth. "Timeline history and the Anzac myth: Settler narratives of local history in a North Australian town," *Oceania* 71, no. 4 (2001): 279–297.

Gay Men and Lesbians Against Discrimination, *Not a Day Goes By: Report on the GLAD Survey into Discrimination and Violence against Lesbians and Gay Men in Victoria* (Melbourne: GLAD, 1994).

Genovese, Ann. "The battered body," *Australian Feminist Studies* 12, no. 25 (1997): 91–103.

George, Jim and Kim Huynh. *The Culture Wars: Australian and American Politics in the 21st Century* (South Yarra: Palgrave Macmillan, 2009).

Gherardi, Silvia and Barbara Poggio, *Gendertelling in Organisations: Narratives from Male-Dominated Environments* (Liber: Copenhagen Business School Press, 2007).

Gleeson, Jessamy. "'Destroying the joint?': Challenging and changing representations of women in mainstream media via online feminist campaigns," in *Creating Space in the Fifth Estate*, ed. Janet Fulton and Phillip McIntyre (Newcastle upon Tyne: Cambridge Scholars Publishing, 2017).

Gleeson, Jessamy. "'(Not) working 9–5': The consequences of contemporary Australian-based online feminist campaigns as digital labour," *Media International Australia* 161, no. 1 (2016): 77–85.

Gleeson, Kate. "From centenary to the Olympics: Gang rape in Sydney," *Current Issues in Criminal Justice* 16, no. 2 (2004): 183–201.

Gleeson, Kate. "From suck magazine to corporate paedophilia. Feminism and pornography—Remembering the Australian way," *Women's Studies International Forum* 38 (2013): 83–96.

Gordon, Linda. *Heroes of Their Own Lives: The History and Politics of Family Violence* (New York: Viking, 1988).

Gordon, Linda. "The politics of child sexual abuse: Notes from American history," *Feminist Review* 28 (1988): 56–64.

Gosztonyi–Ainley, Marianne. *Creating Complicated Lives: Women and Science at English–Canadian Universities, 1880–1980*, ed. Marelene Rayner-Canham and Geoff Rayner-Canham (Quebec: McGill-Queen's University Press, 2012).

Greer, Germaine. *The Female Eunuch* (London: MacGibbon & Kee, 1970).

Grimshaw, Patricia. "Gender, citizenship and race in the Woman's Christian Temperance Union of Australia, 1890 to the 1930s," *Australian Feminist Studies* 13, no. 28 (1998): 199–214.

Grimshaw, Patricia, Charles Fahey, Susan Janson, and Tom Griffiths. "Families and selection in colonial Horsham, Victoria, Australia 1888," *Bulletin* 14 (1984): 27–59.

Grimshaw, Patricia and Lynne Strahan, ed. *The Half–Open Door: Sixteen Modern Australian Women Look at Professional Life and Achievement* (Sydney: Hale & Iremonger, 1982).

Grimshaw, Patricia and Graeme Willett. "Women's history and family history: An exploration of colonial family structure," in *Australian Women: Feminist Perspectives*, ed. Norma Grieve and Patricia Grimshaw (Melbourne: Oxford University Press, 1981).

Haag, Pamela. "The 'ill-use of a wife': Patterns of working-class violence in domestic and public New York City, 1860–1880," *Journal of Social History* 25, no. 3 (1992): 447–477.

Haebich, Anna. *Broken Circles* (Fremantle: Fremantle Arts Centre Press, 2000).

Hall, Barbara. "How will be lean to remember tomorrow? A catalogue of independent women's films," *Lip: A Feminist Journal of Women in the Visual and Performing Arts* (1980): 128.

Hall, Roberta and Bernice Sandler, *The Classroom Climate: A Chilly One for Women?* (Washington, D.C.: Association of American Colleges, 1982).

Hart, Jessica L. and Jeffrey L. Helms. "Factors of parricide: Allowance of the use of battered child syndrome as a defense," *Aggression and Violent Behavior* 8, no. 6 (2003): 671–683.

Haskins, Victoria. "'A better chance'? – sexual abuse and the apprenticeship of Aboriginal girls under the NSW Aborigines Protection Board," *Aboriginal History* 28 (2004): 33–58.

Haskins, Victoria. "'A troublesome gin like Annie': Masculinity, race and intimate violence in Federation-era North Queensland," *law&history* 4, no. 2 (2017): 125–150.
Haskins, Victoria. "'Down in the gully and just outside the garden walk': White women and the sexual abuse of Aboriginal women on a colonial Australian frontier," *History Australia* 10, no. 1 (2013): 11–34.
Haskins, Victoria. "On the doorstep: Aboriginal domestic service as a 'contact zone'," *Australian Feminist Studies* 16, no. 34 (2001): 13–25.
Hatty, Suzanne E. "Preface," in *National Conference on Domestic Violence: Proceedings*, Vol. 1, ed. Suzanne E. Hatty (Canberra: Australian Institute of Criminology, 1986).
Hetherington, Penelope. *Incest and the Community: Australian Perspectives* (Perth: Centre for Western Australian History at the University of Western Australia, 1991).
Heide, Kathleen M. "Parents who get killed and the children who kill them," *Journal of Interpersonal Violence* 8, no. 4 (1993): 531–544.
Heide, Kathleen M. *Understanding Parricide: When Sons and Daughters Kill Parents* (Oxford: Oxford University Press, 2013).
Heide, Kathleen M. and Jessica McCurdy. "Juvenile parricide offenders sentenced to death," *Victims & Offenders* 5, no. 1 (2009): 76–99.
Heide, Kathleen M. and Thomas A. Petee. "Parricide: An empirical analysis of 24 Years of U.S. data," *Journal of Interpersonal Violence* 22, no. 11 (2007): 1382–1399.
Henry, Kristin and Marlene Derlet. *Talking Up a Storm, Nine Women and Consciousness-Raising* (Sydney: Hale and Iremonger, 1993).
Hillbrand, Marc, Jason W. Alexandre, John L. Young, and Reuben T. Spitz. "Parricides: Characteristics of offenders and victims, legal factors, and treatment issues," *Aggression and Violent Behavior* 4, no. 2 (1999): 179–190.
Holland, Alison. "The campaign for women protectors: Gender, race and frontier between the wars," *Australian Feminist Studies* 16, no. 34 (2001): 27–42.
Holt, Amanda. "Parricide in England and Wales (1977–2012): An exploration of offenders, victims, incidents and outcomes," *Criminology & Criminal Justice* 17, no. 5 (2017): 268–287.
Horne, Julia. "Looking from the inside out: Rethinking university history," *Journal of Educational Administration and History* 46, no. 2 (2014): 174–189.
Horne, Julia. "The final barrier? Australian women and the nineteenth century public university," in *Women in Higher Education, 1850–1970: International Perspectives*, ed. E. Lisa Panayotidis and Paul Storz (London: Routledge, 2016).
Horne, Julia and Geoff Sherington. *Sydney: The Making of a Public University* (Sydney: The Miegunyah Press, 2012).
Houlbrook, Matt. *Queer London: Perils and Pleasures in the Sexual Metropolis* (London: University of Chicago Press, 2005).
Howe, Renate and Shurlee Swain. *All God's Children: A Centenary History of the Methodist Homes for Children and the Orana Peace Memorial Homes* (Canberra: Acorn Press, 1989).
Hubbard, Phil. "Sex zones: Intimacy, citizenship and public space," *Sexualities* 4 (2001): 57–71.
Human Rights and Equal Opportunity Commission, *Bringing Them Home: Report of the National Inquiry into the Separation of Aboriginal and Torres Strait Islander Children from Their Families* (Sydney: HREOC, 1997).
Huggins, Jackie. "A contemporary view of Aboriginal women's relationship to the white women's movement," in *Australian Women: Contemporary Feminist Thought*, ed. Norma Grieve and Ailsa Burns (Melbourne: Oxford University Press, 1994).

Hughes, John. "Work in progress: The rise and fall of the Australian filmmakers cooperatives, 1966–86," *Senses of Cinema*, no. 77 (2015), http://sensesofcinema.com/2015/australian-film-history/australian-filmmakers-co-operatives/#fn-25650-9.

Hunt, Susan Jane. *Spinifex and hessian: Women's lives in North-Western Australia, 1860–1900* (Perth: University of Western Australia Press, 1979).

Hunter, Kathryn M. "Silence in noisy archives: Reflections on Judith Allen's 'Evidence and silence – Feminism and the limits of history' (1986) in the era of mass digitisation," *Australian Feminist Studies* 32, no. 91–92 (2017): 202–212.

Jameyson, Karen. "News from down under: Brush strokes with history," *The Horn Book Magazine* 75, no. 3 (1999): 364–368.

Jane, Emma Alice. "'Back to the kitchen, cunt': Speaking the unspeakable about online misogyny," *Continuum* 28, no. 4 (2014): 558–570.

Jebb, Mary Anne. *Blood, Sweat and Welfare: A History of White bosses and Aboriginal Pastoral Workers* (Crawley: UWA Publishing, 2002).

Jeffreys, Sheila. *The Idea of Prostitution* (Melbourne: Spinifex Press, 1997).

Jennings, Karen and David Hollinsworth. "Ways of seeing and speaking about Aboriginal women: II. Shy maids and wanton strumpets," *Hecate* 13, no. 2 (1987/88): 129–133.

Jennings, Rebecca. *Unnamed Desires: A Sydney lesbian history* (Melbourne: Monash University Publishing, 2015).

Johnson, Vivien. "Love will tear us apart: Domestic violence and sexuality," in *National Conference on Domestic Violence: Proceedings* vol. 1, ed. Suzanne E. Hatty (Canberra: Australian Institute of Criminology, 1986).

Johnson, Vivien. *The Last Resort: A Women's Refuge* (Melbourne: Penguin, 1981).

Kaberry, Phyllis M. *Aboriginal Woman: Sacred and Profane* (London: Routledge, 1939).

Kaladelfos, Amanda. "The dark side of the family: paternal child homicide in Australia," *Journal of Australian Studies* 37, no. 3 (2013): 333–348.

Kaladelfos, Amanda. "The 'condemned criminals': Sexual violence, race and manliness in colonial Australia," *Women's History Review* 21, no. 5 (2012): 697–714.

Kaladelfos, Amanda. "The politics of punishment: Rape and the death penalty in colonial Australia, 1841–1901," *History Australia* 9, no. 1 (2012): 155–75.

Kaladelfos, Amanda. "'Until death does part us': Male friendship, intimacy and violence in late colonial Melbourne," in *Intimacy, Violence and Activism: Gay and Lesbian Perspectives on Australasian History and Society*, ed. Graham Willett and Yorick Smaal (Melbourne: Monash University Publishing, 2013).

Kaladelfos, Amanda and Lisa Featherstone. "Editorial: Sexual and gender-based violence: Definitions, contexts, meanings," *Australian Feminist Studies* 29, no. 81 (2014): 233–237.

Kaplan, E. Ann. "Aborigines, film and Moffatt's *'Night Cries: A Rural Tragedy'*: An outsider's perspectives," *Bulletin of the Olive Pink Society* 1, no. 2 (1989): 15.

Kaplan, Gisele. *The Meagre Harvest: the Australian Women's Movement 1950s-1990* (St. Leonards: Allen & Unwin, 1996).

Kerfoot, Deborah and David Knights. *Management, Organisation and Masculinity* (London: Sage, 2004).

Keusch, Nicole. "The phenomenon of the *'Karayuki-san'*: A transnational network of prostitution, 1870–1940," in *Selling Sex in the City: Global history of prostitution*, ed. Magaly Rodríguez García, Lex Heerma van Voss and Elise van Nederveen Meerkerk (Leiden: Brill, 2017).

Kevin, Catherine. "Creative work: Feminist representations of domestic violence in 1970s Australia," in Everyday revolutions: Gender, sexuality and society in 1970s

Australia ed. Michelle Arrow and Angela Woollacott (Canberra: ANU Press, forthcoming 2019).

Kidd, Rosalind. *The Way We Civilise* (St Lucia: University of Queensland Press, 1997).

Kilday, Anne-Marie. "'Sugar and spice and all things nice?': Violence against parents in Scotland, 1700–1850," *Journal of Family History* 41, no. 3 (2016): 318–335.

King, Charlotte, Lorana Bartels, Patricia Easteal, and Anthony Hopkins. "Did defensive homicide in Victoria provide a safety net for battered women who kill: A case study analysis," *Monash University Law Review* 42 (2016): 138–178.

Kingston, Beverley. *My Wife, My Daughter and Poor Mary Ann: Women and Work in Australia* (Melbourne: Thomas Nelson Australia, 1980).

Lake, Marilyn. "Childbearers as rights-bearers: Feminist discourse on the rights of Aboriginal and non-Aboriginal mothers in Australia, 1920–50," *Women's History Review* 8, no. 2 (1999): 347–363.

Lake, Marilyn. *Getting Equal: The History of Australian Feminism* (St Leonards: Allen & Unwin, 1999).

Lake, Marilyn. "Historical reconsiderations IV: The politics of respectability: Identifying the masculinist context," *Historical Studies* 22, no. 86 (1986): 116–131.

Langton, Marcia. *"Well, I Heard it on the Radio and I saw it on the Television… ": An essay for the AFC on the Politics and Aesthetics of Filmmaking by and about Aboriginal People and Things* (Sydney: Australian Film Commission, 1993).

Lanham, David. "Hale, misogyny and rape," *Criminal Law Journal* 7 (1983): 148–166.

Laster, Kathy. "Arbitrary chivalry: Women and capital punishment in Victoria, Australia 1842–1967," *Women & Criminal Justice* 6, no. 1 (1994): 67–95.

Latimore, Jack David Nolan, Margaret Simons, and Elyas Khan. "Reassembling the Indigenous public sphere," *Australasian Journal of Information Systems* 21 (2017): 1–15.

Lee, Alicia. "The foreigner within the walls," in *National Conference on Domestic Violence: Proceedings* vol. 1, ed. Suzanne E. Hatty (Canberra: Australian Institute of Criminology, 1986).

Leonard, William, Marian Pitts, Anne Mitchell, Anthony Lyons, Anthony Smith, Sunil Patel, Murray Couch and Anna Barrett. *Private Lives 2: The second national survey of the health and wellbeing of gay, lesbian, bisexual and transgender (GLBT) Australians* (Melbourne: The Australian Research Centre in Sex, Health & Society, La Trobe University, 2012).

Logan, T.K., Robert Walker and Jennifer Cole. "Silenced suffering: The need for a better understanding of partner sexual violence," *Trauma, Violence and Abuse* 16, no. 2 (2015): 111–135.

Lloyd, Justine. "Women's pages in Australian print media from the 1850s," *Media International Australia* 150, no. 1 (2014): 61–65.

Macintyre, Stuart. *The Reds: The Communist Party of Australia from Origins to Illegality* (Sydney: Allen & Unwin, 1998).

Mackinnon, Alison. *The New Women: Adelaide's Early Women Graduates* (Adelaide: Wakefield Press, 1986).

Madsen, Jane. "Listening at closed doors: A consideration of the use of sound in *Behind Closed Doors*," in *Don't Shoot Darling! Women's Independent Filmmaking in Australia*, ed. Annette Blonski, Barbara Creed and Freda Freiberg (Melbourne: Greenhouse Publications, 1987).

Magarey, Susan. "Feminism as cultural renaissance," *Hecate* 30, no. 1 (2004): 231–246.

Mason, Gail. "Body maps: Envisaging homophobia, Violence and Safety," *Social and Legal Studies* 10, no. 1 (2001): 23–44.

Mason, Gail. "Violence against lesbians and gay men," *Violence Prevention Today* no. 2 (Canberra: Australian Institute of Criminology).

Mason, Gail. "Heterosexed violence: Typicality and ambiguity," in *Homophobic Violence*, ed. Gail Mason and Stephen Tomsen (Sydney: Hawkins Press, 1997).

Mason, Gail. "Reforming the law of rape: Incursions into the masculinist sanctum," in *Sex, Power and Justice*, ed. Diane Kirby (Melbourne: Oxford University Press, 1995).

Mason, Gail. "Violence," in *Australian Feminism: A Companion*, ed. Barbara Caine, Moira Gatens, Emma Grahame, Jan Larbalestier, Sophie Watson, and Elizabeth Webby (Melbourne: Oxford University Press, 1999).

Matthews, Kay Morris. *In Their Own Right: Women and Higher Education in New Zealand before 1945* (Wellington: New Zealand Council for Educational Research, 2008).

Mavin, Sharon and Gina Grandy, "Women elite leaders doing respectable business femininity: How privilege is conferred, contested and defended through the body," *Gender, Work and Organization* 23, no. 4 (2016): 379–396.

May, Ann Mari. *The "Woman Question" and Higher Education: Perspectives on Gender and Knowledge Production in America* (Cheltenham: Edward Elgar, 2008).

Mazerolle, Paul, Li Eriksson, Richard Wortley, and Holly Johnson. "Homicide in Australia and New Zealand: Prescursors and prevention," in *The Handbook of Homicide*, ed. Fiona Brookman, Edward R. Maguire, and Mike Maguire (Chichester: Wiley Blackwell, 2017).

McConnell, Ruth and Steve Mullins. "'We had both been drinking since Christmas': Battered wives and dead abusive husbands in early colonial Rockhampton," *Journal of Australian Colonial History* 5 (2004): 100–119.

McConville, Chris. "Rough women, respectable men and social reform: A response to Lake's 'Masculinism'," *Historical Studies* 22, no. 88 (1987): 432–440.

McDonald, John. "Neo-Liberalism and the pathologising of public issues: The displacement of feminist service models in domestic violence support services," *Australian Social Work* 58, no. 3 (2005): 275–284.

McFerran, Ludo. "Interpretation of a frontline state: Australian women's refuges and the State," in *Playing the State: Australian Feminist Interventions,* ed. Sophie Watson (Sydney: Allen & Unwin 1990).

McFerren [sic], Ludo. "Can men change? What to do with batterers," *Refractory Girl* 33 (1989): 3–4.

McFerrin [sic], Ludo. "Domestic violence: Stories, scandals and serious analysis," *Refractory Girl* 44–45 (1993): 152–159.

McGaha, Johnny E. and Amanda Evans. "Where are the victims? The credibility gap in human trafficking research," *Intercultural Human Rights Law Review* 4 (2009): 239–266.

McGrath, Ann. *Born in the Cattle: Aborigines in Cattle Country* (Sydney: Allen & Unwin, 1987).

McGrath, Ann. "Consent, marriage and colonialism: Indigenous Australian women and coloniser marriages," *Journal of Colonialism and Colonial History* 6, no. 3 (2005).

McGrath, Ann. *Illicit Love: Interracial Sex and Marriage in the United States and Australia* (Lincoln: University of Nebraska Press, 2015).

McGregor, Heather and Andrew Hopkins. *Working for Change: The Movement Against Domestic Violence* (Sydney: Allen & Unwin 1991).

McLaughlin, Megan and Elizabeth H. Pleck. "Editor's note," *Journal of Women's History* 19, no. 4 (2007): 7–11.

McLean, Jessica and Sophia Maalsen. "'We don't want it to be like that for her again': Gendered leadership and online feminism in Australian politics and planning," *Australian Planner* 54, no. 1 (2017): 24–32.

McMahon, Marilyn and Paul McGorrery. "Criminalising emotional abuse, intimidation and economic abuse in the context of family violence: The Tasmanian experience," *University of Tasmania Law Review* 35, no. 2 (2016): 1–22.

Melville, Roselyn. "The external organisational environment and organisational survival and change," *Third Sector Review* 1 (1995): 65–77.

Merewether, Janet. "Fuck the mainstream," in *WomenVision: Women and the Moving Image in Australia*, ed. Lisa French (Melbourne: Damned Publishing, 2003).

Meshkovska, Biljana, Milissa Siegel, Sarah E. Stitterheim and Arjan E.R. Bos, "Female sex trafficking: Conceptual issues, current debates, and future directions," *The Journal of Sex Research* 52, no. 4 (2015): 380–395.

Meyerson, Debra E. and Megan Tompkins, "Tempered radicals as institutional change agents: The case of advancing gender equity at the University of Michigan," *Harvard Journal of Law and Gender* 30, no. 2 (2007): 303–322.

Michaels, Wendy. "The final factor: What political action failed to do," *Lilith: A Feminist History Journal* 19 (2013): 18–31.

Mihalopoulos, Bill. "世界か Women, overseas sex work and globalization in Meiji Japan 明治日本における女性, 国外性労働、海外進出," *The Asia-Pacific Journal* 10, no. 35/1 (2012): 1–24.

Mihalopoulos, Bill. *Sex in Japan's Globalization, 1870–1930: Prostitutes, Emigration and Nation-building* (London: Pickering & Chatto, 2011).

Millward, Liz. *Making a Scene: Lesbians and Community Across Canada, 1964–84* (Vancouver: University of British Columbia Press, 2015).

Mones, Paul. "When the innocent strike back: Abused children who kill their parents," *Journal of Interpersonal Violence* 8, no. 2 (1993): 297–299.

Moore, Catriona. *Indecent Exposures: Twenty Years of Australian Feminist Photography* (Sydney: Allen & Unwin, 1994).

Moore, Catriona. "The more things change… : Feminist aesthetics, then and now," *Artlink* 33, no. 3 (2013): 22–24.

Moreton-Robinson, Aileen. *Talkin' Up to the White Woman: Aboriginal Women and Feminism* (St Lucia: University of Queensland Press, 2000).

Morley, Louise. "Lost leaders: Women in the global academy," *Higher Education Research & Development* 33 no. 1 (2014): 114–128.

Morphy, Howard. "Proximity and distance: Representations of Aboriginal society in the writings of Bill Harney and Bruce Chatwin," in *Popularising Anthropology*, ed. Jeremy McClancy and Christian McDonaugh (London: Routledge, 1996).

Morris, Anne. "Gendered dynamics of abuse and violence in families: Considering the abusive household gender regime," *Child Abuse Review* 18 (2009): 414–427.

Morris, Meagan. "Beyond assimilation: Aboriginality, media history and public memory," *Aedon: Melbourne University Literary Arts Review* 4, no. 1 (1996): 12–26.

Mosmann, Petra. "Encountering feminist things: Generations, interpretations and encountering Adelaide's 'scrap heap'," *Journal of Australian Studies* 40, no. 2 (2016): 172–189.

Mouzos, Jenny and Catherine Rushforth. "Family homicide in Australia," *Trends & Issues in Crime and Criminal Justice* no. 255 (Canberra: Australian Institute of Criminology, 2003).

Mullighan, Hon E.P. *Children in State Care Commission of Inquiry: Allegations of Sexual Abuse and Death from Criminal Conduct* (Adelaide: Children in State Care Commission of Enquiry, 2008).

Muravyeva, Marianna and Raisa Maria Toivo. "'Honor thy father and thy mother': A history of violence against parents," *Journal of Family History* 41, no. 3 (2016): 231–235.

Murdolo, Adele. "Safe homes for immigrant and refugee women: Narrating alternative histories of the women's refuge movement in Australia," *Frontiers: A Journal of Women Studies* 35, no. 3 (2014): 126–153.

Murray, Suellen. *More than refuge: Changing Responses to Domestic Violence* (Perth: University of Western Australia Press, 2002).

Musgrove, Nell. "Abuse of foster children in nineteenth-century Australia: Why did it happen then, and why does it matter now?" *History of Education* 45, no. 4 (2016): 460–476.

Musgrove, Nell. *The Long History of Forgotten Australians and Children's Institutions* (North Melbourne, Vic.: Australian Scholarly Publishing, 2013).

Myers, Christine D. *University Co–Education in the Victorian Era: Inclusion in the United States and United Kingdom* (New York: Palgrave Macmillan, 2010).

Nancarrow, Heather. "In search of justice for domestic and family violence: Indigenous and non-Indigenous Australian women's perspectives," *Theoretical Criminology*, 10, no. 1 (2006): 87–106.

National Council to Reduce Violence against Women and their Children. *Economic cost of violence against women and their children* (Canberra: Commonwealth of Australia, 2009).

Neave, Marcia. "From difference to sameness: Law and women's work," *Melbourne University Law Review* 18 (1992): 768–807.

Nelson, Elizabeth. *Homefront Hostilities: The First World War and Domestic Violence* (Kew, Vic.: Australian Scholarly Publishing, 2014).

Nelson, Elizabeth. "Victims of war: The First World War, returned soldiers, and understandings of domestic violence in Australia," *Journal of Women's History* 19, no. 4 (2007): 83–106.

Nerad, Maresi. *The Academic Kitchen: A Social History of Gender Stratification at the University of California Berkley* (Albany: State University of New York Press, 1999).

Nettelbeck, Amanda. "Intimate violence in the pastoral economy: Aboriginal women's labour and protective governance," in *Intimacies of Violence in the Settler Colony: Economies of Dispossession Around the Pacific Rim*, ed. Penelope Edmonds and Amanda Nettelbeck (Basingstoke: Palgrave Macmillan, 2018).

Newhill, Christina E. "Parricide," *Journal of Family Violence* 6, no. 4 (1991): 375–394.

Nicholas, Lucy, and Christine Aguis. *The Persistence of Global Masculinism: Discourse, Gender and Neo-Colonial Re-Articulations of Violence* (Cham: Palgrave Macmillan, 2018).

Northern Ireland Inquiry into Historical Institutional Abuse 1922 to 1995, Module 2, accessed 29 October 2017, https://www.hiainquiry.org/sites/hiainquiry/files/media-files/hia_312_redacted_opt.pdf.

NSW Government, *NSW Domestic Violence Death Review Team Report, 2015–2017* (Sydney: Domestic Violence Death Review Team, 2017).

NSW Government. "Focus topic: Under-reporting of domestic violence assaults," in *Women in NSW 2013* (Sydney: Family & Community Services, Women NSW, 2013).

O'Connor, Deidre. "Rape law reform – The Australian experience Part 1," *Criminal Law Journal* 1 (1977): 305–319.

O'Connor, Monica and Grainne Healy. *The Links between Prostitution and Sex Trafficking: A Briefing Handbook* (Dublin: Coalitition Against Trafficking in Women, 2006).
O'Donnell, Carol and Jan Craney, eds. *Family Violence in Australia* (Melbourne: Longman Chesire, 1982).
Orr, Liz. "The women's refuge movement in Victoria," in *Women Working Together: Lessons from Feminist Women's Services*, ed. Wendy Weeks (Melbourne: Longman Cheshire, 1994).
Otto, Dianne and Eileen Haley. "Health shelter: A history of Adelaide women's shelter," *Refractory Girl* Winter (1975): 11–16.
Overs, Cheryl and Kate Hawkins. "Can rights stop the wrongs? Exploring the connections between framings of sex workers' rights and sexual and reproductive health," *BMC International Health and Human Rights* 11, no. 3 (2011): S6.
Owen, Chris. *Every Mother's Son is Guilty: Policing the Kimberley Frontier of Western Australian*, 1882–1905 (Crawley: UWA Publishing, 2017).
Paloma, Melody. "Bodies in trouble: On sexual violence and the problem with hashtags," *Overland*, 25 October 2017, accessed 15 November 2017, https://overland.org.au/2017/10/from-hashtag-to-action/.
Panayotidis, E. Lisa and Paul Storz, ed. *Women in Higher Education, 1850–1970: International Perspectives* (London: Routledge, 2016).
Pateman, Carole. *The Sexual Contract* (Polity: Cambridge, 1988).
Pearce, Sharyn. "From bush battler to city editor: Louisa Lawson and the *Dawn*," *Journal of Australian Studies* 21, no. 54–55 (1997): 12–21.
Pearce, Sharyn. "'The best career is matrimony': First-wave journalism and the 'Australian girl'," *Hecate* 18, no. 2 (1992): 64–78.
Penglase, Joanna. *Orphans of the Living: Growing up in "Care" in Twentieth-Century Australia* (Fremantle: Curtin University Books, 2005).
Penhale, Bridget. "Introduction," in *Institutional Abuse: Perspectives across the Life Course*, ed. Nicky Stanley, Jill Manthorpe, and Bridget Penhale (London: Routledge, 1999).
Phillips, Ruth. "Undoing an activist response: Feminism and the Australian government's domestic violence policy," *Critical Social Policy* 26, no. 1 (2006): 192–219.
Piccini, Jon. *Transnational Protest, Australia and the 1960s: Global Radicals* (London: Palgrave Macmillan, 2016).
Pickles, Katie. "Colonial counterparts: The first academic women in Anglo-Canada, New Zealand and Australia," *Women's History Review* 10, no. 2 (2001): 273–297.
Pietsch, Tamson. *Empire of Scholars: Universities, Networks and the British Academic World, 1850–1939* (Manchester: Manchester University Press, 2013).
Pizzey, Erin. *Scream Quietly or the Neighbours will Hear* (Harmondsworth: Penguin, 1974).
Poland, Louise. "Printing presses and protest banners: Feminist presses in Australia," *Lilith: A Feminist History Journal* 10 (2001): 121–136.
Portwood-Stacer, Laura and Susan Berridge. "Introduction: The year in feminist hashtags," *Feminist Media Studies* 14, no. 6 (2014): 1090.
Postmus, Judy L., Sara-Beth Plummer, Sarah McMahon, N. Shaanta Murshid, and Mi Sung Kim, "Understanding economic abuse in the lives of survivors," *Journal of Interpersonal Violence* 27, no. 3 (2012): 411–430.
Povinelli, Elizabeth A. *The Empire of Love: Toward a Theory of Intimacy, Genealogy, and Carnality* (Durham: Duke University Press, 2006).
Powell, Anastasia and Nicola Henry. *Digital Harassment and Abuse of Adult Australians: A Summary Report* (Melbourne: RMIT, 2015).

Powell, Anastasia and Suellen Murray. "Children and domestic violence: Constructing a policy problem in Australia and New Zealand," *Social & Legal Studies* 17, no. 4 (2008): 453–473.

Prentice, Alison. "Bluestockings, feminists, or women workers?: A preliminary look at women's early employment at the University of Toronto," *Journal of the Canadian Historical Association* 2, no 1 (1991): 231–262.

Pringle, Rosemary. "Rape: The other side of Anzac Day," *Refractory Girl*, no. 26 (1983): 31–35.

Pringle, Rosemary and Sophie Watson. "Fathers, brothers, mates: The fraternal state in Australia," in *Playing the State: Australian Feminist Interventions,* ed. Sophie Watson (Sydney: Allen & Unwin 1990).

Puplick, Chris. "Foreword," in *Homophobic Violence*, ed. Gail Mason and Stephen Tomsen (Sydney: Hawkins Press, 1997).

Ramsay, Janet. "Policy activism on a 'wicked issue': The building of Australian feminist policy on domestic violence in the 1970s," *Australian Feminist Studies* 22, no. 53 (2007): 247–264

Ramsey, Carolyn B. "Domestic violence and state intervention in the American West and Australia, 1860–1930," *Indiana Law Journal* 86 (2011): 185–256.

Reavey, Paula and Sam Warner. eds. *New Feminist Stories of Child Sexual Abuse: Sexual Scripts and Dangerous Dialogues* (London: Routledge, 2003).

Reinelt, Claire. "Moving onto the terrain of the state: The battered women's movement and the politics of engagement," in *Feminist Organisations: Harvest of the New Women's Movement*, ed. Myra Marx Ferree and Patricia Yancey Martin (Philadelphia: Temple University Press, 1995).

Report of the Royal Commission and Board of Inquiry into the Protection and Detention of Children in the Northern Territory, vol. 2A (Darwin: Northern Territory Government, 2017).

Renshaw, Lauren, Jules Kim, Janelle Fawkes and Elena Jeffreys. *Migrant Sex Workers in Australia* (Canberra: Australian Institute of Criminology, 2015).

Rentschler, Carrie A. and Samantha C. Thrift. "Doing feminism in the network: Networked laughter and the 'binders full of women' meme," *Feminist Theory* 16, no. 3 (2015): 329–359.

Renzetti, Claire M. *Violent Betrayal: Partner Abuse in Lesbian Relationships* (London: Sage, 1992).

Renzetti, Claire M. and Vivian M. Larkin. "Economic stress and domestic violence," *National Online Resource Center on Violence Against Women*, September 2009, accessed 14 June 2018, https://vawnet.org/material/economic-stress-and-domestic-violence.

Richards, David L. and Jillienne Haglund. *Violence against Women and the Law* (Milton Park: Routledge, 2015).

Ridgeway, Beverly. "Aboriginal women's viewpoint," in *National Conference on Domestic Violence: Proceedings*, Vol. 1, ed. Suzanne E. Hatty (Canberra: Australian Institute of Criminology, 1986).

Rimmer, Peter J. and Lisa M. Allen, ed. *The Underside of Malaysian History: Pullers, Prostitutes, Plantation Workers* (Singapore: Singapore University Press, 1990).

Robert, Hannah. "Disciplining the female Aboriginal body: inter-racial sex and the pretence of separation," *Australian Feminist Studies* 16, no. 34 (2001): 69–81.

Robinson, Shirleene, ed. *Homophobia: an Australian History* (Annandale, NSW: The Federation Press, 2000).

Rossiter, Margaret. *Women Scientists in America: Struggles and Strategies* (Baltimore: The John Hopkins University Press, 1982).

Roth, Paul. "Indigenous voices at work," in *Voices at Work: Continuity and Change in the Common Law World*, ed. Alan Bogg and Tonia Novitz (Oxford: Oxford University Press, 2014).

Rowley, C.D. *The Remote Aborigines* (Ringwood, Vic.: Penguin, 1972).

Rowley, C.D. *The Destruction of Aboriginal Society* (Harmondsworth: Penguin, 1974).

Royal Commission into Family Violence: Report and Recommendations (Melbourne: Victoria Government Printer, 2016).

Royal Commission into Institutional Responses to Child Sexual Abuse. *Final Report: Historical Residential Institutions*, vol. 11 (Sydney: Commonwealth of Australia, 2017).

Royal Commission into Institutional Responses to Child Sexual Abuse. *Final Report: Making Institutions Child Safe*, vol. 6 (Sydney: Commonwealth of Australia, 2017).

Royal Commission into Institutional Responses to Child Sexual Abuse. *Interim Report* (Sydney: Commonwealth of Australia, 2014).

Royal Commission into Institutional Responses to Child Sexual Abuse. *Report of Case Study No. 3: Anglican Diocese of Grafton's Response to Child Sexual Abuse at the North Coast Children's Home* (Sydney: Royal Commission into Institutional Responses to Child Sexual Abuse, 2014).

Royal Commission into Institutional Responses to Child Sexual Abuse. *Report of Case Study No. 5: Response of the Salvation Army to Child Sexual Abuse at Its Boys Homes in New South Wales and Queensland* (Sydney: Royal Commission into Institutional Responses to Child Sexual Abuse, 2015).

Royal Commission into Institutional Responses to Child Sexual Abuse. *Report of Case Study No. 7. Child Sexual Abuse at the Parramatta Training School for Girls and the Institution for Girls in Hay* (Sydney: Royal Commission into Institutional Responses to Child Sexual Abuse, 2014).

Royal Commission into Institutional Responses to Child Sexual Abuse. *Report of Case Study No. 11. Congregation of Christian Brothers in Western Australia Response to Child Sexual Abuse at Castledare Junior Orphanage, St Vincent's Orphanage Clontarf, St Mary's Agricultural School Tardun and Bindoon Farm School* (Sydney: Royal Commission into Institutional Responses to Child Sexual Abuse, 2014),

Royal Commission into Institutional Responses to Child Sexual Abuse. *Report of Case Study No. 17, The Response of the Australian Indigenous Ministries, the Australian and Northern Territory Governments and the Northern Territory Police Force and Prosecuting Authorities to Allegations of Child Sexual Abuse Which Occurred at the Retta Dixon Home* (Sydney: Royal Commission into Institutional Responses to Child Sexual Abuse, 2015).

Royal Commission into Institutional Responses to Child Sexual Abuse. *Report of Case Study No. 26. The Response of the Sisters of Mercy, the Catholic Diocese of Rockhampton and the Queensland Government to Allegations of Child Sexual Abuse at St Joseph's Orphanage, Neerkol* (Sydney: Royal Commission into Institutional Responses to Child Sexual Abuse, 2016).

Royal Commission into Institutional Responses to Child Sexual Abuse. *Report of Case Study No. 30: The Response of Turana, Winlaton and Baltara, and the Victoria Police and the Department of Health and Human Services Victoria to Allegations of Child Sexual Abuse.* (Sydney: Royal Commission into Institutional Responses to Child Sexual Abuse, 2016).

Russell, Lynette, ed. *Colonial Frontiers: Indigenous-European Encounters in Settler Societies* (Manchester: Manchester University Press, 2001).

Russell, Penny and Richard White, ed. *Pastiche I: Reflections on 19th Century Australia* (St Leonards: Allen & Unwin, 1994).

Sallmann, Peter and Duncan Chappell. *Rape Law Reform: A Study of the South Australian Experience* (Adelaide: Australian Criminology Research Council, 1977).
Salter, Michael. "Grace's story: Prologued incestuous abuse from childhood into adulthood," *Violence Against Women* 19, no. 2 (2013): 146–165
Salter, Michael. "Invalidation: A neglected dimension of gender-based violence and inequality," *International Journal of Crime, Justice and Social Democracy* 1, no. 1 (2012): 3–13.
Saunders, Kay. "The study of domestic violence in colonial Queensland: Sources and problems," *Historical Studies* 21, no. 82 (1984): 68–84.
Sawer, Marian. "Governing for the mainstream: Implications for community representation," *Australian Journal of Public Administration* 61, no. 1 (2002): 39–49.
Sawer, Marian. "Misogyny and misrepresentation: Women in Australian Parliaments," *Political Science* 65, no. 1 (2013): 105–117.
Sawer, Marian and Gwendolyn G. Jamieson. "The women's movement and government: Feminist fading," *Australian Feminist Studies* 29, no. 82 (2014): 403–418.
Scates, Bruce and Raelene Frances. *Women and the Great War* (Cambridge: Cambridge University Press, 1997).
Scott, Dorothy and Shurlee Swain. *Confronting Cruelty: Historical Perspectives on Child Abuse* (Carlton South, Vic.: Melbourne University Press, 2002).
Scutt, Jocelynne A. "Domestic violence: The police response," in *Family Violence in Australia*, ed. Carol O'Donnell and Jan Craney (Melbourne: Longman Cheshire, 1982).
Scutt, Jocelynne A. "Consent in rape: The problem of the marriage contract," *Monash University Law Review* 3 (1977): 255–288.
Scutt, Jocelynne A. *Even in the Best of Homes: violence in the family* (Ringwood: Penguin, 1983).
Scutt, Jocelynne A. "Judgements of right thinking men: Marriage, rape and law reform," *Scarlet Woman* 21 (1986): 23.
Scutt, Jocelynne A. "'Still the same old story…': Pornography and violence against women," in *National Conference on Domestic Violence: Proceedings*, Vol. 1, ed. Suzanne E. Hatty (Canberra: Australian Institute of Criminology, 1986).
Scutt, Jocelynne A. ed. *Violence in the Family: a collection of conference papers* (Canberra: Australian Institute of Criminology, 1980).
Sheehy, Elizabeth, Julie Stubbs, and Julia Tolmie. "Defences to homicide battered women: A comparative analysis of laws in Australia, Canada and New Zealand," *Sydney Law Review* 34 (2012): 467–492.
Shimizu, Hiroshi. "Karayuki-san and the Japanese economic advance into British Malaya, 1870–1920," *Asian Studies Review* 20, no. 3 (1997): 107–132.
Shon, Phillip C. and Shannon M. Barton-Bellessa. "Pre-offense characteristics of nineteenth-century American parricide offenders: An archival exploration," *Journal of Criminal Psychology* 2, no. 1 (2012): 51–66.
Shon, Phillip C. and Michael A. Roberts. "Post-offence characteristics of 19th-century American parricides: An archival exploration," *Journal of Investigative Psychology and Offender Profiling* 5, no. 3 (2008): 147–169.
Shon, Phillip C. and Christopher R. Williams. "An archival exploration of 19th-century American adult female offender parricides," *OMEGA — Journal of Death and Dying* 67, no. 3 (2013): 247–268.
Simmel, Georg. "The poor," in *On Individuality and Social Forms*, ed. Don Levine (Chicago: University of Chicago Press, 1971).
Simone, Tauri. "Aboriginal stockwomen: Their legacy in the Australian pastoral industry" (Doctor of Philosophy, Deakin University, 2016).

Smaal, Yorick. "Boys and homosex: Danger and possibility in Queensland, 1890–1914," in *Children, Childhood and Youth in the British World*, ed. Shirleene Robinson and Simon Sleight (Basingstoke: Palgrave Macmillan, 2015), 221–236
Smaal, Yorick. "Historical perspectives on child sexual abuse, Part 1," *History Compass* 11, no. 9 (2013): 702–714.
Smaal, Yorick. "Historical perspectives on child sexual abuse, Part 2," *History Compass* 11, no. 9 (2013): 715–726.
Smaal, Yorick. "Keeping it in the family: Incest in colonial Australia," *Journal of Australian Studies* 37, no. 3 (2013): 316–332.
Smaal, Yorick, Andy Kaladelfos, and Mark Finnane, ed. *The Sexual Abuse of Children: Recognition and Redress*, ed. (Clayton, Vic.: Monash University Publishing, 2016).
Smallwood, Emma. *Stepping Stones: Legal Barriers to Economic Equality After Family Violence* (Melbourne: Women's Legal Service Victoria, 2015).
Smart, Judith. "The Great War and the 'scarlet scourge': Debates about venereal diseases in Melbourne during World War I," in *An Anzac Muster: War and Society in Australia and New Zealand 1914–18 and 1939–45*, ed. Judith Smart and Tony Wood (Clayton: Monash University Press, 1992).
Smith, Philippa Mein. *A Concise History of New Zealand* (Cambridge: Cambridge University Press, 2005).
Sobsey, Dick, Wade Randall, and Rauno K.Parrila. "Gender differences in abused children with and without disabilities," *Child Abuse and Neglect* 21, no. 8 (1997): 707–720.
Sousa, Cindy, Todd I. Herrenkohl, Carrie A. Moylan, Emiko A. Tajima, J. Bart Klika, Roy C. Herrenkohl, and M. Jean Russo. "Longitudinal study on the effects of child abuse and children's exposure to domestic violence, parent-child attachments, and antisocial behavior in adolescence," *Journal of Interpersonal Violence* 26, no. 1 (2011): 111–136.
Spearritt, Katie. "The sexual economics of colonial marriage," in *On the Edge: Women's Experiences of Queensland*, ed. Gail Reekie (St Lucia: University of Queensland Press, 1994).
Spivak, Gayatri Chakravorty. "Can the Subaltern Speak?" in *Marxism and the Interpretation of Culture*, ed. Cary Nelson and Lawrence Grossberg (Houndmills: Macmillan, 1988).
Stage, Sarah and Virginia Vincenti, ed. *Rethinking Home Economics: Women and the History of a Profession* (Ithaca: Cornell University Press, 1997).
Stebbins, Robert A. *Serious Leisure: A Perspective for our Time* (New Brunswick: Transaction, 2007).
Stevenson, Ana. "Making gender divisive: 'Post-feminism', sexism and media representations of Julia Gillard," *Burgmann Journal* 2 (2013): 53–66.
Stevenson, Ana. *The Woman as Slave in Nineteenth-Century American Social Movements* (Palgrave Macmillan, *forthcoming*).
Stevenson, Kim. "'These are cases which it is inadvisable to drag into the light of day': Disinterring the crime in incest in early twentieth-century England," *Crime, History and Societies*, 20, no. 2 (2016): 6–28.
Stott, Jennifer. "Celluloid maidens: All teched-up and nowhere to go," in *Don't Shoot Darling! Women's Independent Filmmaking in Australia*, ed. Annette Blonski, Barbara Creed and Freda Freiberg (Melbourne: Greenhouse Publications, 1987).
Strange, Carolyn. "Masculinities, intimate femicide and the death penalty in Australia, 1890–1920," *British Journal of Criminology* 43, no. 2 (2003): 310–339.
Strange, Carolyn. "The unwritten law of executive justice: Pardoning patricide in Reconstruction-era New York," *Law and History Review* 28, no. 4 (2010): 891–930.

Stubbs, Julie and Julia Tolmie. "Battered woman syndrome in Australia: A challenge to gender bias in the law?" in *Women, Male Violence and the Law*, ed. Julie Stubbs (Sydney: The Institute of Criminology, 1994).

Summers, Anne. *Damned Whores and God's Police* (Ringwood: Penguin, 1975).

Summers, Anne. *Damned Whores and God's Police*, updated edition, (Ringwood: Penguin, 1994).

Summers, Anne. "Her rights at work: The political persecution of Australia's first female Prime Minister," *The Economic and Labour Relations Review* 23, no. 4 (2012): 115–126.

Swain, Shurlee. "Confronting cruelty: Writing a history of the detection and treatment of child abuse," *Victorian Historical Journal* 71, no. 1 (2000): 7–18.

Swain, Shurlee. *History of Institutions Providing out-of-Home Care for Children* (Sydney: Royal Commission into Institutional Responses to Child Sexual Abuse, 2014).

Teo, Hsu-Ming. "'We have to learn to love imperially': Love in late colonial and federation Australian romance novels," *Journal of Popular Romance Studies* 4, no. 2 (2014): 1–20.

Terami-Wada, Motoe. "Karayuki-san of Manila: 1880–1920," *Philippine Studies*, no. 34 (1986): 287–316.

Timmerman, Margaretha C. and Pauline R. Schreuder. "Sexual Abuse of Children and Youth in Residential Care: An International Review," *Aggression and Violent Behavior* 19 (2014): 715–720.

Theobald, Jacqui. "Feminist oral history and the Victorian domestic violence services movement," *Australian Feminist Studies* 28, no. 78 (2013): 364–374.

Theobald, Jacqui. "The beginnings of the Victorian women's refuge movement: Difference, equality and protectionism, 1974–1979," *Lilith: A Feminist History Journal* 21 (2015): 48–62.

Theobald, Jacqui. "Women's refuges and the state in Victoria, Australia: A campaign for secrecy of address," *Women's History Review* 23, no. 1 (2014): 60–81.

Theobald, Jacqui, Suellen Murray and Judith Smart. *From the Margins to the Mainstream: The Domestic Violence Services Movement, Victoria, 1974–2016* (Melbourne: Melbourne University Press, 2017).

Theobald, Marjorie. *Knowing Women: Origins of Women's Education in Nineteenth Century Australia* (Cambridge: Cambridge University Press, 1996).

Thrift, Samantha C. "#Yesallwomen as Feminist Meme Event," *Feminist Media Studies* 14, no. 6 (2014): 1090–1092.

Tomsen, Stephen and Gail Mason. "Engendering homophobia: violence, sexuality and gender conformity," *Journal of Sociology* 37, no. 3 (2001): 257–273.

Tomsic, Mary. *Beyond the Silver Screen: A history of women, filmmaking and film culture in Australia, 1920–1990* (Melbourne: Melbourne University Press, 2017).

Tomsic, Mary. "'We will invent ourselves, the age of the new image is at hand': Creating, learning and talking with Australian feminist filmmaking," *Australian Feminist Studies* 22, no. 53 (2007): 287–306.

Tually, Selina, Debbie Faulkner, Cecile Cutler and Michele Slatter. *Women, Domestic and Family Violence and Homelessness: A Synthesis Report* (Adelaide: Flinders Institute for Housing, Urban and Regional Research, 2008).

Twomey, Christina. *Deserted and Destitute: Motherhood, Wife Desertion and Colonial Welfare* (Kew: Australian Scholarly Press, 2002).

Tyson, Danielle, Deborah Kirkwood, and Mandy McKenzie. "Family violence in domestic homicides: A case study of women who killed intimate partners post-legislative reform in Victoria, Australia," *Violence Against Women* 23, no. 5 (2017): 559–583.

United Nations Human Rights Office of the High Commissioner, "Protocol to prevent, suppress and punish trafficking in persons especially women and children, supplementing the United Nations convention against transnational organized crime," *Office of the United Nations High Commissioner*, accessed 15 September 2017 http://www.ohchr.org/EN/ProfessionalInterest/Pages/ProtocolTraffickingInPersons.aspx.

Walker, Garthine. "Imagining the unimaginable: Parricide in early modern England and Wales, c. 1600–c. 1760," *Journal of Family History* 41, no. 3 (2016): 271–293.

Walker, Gillian. *Family Violence and the Women's Movement: The Conceptual Politics of Struggle* (Toronto: University of Toronto Press, 1990).

Walker, Sonia. "Battle-axes and sticky-beaks: Women and jury service in Western Australia 1898–1957," *Murdoch University Electronic Journal of Law* 11, no. 4 (2004).

Walsh, Jeffrey A., Jessie L Krienert, and Danielle Crowder. "Innocence lost: A gender-based study of parricide offender, victim, and incident characteristics in a national sample, 1976–2003," *Journal of Aggression, Maltreatment & Trauma* 16, no. 2 (2008): 202–227.

Warren, James F. *Ah Ku and Karayuki-San: Prostitution and Singapore Society, 1870–1940* (Oxford: Oxford University Press, 1993).

Waseem, Saba. *Policy Research Paper no. 23: Household Monies and Decision-making*, Australian Government Department of Family and Community Services (Sydney: Social Policy Research Centre, University of New South Wales, 2004).

Webster, Amy. "The Re-conceptualisation of Domestic Violence Under the Howard Government Since 1996," *Lilith: A Feminist History Journal* 16 (2007): 57–68.

Weeks, Wendy, ed. *Women Working Together: Lessons from Feminist Women's Services*, (Melbourne: Longman Cheshire, 1994).

Weitzer, Ronald. "The movement to criminalize sex work in the United States," *Journal of Law and Society* 37, no. 1 (2010): 61–84.

Weitzer, Ronald. "The social construction of sex trafficking: Ideology and institutionalization of a moral crusade," *Politics and Society* 35 (2007) 447–475.

Whitehead, Kay. "Higher education, work and 'overstrain of the brain': Amy Marion Elliott MSC, University of Tasmania 1900," *History of Education Review* 29, no 1 (2000): 16–31.

Willett, Graham and Yorick Smaal, ed. *Intimacy, Violence and Activism: Gay and Lesbian Perspectives on Australasian History and Society* (Melbourne: Monash University Publishing, 2013).

Wilson, Alex, Bronwyn Lee Carlson, and Acushla Sciascia. "Reterritorialising social media: Indigenous people rise up," *Australasian Journal of Information Systems* 21 (2017): 1–4.

Wilson, Emily. "'Someone who is sick and in need of help': Medical attitudes to homosexuality in Australia, 1960–1979," in *Homophobia: An Australian History*, ed. Shirleene Robinson (Sydney: The Federation Press, 2008).

Wilson, Tikka Jan. "Feminism and institutionalized racism: Inclusion and exclusion at an Australian feminist refuge," *Feminist Review* 52, no. 1 (1996): 1–26.

Wilson, Paul. *The Other Side of Rape* (St. Lucia: University of Queensland Press, 1978).

Wolfe, Patrick. "Land, labour, and difference: Elementary structures of race," *American Historical Review* 103, no. 3 (2001): 866–905.

Wolfe, Patrick. "Settler colonialism and the elimination of the native," *Journal of Genocide Research* 8, no. 4 (2006): 387–409.

Wolfe, Patrick. *Settler Colonialism and the Transformation of Anthropology: The Politics and Poetics of an Ethnographic Event* (London: Cassell, 1999).

Woollacott, Angela. "Ambiguity and necessity: Settlers and Aborigines in intimate tension in mid-nineteenth century Australia," in *Intimacies of Violence in the Settler Colony: Economies of Dispossession Around the Pacific Rim*, ed. Penelope Edmonds and Amanda Nettelbeck (Basingstoke: Palgrave Macmillan, 2018).

World Health Organisation, Department of Reproductive Health and Research, London School of Hygiene and Tropical Medicine and South African Medical Research Council. *Global and regional estimates of violence against women: prevalence and health effects of intimate partner violence and non-partner sexual violence* (Italy: World Health Organisation Reports, 2013).

Yamazaki, Tomoko. "Sandakan no. 8 brothel," *Bulletin of Concerned Asian Scholars* 7, no. 4 (1975): 52–60.

Yeatman, Anna. *Bureaucrats, Technocrats, Femocrats: Essays on the Contemporary Australian State* (Sydney: Allen & Unwin, 1990).

Yuriko, Nagata. "The Japanese in the Torres Strait," in *Navigating Boundaries: The Asian Diaspora in Torres Strait*, ed. Anna Shnukal, Guy Ramsay and Yuriko Nagata (Canberra: Pandanus Books, 2004).

Zainu'ddin, Ailsa. "The admission of women to the University of Melbourne, 1869–1903," *Melbourne Studies in Education* 15, no. 1 (1973): 50–106.

ABOUT THE CONTRIBUTORS

Dr Liz Conor is an ARC Future Fellow at La Trobe University. She is the author of *Skin Deep: Settler Impressions of Aboriginal Women*, (UWA Publishing, 2016) and *The Spectacular Modern Woman: Feminine Visibility in the 1920s* (Indiana University Press, 2004). She is former editor of the journal Aboriginal History and has published widely in academic and mainstream press on gender, race and representation.

Dr Lisa Durnian is a recent Griffith Criminology Institute PhD graduate on the ARC Laureate Fellowship "The Prosecution Project". Her doctoral research explores the guilty plea phenomenon, whereby traditional criminal jury trials where replaced by defendants pleading guilty. This mixed-methods research analyses large-scale data of cases prosecuted in Australian Supreme Courts between 1901 and 1961.

Associate Professor Tanya Evans teaches history at Macquarie University Sydney, Australia where she directs the Centre for Applied History. Her publications include: *Fractured Families: Life On The Margins in Colonial New South Wales* (2015); with Pat Thane, *Sinners, Scroungers, Saints: Unmarried Motherhood in Modern England* (2012). She also works as a consultant for the television series *Who do you think you are?*

Associate Professor Lisa Featherstone is an Associate Professor in Australian History at the University of Queensland. Lisa researches sexual violence in Australia's past, with a focus on legal and medical history. She has published widely in the field in leading journals. Her most recent book, co-authored with Andy Kaladelfos, *Sex Crimes in the Fifties* (2016) was shortlisted for the prestigious NSW Premier's Prize for History. She holds an interdisciplinary ARC Discovery Project, "Sexual Offences, legal responses, and public perceptions, 1880s–1980s" with Andy Kaladelfos, Carolyn Strange and the late Nina Westera.

Professor Tanya Fitzgerald is Professor of History of Education at La Trobe University. Her research interests span the of history of women's higher education, and higher education policy and leadership. Tanya is currently working on an ARC-funded project: *Fostering women leaders through* *educational exchange 1930–1980* (with Diane Kirkby and Vera Mackie). Publications in progress include a major reference work *International Handbook of Historical Studies in Education: Debates, tensions and directions* (Springer, 2018) and *New beginnings: Historical perspectives on teacher preparation in Aotearoa New Zealand* (with Sally Knipe, Emerald, 2019).

Professor Raelene Frances is Dean of the College of Arts and Social Sciences at the Australian National University. She is also a professor of history, with prize-winning books on the history of women, work and war. Prior to taking up her role at ANU in mid-2017 she was Dean of Arts at Monash University for 10 years and before that had teaching, research and leadership roles at UNSW, the University of Auckland and Murdoch University. Her 2007 book, *Selling Sex: a Hidden History of Prostitution*, was short-listed for the Ernest Scott Prize in Australian and New Zealand History.

Dr Rebecca Jennings is a Lecturer in Modern Gender History at University College, London. Her research focuses on British and Australian lesbian history and she is the author of *Tomboys and Bachelor Girls: A Lesbian History of Post-war Britain* (Manchester University Press, 2007) and *Unnamed Desires: A Sydney Lesbian History* (Monash University Publishing, 2015). She is currently completing her forthcoming book, "Sisters, Lovers, Wives and Mothers: Lesbian Intimacy in Britain and Australia 1945–2000", based on Australian Research Council-funded research into lesbian relationship models and parenting practices in post-war Britain and Australia.

Dr Andy Kaladelfos is Lecturer in Criminology in the School of Social Sciences at the University of New South Wales. Prior to UNSW, Andy was Senior Research Fellow with the ARC Laureate Fellowship Project "Prosecution and the Criminal Trial in Australian History" at the Griffith Criminology Institute, Griffith University (2012-2018).

Dr Brigitte Lewis researches and writes on feminist digital activism, lesbian identity, female desire, and all things tech. She has a PhD on twenty-first century identity creation and the limits of rationality from the University of Melbourne. Her most recent piece was "Women Want to (Fuck) too", in a feminist anthology published by Penguin. Brigitte is an Ethical Hacker for Deloitte.

Professor Suellen Murray is Associate Dean, Research and Innovation, in the School of Global, Urban and Social Studies at RMIT University in Melbourne, Australia. Suellen has specialised in research concerning violence against women and its related policy and practice responses. She is the author of *More than Refuge: Changing Responses to Domestic Violence* (2002) and co-author with Jacqui Theobald of *From the Margins to the Mainstream: The Domestic Violence Services Movement in Victoria, Australia, 1974–2016* (2017) and with Anastasia Powell, *Domestic Violence: Australian Public Policy* (2011)

Dr Alana Piper is a Postdoctoral Research Fellow in the Australian Centre for Public History at the University of Technology Sydney. She has published widely on gender, crime and legal history. Alana's work also draws on digital humanities approaches, both in her previous role as a Research Fellow on the ARC Laureate Fellowship "The Prosecution Project" (2014–2018), and her current Chancellor's Fellowship project "Criminal Characters" (2018–2022).

Dr Zora Simic is a Senior Lecturer in History and Women's and Gender Studies in the School of Humanities and Languages at the University of New South Wales. She has published widely on past and present feminisms and is currently undertaking a history of domestic violence in Australia with Professor Ann Curthoys and Dr Catherine Kevin.

Dr Ana Stevenson is a Postdoctoral Research Fellow in the International Studies Group at the University of the Free State. Her research about women's movements in Australia and the United States appears in journals such as the *Women's History Review*, *Cultural & Social History*, and *Pacific Historical Review*.

Professor Shurlee Swain is Emeritus Professor of Humanities at Australian Catholic University. She has published widely in the area of Australian social history and her research has informed several of Australia's inquiries into historical institutional abuse.

Dr Jacqui Theobald is a Lecturer in social work and social policy at La Trobe University Bendigo. Jacqui's primary areas of research interest includes violence against women and homelessness. She is co-author with Suellen Murray of *From the Margins to the Mainstream: The Domestic Violence Services Movement in Victoria, Australia, 1974–2016* (2017).

Dr Mary Tomsic is a Postdoctoral Research Associate at The University of Melbourne. She is part of an ARC Laureate project on the history of child refugees and Australian internationalism (FL140100049). Her research interest is in gender, sexualities, film and visual forms generally, with particular focus on the political nature of these forms of creative expression. Her book *Beyond the Silver Screen: A History of Women, Filmmaking and Film Culture in Australia 1921–1990* was published by Melbourne University Press in 2017.

CPSIA information can be obtained
at www.ICGtesting.com
Printed in the USA
BVHW031323271019
562137BV00002B/7/P

9 781925 835304